DIFFERENTIATING INSTRUCTION

To all the students whose teachers
have collaborated to bring their students differentiated
instruction so that everyone learns

DIFFERENTIATING INSTRUCTION

COLLABORATIVE PLANNING and TEACHING for UNIVERSALLY DESIGNED LEARNING

Jacqueline S. Thousand
Richard A. Villa
Ann I. Nevin

CORWIN PRESS
A SAGE Publications Company
Thousand Oaks, CA 91320

For information:

Corwin Press
A Sage Publications Company
2455 Teller Road
Thousand Oaks, California 91320
www.corwinpress.com

Sage Publications Ltd
1 Oliver's Yard
55 City Road
London EC1Y 1SP
United Kingdom

Sage Publications India Pvt Ltd
B 1/I 1 Mohan Cooperative
Industrial Area
Mathura Road, New Delhi 110 044
India

Sage Publications Asia-Pacific Pte Ltd
33 Pekin Street #02-01
Far East Square
Singapore 048763

Printed in the United States of America

Library of Congress Cataloging-in-Publication Data

Thousand, Jacqueline S., 1950-
Differentiating instruction: Collaborative planning and teaching for universally designed learning/Jacqueline S. Thousand, Richard A. Villa, Ann I. Nevin.
    p. cm.
Includes bibliographical references and index.
ISBN-13: 978-1-4129-3860-0 (cloth : alk. paper)
ISBN-13: 978-1-4129-3861-7 (pbk. : alk. paper) 1. Individualized instruction. 2. Teaching teams. I. Villa, Richard A., 1952- II. Nevin, Ann. III. Title.

LB1031.T56 2007
371.39'4--dc22

2006031971

This book is printed on acid-free paper.

10 11 10 9 8 7 6 5 4

Acquisitions Editor:	Allyson P. Sharp
Editorial Assistant:	Nadia Kashper
Production Editor:	Beth A. Bernstein
Copy Editor:	Thomas Burchfield
Typesetter:	C&M Digitals (P) Ltd.
Proofreader:	Andrea Martin
Indexer:	Molly Hall
Cover Designer:	Scott Van Atta
Graphic Designer:	Karine Hovsepian

Contents

Special Features Listing of Tables & Figures

TABLES

FIGURES

A Letter to Our Readers

Dear Colleague:

We are so excited to be able to share the content of this book with you. We, like many of you, have worked tirelessly for many years to inspire, relate to, and meet the needs of our students. We have at times been very successful while, at other times, we have been less effective than we would like. In this book, we share two approaches that we have used, and have seen used, to differentiate instruction in elementary, middle, and secondary classes. When we (or our colleagues) have used either the retrofit approach or the universal design for learning approach, we have witnessed success for both the teachers and the students. And there is not much that can beat the "rush" you feel when you know that you are teaching effectively.

We recognize that the students who comprise today's classrooms are much more diverse than those who were students when we first began our teaching careers. Many of the practices that made a teacher effective when we were the students or just beginning our careers as teachers—content mastery, human relations, use of materials, planning, classroom management—remain the same. However, today there is a greater need for effective teachers than at any other time in the history of our profession. Today's effective teachers must differentiate instruction to facilitate their students' mastery of the goals of education. Today's effective teachers must relate to and inspire their students from various backgrounds and life circumstances. They must create communities of learners, facilitate student acquisition of core curriculum content, prepare students for independence and self-determination, and provide opportunities for learners to support one another to solve problems and to acquire and analyze information. Today's teachers can accomplish all of this through the use of high-yield instructional strategies and by using either the retrofit or the universal design for learning approaches to differentiated instruction that are detailed in this book.

The likelihood of success by using differentiated instruction will be enhanced when you collaborate with others to learn the content, plan and teach for differentiation, reflect about the successes of the lessons that you teach, and redesign your approach to refine and improve teaching effectiveness. Strategies for collaborative planning and teaching to accomplish the goals of differentiated instruction are also offered throughout this book.

We have experienced the joy of being life-long learners; we want that joy for you as well. We feel confident that when you are armed with the strategies and approaches found in this book, you will feel that "rush of success" when you apply these techniques in your lesson planning and implementation. We are also confident that when you see your students succeed you will feel yourself to be a more effective teacher. We encourage you to let us know how you are doing as you use the information offered in this book, while you continue your journey toward being the most effective teacher that you can be for all of the students in your classroom.

Acknowledgments

Corwin Press gratefully acknowledges the contributions of the following reviewers:

Douglas Fisher
Co-Director
Center for the Advancement
  of Reading
San Diego, CA

Bee Gallegos
Research Librarian
Fletcher Library
Arizona State University
  at the West Campus
Phoenix, AZ

Teresa Hamm
Director of Student Services
Old Rochester Regional School
  District
Mattapoisett, MA

Mandy Hollenbacher
Math Teacher
Twin Oaks Valley High School
Morgantown, PA

Paula Kluth, PhD
Consultant and Independent Scholar
Oak Park, IL

Robi Kronberg, PhD
Educational Consultant
Littleton, CO

Jay McTighe
Education Author and Consultant
Jay McTighe and Associates
  Educational Consulting
Columbia, MD

Carol Ann Tomlinson
Professor and Program Coordinator
  for the Educational
  Psychology/Gifted
  Education Program Area
Curry School of Education
University of Virginia
Charlottesville, VA

Gwendolyn Webb-Johnson
Assistant Professor
Department of Educational
  Administration and
  Human Resources
Texas A&M University
College Station, TX

In addition, the authors wish to acknowledge the following individuals whose work we have referenced and used in this book.

Dr. Alice Udvari-Solner
University of Wisconsin–Madison
Madison, WI

Ruth Beecher
Teacher
Robinson Elementary School
Starksboro, VT

Rebecca Shuflitowski
School Psychologist
11244 Southwest 128 Court
Miami, FL

Dr. Shirley Ritter
Dr. Stephanie Morris
School of Education
Furman University
Greenville, NC

Carrie Kizuka
Mathematics Co-teacher
Twin Valley High School
Morgantown, PA

Francis Duff
High School Language Arts Teacher
Cibola High School
Albuquerque, NM

About the Authors

Jacqueline Thousand is a professor in the College of Education at California State University–San Marcos and co-coordinates the special education professional preparation and masters programs. Prior to coming to California, she taught at the University of Vermont, where she directed the Inclusion Facilitator and Early Childhood/Special Education graduate and post-graduate professional preparation programs and coordinated federal grants, all of which were concerned with inclusion of students with disabilities in local schools. Dr. Thousand is a nationally known teacher, author, systems change consultant, and disability rights and inclusive education advocate. She has authored numerous books, research articles, and book chapters on issues related to inclusive schooling, organizational change strategies, differentiated instruction and universal design for learning, cooperative group learning, collaborative teaming and teaching, creative problem solving, and positive behavioral supports. She is actively involved in international teacher education and inclusive education endeavors and serves on the editorial boards of several national and international journals.

Richard A. Villa is President of Bayridge Consortium, Inc., in San Diego, California. His primary field of expertise is the development of administrative and instructional support systems for educating all students within general education settings. Dr. Villa is recognized as an educational leader with the commitment and the conceptual, technical, and interpersonal skills to inspire and work collaboratively with others in order to implement current and emerging exemplary educational practices. Dr. Villa has been a classroom teacher, special education administrator, pupil personnel services director, and director of instructional services. Dr. Villa has made presentations at international, national, and state educational conferences and has provided technical assistance to the U.S., Canadian, Vietnamese, Laotian, and Honduran departments of education, and to university personnel, public school systems, and parent and advocacy organizations. He has authored nine books and over 100 articles and chapters. Dr. Villa is known for his enthusiastic, knowledgeable, and humorous style of presentation.

 **Ann Nevin**, author of books, research articles, and numerous book chapters, is a scholar and teacher educator who graduated *magna cum laude* from the University of Minnesota with a PhD in Educational Psychology. Her doctoral research focused on how teachers and administrators can integrate students with special learning needs. She also earned advanced degrees in special education and educational administration and has participated in the development of innovative teacher education programs since the 1970s. Her advocacy, research, and teaching includes more than thirty years of working with a diverse array of people to help students with disabilities succeed. As Dr. Nevin explains, "I believe that the purpose of education is to empower others."

1

Why Differentiation of Instruction Now?

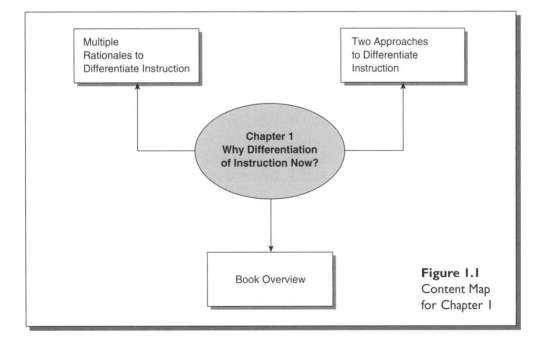

Multiple Rationales to Differentiate Instruction

Two Approaches to Differentiate Instruction

Chapter 1
Why Differentiation
of Instruction Now?

Book Overview

Figure 1.1
Content Map
for Chapter 1

Learning is the process of preparing to deal with new situations.

—Alvin Toffler

Why did we decide to write this book? We wrote this book for you—classroom teachers, special educators, curriculum coordinators, administrators, and teacher trainers—because we wanted to provide you with a valuable resource to meet the needs of an increasingly diverse student body. We believe that you, as echoed by Alvin Toffler's wise remark, are in a constant process of learning to prepare yourselves and your students to deal with new situations.

Differentiated instruction has been described as a teaching philosophy based on the premise that teachers should adapt instruction to student differences, because "one size does not fit all" (Willis & Mann, 2000).

According to Starr (2004):

> At its most basic level, differentiating instruction means shaking up what goes on in the classroom so students have multiple options for taking in information, making sense of ideas, and expressing what they learn. In other words, a differentiated classroom provides different avenues to acquiring content, processing or making sense of ideas, and developing products.

Differentiated instruction can be defined as a way for teachers to recognize and react responsively to their students' varying background knowledge, readiness, language, preferences in learning, and interests (Hall, 2002).

Fortunately, we have learned a great deal about differentiating instruction through our experiences as teachers, teacher educators, and advocates for personalized and differentiated instruction. Our work with each other (in addition to our work with many other educators) over the years has helped us to integrate principles from both psychology and the curriculum so that students' unique needs can be addressed by their teachers. While there are many reasons to advocate for differentiating instruction on behalf of K–12 students in all schools, the arguments we outline below will focus on giving you information to support your own practice, beliefs, and feelings about the benefits of differentiated instruction.

■ RATIONALES FOR DIFFERENTIATED INSTRUCTION

We will offer five reasons for why differentiated instruction should be implemented now. As illustrated in Figure 1.2, differentiated instruction helps teachers (1) to meet the needs of diverse students, (2) to meet legal mandates, (3) to be ethical in implementing democratic values, (4) to dispel myths that abound in education, and (5) to be more effective in teaching all students. As we explain each rationale below, ask yourself to what extent do you agree or disagree with these reasons. You may want to make your own list of reasons for differentiating instruction.

Figure 1.2   The Multiple Rationales for Differentiated Instruction

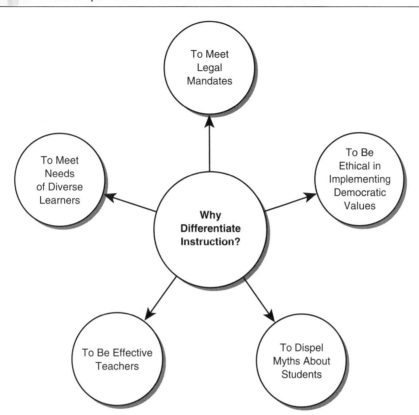

RATIONALE #1: MEET ■
NEEDS OF DIVERSE STUDENTS

Do you wonder how you will meet the diverse needs of the children who enter your classroom? You are not alone. The demographics of America's classrooms reflect increasing diversity, as shown in Figure 1.3.

Moreover, there is an increase of children from culturally and linguistically diverse heritages in classrooms all over the United States. In addition to the presence of African Americans and Hispanic Americans, ethnicity itself has become increasingly diverse with the advent of immigrants from Southeast Asia, Haiti, and other areas of the globe. As cited by Paige (2004), 4.1 million students (8.5 percent) were English language learners.

By the year 2010, according to Schwartz and Exeter (1989), immigration, migration, and fertility patterns indicate that about 38 percent of people under the age of 18 in the United States will be African, Asian, or Hispanic American. By 2010, more than half of the children will be from minority and ethnically diverse heritages in Hawaii (80 percent), New Mexico (77 percent), California (57 percent), Texas (57 percent), New York (53 percent), Florida (53 percent), Louisiana (50 percent), and the District of Columbia (93 percent).

Figure 1.3   Racial Profile of U.S. Schools

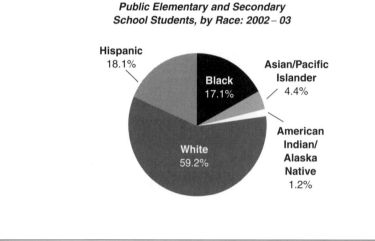

In an additional nineteen states, children from African, Hispanic, Native, or Asian American heritage will make up 25 percent of the population.

Add to this the notion that the number of children with disabilities from culturally and linguistically diverse families has increased from 33 percent in 1992 to 46.7 percent in 2001 (U.S. Department of Education, 2001). Paige (2004) emphasizes these demographics when citing the 6.4 million students (13.4 percent) who are served in federally supported programs for students with disabilities.

In other words, we can say with confidence that diversity in America's classrooms is here to stay. Differentiated instruction can help teachers meet the needs of children with diverse characteristics.

■ RATIONALE #2: MEET LEGAL MANDATES

Do you ponder how you will meet all the legal demands of the teaching profession? Legal mandates such as the 2001 No Child Left Behind (NCLB) Act and the 2004 Individuals with Disabilities Education Improvement Act (IDEIA) are replete with requirements to individualize instruction. Both NCLB and IDEIA promote the inclusion of increasing numbers of students with disabilities as full participants in rigorous academic and general education curriculum and assessment. The stated goal of the 2001 NCLB Act is to close the achievement gap with accountability, flexibility, and choice, so that no child is left behind.

Like IDEIA, the NCLB Act's requirements for high standards and student performance are intended to foster conditions that lead to better instruction and learning, equality of opportunity to learn, and excellence in performance for all children. NCLB emphasizes accountability for all learners by requiring the disaggregation and review of data for all learners (e.g., students in poverty, students who are English language learners, students with disabilities).

Additionally, the NCLB Act requires teachers to meet the standards that would certify them as highly qualified in every subject area they teach. The result has been an increase in the number of students with disabilities being taught in co-taught classrooms by two types of teachers whom we call "Masters of Curriculum" (e.g., classroom teachers) and "Masters of Access" (e.g., special educators, English language learning teachers, teachers of students who are gifted and talented).

IDEIA requires that students with disabilities be given the opportunity to participate in the same general curriculum taught to all other students in the public educational system. You may ask, "What is meant by the general education curriculum?" The U.S. *Federal Register* (March 12, 1999) defined it as "curriculum that is used with nondisabled children" (p. 1470). This means the whole educational experience, not just the curricular content! It includes content, process, and products. It means access to everything—information, teaching, and assessment—that students without disabilities already enjoy. The U.S. Department of Education Office of Special Education and Rehabilitative Services (1999, p. 1470) emphasizes, "Access to the general education curriculum must not be viewed as exclusively a special education concern; . . . *all* students benefit when the general education curriculum becomes more accessible."

RATIONALE #3: BE ETHICAL IN ■ IMPLEMENTING DEMOCRATIC VALUES

Are there moral and ethical arguments to support the use of differentiated instruction?

Yes. In fact, differentiated instruction can advance the continued evolution toward democracy in the American classroom. Many groups, including women, Native Americans, African Americans, Latino Americans, and people with differing abilities, have struggled to receive an education. As noted by Blankenship and Lilly (1981), "Throughout history education has been for the elite and educational practices have reflected an elitist orientation" (p. 18).

When teachers differentiate instruction, they are consciously and conscientiously making the content, processes, and outcomes of instruction more accessible to all students—regardless of the students' race, gender, ethnicity, language, or differing abilities. Through culturally responsive instructional and assessment techniques, teachers can design differentiated instruction lessons that represent the cultural and linguistic strengths of their students and communities (Dill & Boykin, 2005; Duda & Utley, 2006a; Webb-Johnson, 2003).

Differentiated instruction can be considered part of a larger reform movement derived from notions of education in a democratic society. As explained by Apple and Beane (1995)

> democratic classrooms are comprised of students and teachers who see themselves as participants in communities of learning. By their very nature, these communities are diverse, and that diversity is prized,

not viewed as a problem. Such communities include people who reflect differences in age, culture, ethnicity, gender, socioeconomic class, aspirations, and abilities. These differences enrich the community and the range of views it might consider. Separating people of any age on the basis of these differences or using labels to stereotype them simply creates divisions and status systems that detract from the democratic nature of the community and the dignity of the individuals against whom such practices work so harshly. While the community prizes diversity, it also has a sense of shared purpose. . . . The common good is a central feature of democracy. (p. 10)

In the United States, democratic values are embedded in federal legislation, mission statements of school systems, and the oft-stated goal of helping students to become citizens who can make decisions and effectively engage in multiple adult roles. Teachers who use differentiated instruction can offer their students opportunities to make choices, solve problems among a group, develop consensus, and deal with conflict of ideas. Students with a great variety of differences can have an effective voice. Giving students power and control in the classroom can both prevent problematic behaviors and promote higher levels of learning (Apple & Beane, 1995).

■ RATIONALE #4: DISPEL MYTHS

Do you question the truth of several myths that pervade education today?

Although there is ample data to show that children such as those who learn English as a second language, those with disabilities, and those who live in poverty score low on achievement tests compared to their peers, it is not true that these children cannot learn. Teachers (and families) often make assumptions about what our students can and cannot achieve based on our perceptions of them and the beliefs we have about the labels we give them or their perceived abilities and disabilities.

However, these assumptions about students and their potential are often wrong. For example, throughout history we have assumed that several different populations of people who behaved differently were unable to learn, including people with cerebral palsy, people with autism, and the deaf (Crossley, 1997). Historically, educators have also made damaging negative assumptions that have subsequently been proven to be false about the learning potential of girls, students of color, and students who are learning English as a second language.

Making assumptions about an individual based upon a classification (such as language proficiency, social or economic class, race, or ability and disability) is dangerous, as it can lead to tunnel vision. Specifically, it can blind others to an individual's strengths and abilities and cause them to see only the person's disability—a phenomenon described as "disability spread" (Van der Klift & Kunc, 2002, p. 26), where people see only the limitations of the student. When students' strengths and abilities are ignored, it is easy to limit expectations or ignore ways in which strengths and abilities can be employed to motivate and support their learning.

Differentiated instruction can help dispel the myth that English language learners cannot learn. It can dispel the myth that students with disabilities, children of color, and students in poverty cannot learn. Teachers all across America dispel the myths about these students every time they successfully teach a differentiated instruction lesson.

How does differentiated instruction dispel these myths? When teachers use differentiated instruction, they are using a process to address the needs of students who need extra help or enrichment and that allows them to assess the impact of the lessons they are teaching. The immediate feedback shows teachers which students need extra help, which ones need more challenging assignments, and those who can move on to the next level of difficulty.

RATIONALE #5: BE EFFECTIVE ■

Many people adopt differentiated instruction because of the research evidence that shows positive academic and behavioral outcomes for diverse learners, increased capability to personalize support for students, and the increased effectiveness of instruction. When differentiated instruction and co-teaching are combined, results can be seen in increased student performance on high stakes assessments.

For example, the *Commercial Appeal* (Noeth, 2004) reported that when co-teaching was used in all Shelby County, Tennessee, high schools, 70 percent of the county's special education students were included in general education classrooms through support of a special educator and a general education teacher certified in either English or mathematics. After one year of co-teaching, teachers were better able to meet the unique learning needs of their students. The percentage of participating special education students who passed the Gateway English test increased from 20 to 40 percent. Because of these test score gains, several high schools were removed from the troubled schools list. Although the author of the article does not explain how the co-teachers differentiated their instruction as co-teachers, other researchers have explained the differentiation that can occur within a co-teaching environment (e.g., Cramer, Nevin, Voigt, & Salazar, 2006; Cramer, Nevin, Salazar, & Landa, 2004; Garrigan & Thousand, 2006).

What do teachers have to say about differentiated instruction? As they explain it, they meet the needs of the diverse learners in their classrooms through "differentiated instruction, breaking the curriculum into smaller chunks, and curriculum mapping" (Cramer & Nevin, 2007). They describe how they use differentiated instructional processes such as hands-on activities, cooperative learning groups, peer tutoring, and increased visual aids in the classroom. They also described using audio texts and English for speakers of other languages (ESOL) techniques for reading and writing (such as sentence strips and word walls).

Differentiated instruction encouraged both general and special educators to try new arrangements in the presentation of curricular content. Consider the testimony of high school teachers who reported their experiences in implementing differentiated instruction. One special educator emphasized that students enjoyed having multiple educators in the classroom. "It breaks up the presentation style, and the monotony that can happen when just one educator presents for the entire period." Instructional responsiveness to the individual learning needs of all students can occur, as one general educator reported, through her "hands-on experiences where students are engaged in helping one another, teaching one another, and sharing their talents." She further commented, "This far surpasses the outcomes when a student is assigned a one-on-one aide." All interviewees said that they experienced an "increased sensitivity to the emotional, academic, and physical needs of the students" and that this led to "increased opportunities for students to succeed" (Villa, Thousand, Nevin, & Liston, 2005).

Elementary teachers who co-teach report similar results. Salazar and Nevin (2005) described the implementation of a co-teaching initiative that resulted in an increase in the percentage of children with disabilities who were being effectively educated within their general education classrooms along with children without disabilities. That study reported class-by-class enrollment data and achievement data for the children with disabilities in the co-taught classrooms. Both general and special educators identified the importance of differentiated instruction, as well as training teachers to use this approach, as a major factor for its success.

What happens to children in classrooms where teachers collaborate by using differentiated instruction techniques? In a follow-up in-depth case study of one co-teacher team who "looped"—moved to the next grade along with their class—with their third graders when those students were promoted to fourth grade, Cramer et al. (2005) described the effects of teacher collaboration on student achievement. Their scores on the Florida statewide achievement tests in reading, along with feedback from school personnel, indicated that students with disabilities, as well as their peers, showed strong gains in reading and social skills.

As one of the teachers explained, "We share responsibility for differentiating instruction." The classroom teacher elaborated, "It's beneficial [co-teaching] to the students. It's not always easy to work with another adult, but because it is so powerful for the students, I think it's worthwhile whatever inconvenience it might be for the teachers" (Cramer, Nevin, Salazar, & Landa, 2006).

Similarly, co-teachers who differentiated instruction in a California school reported academic gains in literacy for students both with and without disabilities. Garrigan and Thousand (2005) used a computer assisted instructional program that was developed using UDL principles to meet the needs of advanced learners, challenged learners, and English language learners. The differentiated instruction arranged by the co-teachers made it possible for students with and without disabilities to thrive:

> . . . the literacy performance of the four students with identified disabilities increased dramatically over the five months of the co-teaching intervention. . . . Pre-post intervention gains exceeded what might be expected, given their low starting performances. (Garrigan & Thousand, 2005, p. 59)

What happens to students who are gifted and talented when their teachers use differentiated instruction? Tomlinson encourages teachers to think of differentiated instruction as a way to create "classroom escalators" that take students to higher and higher levels, rather than as "stairwells" that take students to a certain grade-level landing where they stop (cited in Hess, 1999, p. 24).

In differentiated instruction, teachers provide multiple avenues to learning so that the classroom is a good fit for varied learners—including those who are advanced (Gregory & Chapman, 2002; Tomlinson, 1999).

RETROFIT AND UNIVERSAL DESIGN: ■ TWO APPROACHES TO DIFFERENTIATED INSTRUCTION

What is differentiated instruction?

We will begin to answer this question by explaining what differentiated instruction is *not*. A curriculum is not differentiated when assignments arc the same for all learners. Nor does it involve adjustments that consist of varying the level of difficulty of questions for certain students, grading some students harder than others, or letting students who finish early play games for enrichment.

Instead, differentiated instruction is a process where educators vary the learning activities, content demands, modes of assessment, and the classroom environment to meet the needs and support the growth of each child. With differentiated instruction, teachers plan different learning experiences in response to each student's needs. They develop individualized learning goals, define curricular content, structure learning activities, and conduct varied assessments that allow students to choose how to achieve the goals. Using differentiated instruction enables teachers to develop methods of teaching and learning for students of differing abilities within the same class. Teachers can maximize their students' growth and individual success by teaching each student at his or her skill level, *and* therefore assisting in the learning process. Teachers mesh their skills and knowledge about their curriculum with the training, skills, and knowledge that special educators have learned in individualizing instruction by suggesting and teaching their partner teachers to use accommodations and adaptations.

Other school personnel can add their specialized knowledge and skills to the development of differentiated instruction lessons: teachers whose students speak languages other than English, reading teachers, speech and language therapists, school psychologists, gifted and talented teachers, teachers in schools with high populations of economically disadvantaged students, guidance counselors, and so on.

As shown in Table 1.1, teachers can differentiate instruction using two major approaches: (1) *retrofitting*, or (2) *universal design for learning.*

We recognize that the inclusion of a **retrofitting** process in a discussion of differentiation of instruction might not mesh with everyone's concept of differentiation because it is a reactive rather than a proactive approach. Retrofitting is what happens when we realize that a process is not working and so decide to remodel rather than gather facts about our students and reconceptualize or redesign the content, process, and product demands from scratch (i.e., older buildings that are retrofitted with ramps to make them accessible for people in wheelchairs).

Table 1.1   Two Approaches to Differentiated Instruction

Reactive Retrofit	Proactive Universal Design for Learning
Content Demands	Gather Facts About the Learner(s)
Process Demands	Use differentiated instruction to design:
Product Demands	Content Demands
Facts About the Learner(s)	Product Demands
Discover mismatches & use differentiated instruction to address any mismatches between facts about the learners and the content, process, and product demands of the classroom	Process Demands

Retrofitting the preexisting curriculum and methods is what most teachers try to do to meet the needs of their students with disabilities. But retrofitting the curriculum tries to find a solution *after* the fact in order to fit the student into the existing program. We acknowledge that the readers of this book may be in different stages in terms of creating differentiated classrooms. Retrofitting provides a process and place to begin for those of you who are just beginning to think about differentiation. We celebrate your decision to employ a retrofit approach rather than sending students away to other environments. (Chapter 2 illustrates the use of a retrofit approach in elementary, middle, and secondary school classrooms.)

In contrast, differentiating instruction can now benefit from what is known as *universal design for learning* (UDL). UDL is an educational application of universal design principles developed and used by architects, product designers, engineers, and environmental design researchers to make products, communications, and the physical environment usable to as many people as possible at little or no extra cost.

Here, UDL will be used to refer to the creation of differentiated learning experiences that minimize the need for modifications for particular circumstances or individuals (Meyer & Rose, 2002; Udvari-Solner, 1996). Because of the unique levels of readiness, differing interests, and varying learning styles of the students who enter our classrooms every day, Tomlinson (1999) encourages the use of instruction by design in curriculum development, instructional delivery, and assessment to facilitate meaningful and effective differentiated instruction not only for students perceived as disabled, at risk, or gifted, but also for "allegedly average" students. In this way, a universal design approach to differentiated instruction can be seen to extend the promise of individualized goals for instruction to all students.

According to Hall (2002), teachers who use differentiated instruction recognize and react *responsively* to their students' varying background knowledge, readiness levels, language skills, preferences in learning, and interests. Using the

UDL approach creates and designs products and environments so that they can be used *without* modifications. In Chapters 3 through 7 of this book, we take you through a step-by-step process developed by the Center for Applied Special Technology (CAST) (2006) and elaborated for teacher educators by Udvari-Solner (1996) at the University of Wisconsin. This process will help you apply UDL principles to help provide all students with multiple means of *representation,* multiple means of *engagement,* and multiple means of *expression.*

To initiate a universal design approach, educators first gather facts about their learners and think about three distinct curriculum access points—content, process, and product (Tomlinson, 1999).

The *content* access design point concerns what is taught and what we want students to learn, know, and do. Educators must keep content standards front and center as they consider how to facilitate access at the curriculum content design point. A key aspect of content is determining the appropriate entry point for various learners into the content. Here, educators may consider how to integrate curriculum across the disciplines, or how to include the teaching of responsibility, peacemaking, and self-determination as part of the curriculum.

The *product* access design point concerns how students demonstrate what is learned and how their products are assessed. At this point, instructors may consider how student learning preferences can be used by students to show what they have learned and how to augment standardized assessment with authentic assessment approaches.

The *process* access design point concerns how students go about making sense of what they are learning. Here, teachers may consider how technology and peer-mediated instructional approaches could be incorporated into instruction.

Table 1.1 summarizes the differences and similarities between the retrofit and the UDL approaches. The basic and most salient difference is that the retrofit process begins after the lesson plans have already been completed and the lesson is underway.

In contrast, the UDL approach starts with facts about the learners and designs content, product, and process to match the learners' characteristics, thus decreasing the need for retrofitting. This can be done at any time during the school year. Typically the level of planning is more intensive at the beginning when teachers are "getting to know" their students. However, with increased mobility of the student population, teachers can expect to handle "new students" at any time during the year—thus requiring a continuous process of getting to know students.

When teachers use UDL to differentiate instruction, they are assured that their curriculum has been designed based on the individual needs of the students in their diverse classrooms. The curriculum has built-in means for the teacher to present the subject matter so that each student can have meaningful access to it using his or her abilities and strengths, without first having to overcome the usual physical, affective, or cognitive barriers, or without having to be stigmatized by, or isolated from, the other students.

With UDL, teachers are assured that even those students who have physical, sensory, or cognitive disabilities will be able to learn some or all of the same lessons as the other students. From the teacher's point of view, having materials with built-in accommodations saves time and energy. When adaptations or accommodations are not provided to teachers, they must resort to retrofitting by either creating all the accommodations themselves—an unrealistic expectation—or experiencing much more difficulty in teaching their students.

■ OVERVIEW OF THE BOOK

The remaining chapters in this book will lead you through the process of how to differentiate instruction. Chapter 2 will follow the school lives of several students whose teachers use the retrofit approach. Chapter 3 will discuss the UDL approach as well as a lesson plan format that has been helpful in designing, implementing, and evaluating differentiated instruction lessons.

Chapter 4 will serve as a guide as to how to gather facts about the learners you teach. Chapter 5 will discuss how to differentiate access to the content of learning. Chapter 6 will discuss differentiating the products of learning or how the students will show what they know. Chapter 7 will detail the methods to differentiate the process of learning.

In Chapter 8, we emphasize the importance of collaborative planning, while in Chapter 9 we discuss collaborative teaching to accomplish differentiation of instruction using the UDL approach.

In Chapters 10 through 13, we put it all together by examining the UDL approach to differentiating education for lessons through four different scenarios involving those students introduced in Chapter 2: elementary social studies for Kevin (Chapter 10), middle school mathematics for Rosa (Chapter 11), middle school science for Tina (Chapter 12), and high school language arts for Chang (Chapter 13).

Chapter 14 summarizes our basic assumptions and offers advice for sustaining the work involved in differentiating instruction. We hope that as a result of reading this book and working in collaboration with others, both retrofitting and the UDL processes will help make differentiated instruction more manageable for both teachers and administrators.

Throughout the book, we utilize tables and charts as one method to explain differentiated instruction. The tables and charts can be used to provide visual referents for the text information—an accommodation to assist in comprehension.

Textual scaffolding may be found in the organization of a text and includes features such as content webs for each chapter, headings, introductions, summaries, and tables. We hope the text-scaffolding techniques will help to make the selection more reader-friendly (Van Den Broek & Kremer, 2000) in addition to providing a model of how teachers might use text scaffolding for their own learners.

We hope as you complete your journey toward differentiating instruction that you will be better prepared to address the instructional needs of today's diverse array of learners. In this way, all of us can agree with Alvin Toffler's remark that introduced this chapter: "Learning is the process of preparing to deal with new situations."

EMERGING RESEARCH AND RESOURCES ■

There is an emerging research base that supports the UDL approach. CAST (2006) has sponsored several projects to implement UDL in K–12 settings. Some research studies that assess UDL techniques in the classroom indicate promising results to more fairly determine what students with disabilities really know. The database for differentiated instruction builds on the well-established research basis for effective teaching practices. In fact, if teachers design assessments using universal design principals, they may obtain more fair and accurate tests of what their students with disabilities actually know.

Teachers and researchers worked together to compare and contrast two delivery methods (the pencil and paper method versus computer-assisted read-a-loud method) for two equivalent forms of a National Assessment of Educational Progress United States history and civics test (Dolan, Hall, Banerjec, Chun, & Strangman, 2005). For questions with reading passages greater than 100 words in length, students with learning disabilities who took the computer-assisted read-aloud version of the tests did better than their counterparts who used pencil and paper.

While UDL materials need not be digital, there are two well-known examples of digital designs. *WiggleWorks,* an early literacy program from Scholastic (http://teacher.scholastic.com/products/wiggleworks/index.htm), builds and design features that allow children with many different abilities and disabilities to learn together. For example, all of the text can be enlarged, changed in color or highlighting, or read aloud by the computer. With *WiggleWorks,* children can navigate the software's learning activities via mouse or keyboard, and children with significant motor disabilities can turn on a built-in scanning feature via a single switch.

In Microsoft's *Encarta '98 for Windows,* video and audio are used to make many concepts clearer than text alone could do. Moreover, for students who are deaf, every video and audio is captioned using Microsoft's SAMI technology.

2

Accessing the General Education Curriculum Through a Retrofit Framework

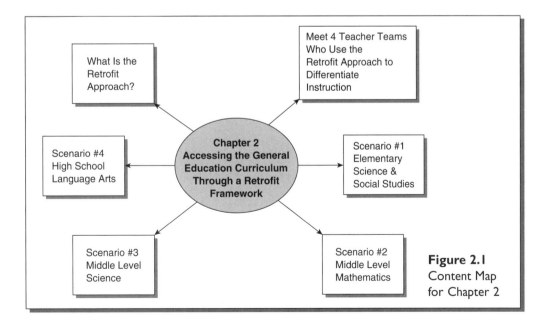

Figure 2.1 Content Map for Chapter 2

Learning results should be considered in terms of understanding the "big ideas" and core processes within the content standards.

—Wiggins and McTighe (2005)

The kinds of students that we have in our nation's classrooms are becoming increasingly diverse. Educators who were once accustomed to sending students with different learning preferences and academic, communication, and behavioral differences to separate classes and programs are now wrestling with how to absorb these students into their classrooms and facilitate their access to, and progress in, core curriculum content and standards. We believe that it is our responsibility as teachers to ensure that *all* learners grasp the big ideas and experience the core instructional processes within the content standards, as suggested by Wiggins and McTighe (2005).

In this chapter, you will find the answers to the following questions:

- What should you know about using a retrofit approach to provide students with access to the general education curriculum?
- In what ways might classroom teachers differentiate instruction for students using the retrofit approach?

Retrofit is one of two approaches used by educators to meet the diverse needs of learners in mixed-ability classrooms. A retrofit approach assists educators in designing ways to correct the mismatch between the skills of particular learners and the way we traditionally have made the content, process, and products of education accessible to students in general.

Since the word "retrofit" is derived from architecture, an architectural analogy may help to clarify the term. Think of a school building that was built in the 1960s. Was that building constructed to be accessible to all learners? Of course, the answer is no. Today, however, that building would be made accessible performing a retrofit: widening the doorways, changing the bathroom configurations, adding an elevator, and so on. A retrofit approach works but it is costly in labor, material, time, and dollars because you are redoing much of the work that was done when the building was first constructed.

Similarly, educators may need to apply a retrofit approach when students enter a classroom and encounter preexisting conditions that do not allow them to access the general education curriculum (for example, when a student who reads independently at a third grade reading level encounters a textbook that is written at a sixth grade reading level). In a retrofit approach, teachers alter preexisting curriculum and instructional and assessment methods to assist students to access the curriculum. Educators are making accommodations and modifications to support learners who enter a classroom where there are preexisting conditions such as particular materials, and a typical way of delivering instruction and assessing students.

In order for educators to maximize the retrofit approach to correct the mismatch between learners and the demands of a classroom, they must compare information about the particular student with the content, process, and product demands of their classroom.

It is important to note that in order to be successful, they must gather facts about the student's strengths as well as his or her challenges. Historically, many educators have gathered facts about the student's perceived deficits and either ignored or downplayed gathering of positive information about that same student. We contend that so long as educators focus only on a student's perceived deficits, they will not have all the information that they need to motivate and educate someone who is struggling to learn. By gathering information about a student's strengths, learning styles and preferences, multiple intelligences, and interests as well as about the demands of their classroom, they will then have the facts necessary to identify and address potential mismatches. Table 2.1 illustrates the data that a team might collect and use to help them identify and address any potential mismatches through a retrofit approach.

To illustrate the power of a retrofit approach in addressing mismatches between the facts about learners and the classroom's demands, we introduce you to four co-teaching teams and one student of each team who is struggling to learn. We then discuss how the co-teaching team addresses the mismatches by examining the facts about the learner and retrofitting the content, process, or product demands.

All four teams eventually recognized that they could not change the facts about the learners overnight, but that they could adapt content, process, and product demands so that each of these learners could successfully participate and learn in a general education classroom. Table 2.2 introduces you to these four pairs of co-teachers at a glance, as well as their respective student of concern.

SCENARIO #1: ELEMENTARY SCIENCE ■ AND SOCIAL STUDIES

Mr. Gleason is a fourth grade science and social studies teacher. He has been teaching for eight years and has recently relocated from another state and is

Table 2.1   Gathering the Facts About the Learner and the Classroom Demands

Facts About the Learner	Facts About the Classroom Demands
Strengths Background Knowledge & Experiences Interests Learning Style(s) Multiple Intelligences Important Relationships Other: _____ Other: _____	Content Demands How is the content made available 　to the learners?
	Process Demands What processes do the teachers use 　to facilitate student learning?
Goals Does this learner have any unique goals 　related to academic learning, communication, 　English language acquisition, and/or 　social-emotional functioning? Are there particular concerns about this learner?	Product Demands How do the students demonstrate 　what they have learned? How are they graded?

Table 2.2   Meet the Co-teachers and Students

Co-teachers	Grade Level	Subject Area(s)	Student
Mr. Gleason, Classroom Teacher; Ms. Villalobos, Special Education Teacher	Fourth	Science Social Studies	Kevin
Mr. Jupp, Math Teacher; Mr. Dondero, Gifted & Talented Teacher	Middle Level	Math	Rosa
Ms. Swanson, Classroom Teacher; Ms. Tac, Speech/Language Therapist	Middle Level	Science	Tina
Ms. Griffith, Classroom Teacher; Ms. Lang, English Language Learning Teacher	High School	Language Arts	Chang

beginning his first year in a new elementary school. He has had some prior co-teaching experience in his previous school and was informed that co-teaching played a large part in his new school. Mr. Gleason is looking forward to establishing a collegial relationship with his co-teacher, Ms. Villalobos.

Ms. Villalobos is a special education teacher who has worked in the school for ten years. She has been actively collaborating with general education teachers in planning and co-teaching at the school for the past five years. The various teachers with whom she has collaborated during this time have differed in their willingness and capacity for co-teaching and making adaptations for struggling learners.

At their first planning meeting, Ms. Villalobos asks Mr. Gleason to identify students in his class with whom he is concerned. Mr. Gleason names several students. However, he is particularly concerned about Kevin. Kevin frequently walks out of class, never completes homework, refuses to participate in some activities, and is failing the class. Mr. Gleason notes that he sees the same problematic behaviors from Kevin in both his science and social studies classes.

Ms. Villalobos asks Mr. Gleason what Kevin *can do,* how he learns, what he likes about school, which students in the class are his friends, what kinds of activities support his learning, and what his interests and strengths are. Mr. Gleason replies that because it is relatively early in the school year, he does not know Kevin well, and so cannot answer those questions.

Mr. Gleason asks Ms. Villalobos if Kevin might have a disability or a low IQ. Ms. Villalobos responds that Kevin does indeed have a learning disability and is eligible for special education. Ms. Villalobos encourages Mr. Gleason to find a solution by focusing on Kevin's strengths rather than his perceived deficits. Ms. Villalobos notes they will never have enough information to help Kevin learn if they focus only on the areas where he is struggling. She suggests that they gather information about his strengths, interests, and how he best learns. They agree to this approach and a further meeting.

At their next meeting, they discuss the results of their information gathering, including Kevin's strengths, and their ongoing concerns. Ms. Villalobos shows Mr. Gleason Kevin's IEP goals for reading, his small group social skills, and how he manages stress. They agree that these goals are appropriate for Kevin, based on what they have learned about him. Ms. Villalobos asks Mr. Gleason to describe how he makes the classroom content available, the processes he uses to teach, and how students in his classes demonstrate what they have learned. The co-teachers then address the questions that appear in Table 2.1 and then summarize this information in four columns as shown in Table 2.2.

(Note that the first two columns of Table 2.3 are abbreviated forms of the "Facts About the Learner" and "Facts About Class Demands" from Table 2.1. The third column is for the co-teachers to identify potential mismatches between facts about Kevin and facts about class demands. The fourth column is for recording ideas for resolving mismatches.)

Upon review of the facts about Kevin and the classroom demands, Mr. Gleason and Ms. Villalobos note several mismatches.

What mismatches do you identify? Please feel free to record your own observations of mismatches in the third column of Table 2.3.

After recording mismatches, Mr. Gleason and Ms. Villalobos agree to brainstorm at least three possible solutions for each of the mismatches between the facts about Kevin and the content, process, and product demands of the classroom. You can help them by listing your own solutions to the following challenges. Again, feel free to record your ideas and your answers to the following questions in the fourth column of Table 2.3.

- In what ways might they address the mismatch between Kevin's failure to do homework and the types and amount of homework assigned?
- In what ways might you handle Kevin when he walks out of class?
- In what ways might you use Kevin's strengths to remedy the mismatches?
- In what ways might you address the mismatch between the task demands associated with oral reading, the independent research paper, and Kevin's outcome measures as is indicated by his failing grades on the tests and quizzes? (The task demands on tests and quizzes might need to be adjusted.)

The list of solutions brainstormed by Mr. Gleason and Ms. Villalobos appears in Table 2.4.

Following the brainstorming activity, Ms. Villalobos and Mr. Gleason compare Kevin's strengths to their brainstormed list to be sure that they have capitalized upon his strengths in order to capture his interests. Also, they want to allow him to learn and demonstrate what he learns in ways that represent his learning preferences.

Please review Kevin's strengths and the brainstormed list in Table 2.4:

- Which of Kevin's strengths are used to address the mismatch between the facts about Kevin and facts about the classroom demands?
- What are additional ways to use his strengths and learning preferences to support his learning in Mr. Gleason's classroom?

Table 2.3 Student and Class Summary for Kevin

Facts About the Student Name: Kevin	Facts About the Class/Lesson Class: Science/Social Studies	Mismatches Between Student Facts and Class/Lesson Facts	Potential Solutions to Mismatches Between Facts
Strengths/Interests: Stamp collecting Story telling **Learning Style(s):** Auditory learner **Multiple Intelligences:** Visual/spatial Interpersonal **Important Relationships:** Jose and Francisco, both of whom are in the class **Other:** Relates well with younger students Likes being in a leadership role Good decision maker when given choices **Goals/Concerns:** Reads and writes independently at second grade level Walks out when frustrated Refuses to participate in oral reading activities Fail quizzes and tests Doesn't do homework	**Content Demands:** Both science and social studies texts have a fourth grade readability level. Following teacher lecture, the students take turns reading orally, up and down the rows, from the textbook. **Process Demands** Teacher lecture Oral reading Independently answering, with short written answers, the questions from the textbook Small group activities one day a month to review previously taught content **Product Demands:** Published tests Teacher-designed quizzes Short written answers to questions from text. Start in class; complete unfinished as homework Each student selects a topic for an independent report from either science or social studies. **How are students graded?** Quizzes and tests with preset mastery criteria Homework and report reviewed by teacher; grades assigned		

Table 2.4   Brainstormed Solutions to Address Mismatches Between Kevin and the Content, Process, and Product Demands of the Fourth Grade Science and Social Studies Classes

Doesn't Do Homework

Don't assign Kevin homework.

Change the name from homework to "home fun."

Ask him why he doesn't do the homework.

Provide him with material he can read for homework.

Give him the questions on audiotape and allow him to dictate his answers.

Provide him with support through a homework club or homework buddy before school, at lunchtime, or after school.

Create a homework menu from which he selects a homework option.

Create a contingency contract and reward him for doing his homework.

Make him the homework monitor.

Assign him a homework buddy who calls him on the phone and records their collective answers to the questions.

Hold a student-parent-teacher conference.

Walks Out of Class When Frustrated

When you sense that he is frustrated, send him on a mission; legitimize his leaving class.

Teach him to monitor breathing, pulse rate, sweating in his palms and have him signal when he is frustrated so he can think about what has led up to the frustration and change it.

Initially allow him to leave four times a week and gradually decrease the amount of times he can leave the class.

Assign him more leadership roles within the class.

Create an in-class time-out space where he can go rather than leaving the class.

Structure more cooperative group assignments.

Oral Reading From a Textbook That is Too Difficult

Stop oral reading up and down the rows.

Rehearse with Kevin the content that he will be assigned to read.

Arrange for him to read with a partner

Use "Literature Circles."

Do choral or echo reading.

Ask him to paraphrase or summarize what has been said thus far when it is his turn to read.

Teach reading in the content area.

Assign him the role of randomly calling on students to read thereby breaking up the predictability of who will read when.

Independent Research Paper

Assign the paper as a partner or group product.

Change the format—allow oral or PowerPoint presentations, create posters or other visual representations.

Allow Kevin to teach what he has learned to younger students.

Chunk it—meet with him periodically throughout the year to review the parts that are done.

Failing Grades on Tests and Quizzes

Test Kevin orally.

Hold him accountable for less information.

Place less weight on tests and quizzes.

Refuses to Do Some Tasks

Ask Kevin why he does not do those tasks.

Collect data to see which tasks he refuses to participate in.

Increase the use of partner and group work.

Allow him to select one task a day that he does not want to do.

Vary tasks and allow choice so that students with various strengths have an opportunity to use them.

As they discuss their solutions for Kevin, Mr. Gleason tells Ms. Villalobos that knowing Kevin's disability type and his IQ score would not help him address mismatches between Kevin and classroom demands. He acknowledges that comparing the content, process, and product demands of his class with the strength-based and goal-related information they have about Kevin has provided them the information they need to address Kevin's difficulties.

Ms. Villalobos and Mr. Gleason then develop criteria for selecting from among their brainstormed list the best strategies for helping Kevin. What criteria would you develop to judge an idea to be "good" for an accommodation, modification, or change in class demands?

Ms. Villalobos and Mr. Gleason developed the following criteria and applied them to their list:

- Is the accommodation reasonable and manageable?
- Will the idea empower and not humiliate the student?
- Will the idea be neutral or positive in terms of its impact on the learning of other students in the class?
- Is the idea likely to work?
- Is the idea student generated or student validated?

To ensure that the fifth criterion—whether the idea was student generated or student validated—would be used, Mr. Gleason suggests that he and Ms. Villalobos meet with Kevin to share their brainstormed list and ask Kevin which ideas he thought would work for him and to see what additional ideas of his own he might have. Mr. Gleason thanks Ms. Villalobos for guiding him through the strength-based retrofit approach and says he is eager to meet with Kevin to create a "short list" to put into action.

■ SCENARIO # 2: MIDDLE LEVEL MATHEMATICS

Mr. Jupp is a veteran middle level math teacher who prefers to teach alone. To help reach the school district's goal of complying with the No Child Left Behind Act's requirement that all students have access to highly qualified teachers, he is welcoming a more diverse group of students to his classroom, as well as support personnel to assist both him and his students through collaborative planning and teaching.

Mr. Dondero, a teacher who is certified to work with students who are gifted and talented, has had a variety of jobs in the district. He has been assigned to co-teach with Mr. Jupp. While Mr. Dondero is an upbeat professional who is quite popular with the administration, families, students, and faculty, he has, however, never co-taught. Therefore, he looks forward with some trepidation to co-teaching with Mr. Jupp.

After their first three days of teaching together, they realize that one of the students, Rosa, is disrupting the entire class, requires a fair amount of both teachers' time, and is not doing well on the class assignments. They both acknowledge that having two teachers in the classroom allows one of them to continue to teach while the other intervenes with Rosa. They decide to gather information about Rosa and compare it with their content, process, and product demands to discover if a mismatch exists. They used the same four-column format as Kevin's co-teachers used. (See Table 2.5 for the information they gathered.)

After reviewing the data, they discover several mismatches. They decide to change some of the content, process, and product demands in hopes of reducing Rosa's disruptive behavior and enhance her and the other students' learning experience.

- What mismatches do you identify? Please feel free to record your own observations of mismatches in the third column of Table 2.5.
- In what ways might they address each of the mismatches? Please feel free to record your ideas for resolving mismatches in the fourth column of Table 2.5.

Using the information in Table 2.5 and their own list of mismatches, Mr. Jupp and Mr. Dondero brainstorm the ideas listed in Table 2.6.

- What criteria would you use to judge which of these ideas to implement with Rosa in Mr. Jupp's mathematics class?
- Which ideas are ones that meet your criteria and capitalize upon Rosa's interests and strengths?

SCENARIO #3: MIDDLE LEVEL SCIENCE ■

Ms. Swanson, a middle level science teacher in her second year of teaching, has firm mastery of the curriculum content. She has, however, great difficulty establishing discipline and facilitating her students' learning of the content. She is concerned about poor test results, daily discipline referrals to the office, parental and administrative complaints about her classroom, and the sheer exhaustion she feels at the end of the day. She had taught a different science course to most of the students in her class the previous year. She is upset to hear that this year she will not only be assigned a co-teacher to help her establish better discipline and ensure more effective teaching, but she will also be assigned Tina, a student who has more significant disabilities than any student Ms. Swanson has ever taught.

Ms. Tac is a speech-language therapist who has been assigned to co-teach with Ms. Swanson. She has previously co-taught with both math and science teachers at the middle level. She has experience teaching a wide range of students with communication, cognitive, academic, and behavioral difficulties. She knows that Ms. Swanson is reticent about co-teaching with another professional.

At their first planning meeting, Ms. Swanson states that she does not believe a student like Tina should be in a general education classroom. Having taught most of the students the previous year, Ms. Swanson shares with Ms. Tac that these students are probably the "dumbest group of students" that Ms. Tac

Table 2.5 Student and Class Summary for Rosa

Facts About the Student Name: _Rosa_	Facts About the Class/Lesson Class: _Mathematics_	Mismatches Between Student Facts and Class/Lesson Facts	Potential Solutions to Mismatches Between Facts
Strengths Background Knowledge & Experiences: Recently arrived from Nicaragua Interests and Skills: Bilingual & bi-literate in Spanish & English Sense of humor Empathetic Relates well with younger students Multiple Intelligences: Verbal/linguistic Musical/rhythmic Bodily/kinesthetic Important Relationships: Best friend, Chris, not in any of her classes Grandmother (_abuela_) Other: Refuses to do board work Outbursts place herself and others in danger; throws objects (e.g., emery board, nail polish, pens) Surreptitiously listens to iPod Primps (e.g., polishes nails in class) Bilingual cursing and swearing New to the community **Goals/Concerns** Difficulty with impulsivity control Forgets social skills when frustrated with either students or adults. Easily frustrated Has difficulty completing work Reads English 2 years below grade level Math skills spotty due to frequent moves. Tests 2–3 years below grade level	**Content Demands** Content made available by teacher lecture and teacher and student demonstration on board or overhead transparency State adopted grade-level math textbook in English **Process Demands** Teacher models solving new material Student volunteers selected to put answers on the board. Two or three high-achieving students usually selected to model solving of problems similar to those solved by the teacher on the board, with immediate public correction, if needed. Students begin independent practice in class. Uncompleted portions assigned for homework. **Product Demands:** Four nights a week, assigned odd-numbered homework problems from the book (20 problems a night) **How are students graded?** Weekly quizzes on Friday Unit exams Statewide math assessment exam		

24

Table 2.6   Brainstormed Solutions to Address Mismatches Between Rosa and Facts About Demands of the Middle Level Mathematics Classroom

1. Meet with Rosa and her grandmother to determine the communicative intent of her behavior.

2. Develop a behavioral contract with Rosa, with grandmother's involvement.

3. Contract has an element where she can listen to her iPod at the end of the class, contingent upon behavioral success.

4. Rosa could earn time for the entire class to listen to music at the end of the class.

5. Supply her with an algebra text with a lower readability level.

6. Supply her with a grade-level algebra text in Spanish.

7. During study period, tutor Spanish-speaking students who are struggling in math.

8. Consider transferring Chris into this algebra section and seating him next to Rosa.

9. Start small with some cooperative group learning activities such as think-pair-share activities.

10. Play music of student choice for groups during group work.

11. Strategically seat students with Rosa who are proficient and supportive.

12. Rehearse board problems with her to prepare her.

13. Move her seat to the front of the room.

14. Have the co-teacher observe Rosa to determine the antecedents, frequency of behaviors, and consequences.

15. Consider alternate ways for students to show what they learn in ways that tap into musical talents (e.g., show equation solutions via bodily/kinesthetic or music such as a rap).

16. Set class norms regarding iPods, cosmetics, and perfumes.

17. Because she is empathetic, talk to Rosa about the negative impact of perfume on classmates who are sensitive or allergic.

18. Set class norms for "respectful" language.

19. Reduce the number of homework problems for Rosa, at least in the short term, to get her going on doing some homework.

20. Get white boards for all the students to use for recording and showing their work.

21. Create homework groups and distribute the number of problems (i.e., each group of 4 students is assigned 5 out of a group of 20 problems to solve and then prepare to model and explain the next day during homework review).

22. Infuse social skills into instruction through setting up of cooperative groups.

23. Podcast some of the lessons.

will ever be likely to encounter. Ms. Tac asks why Ms. Swanson feels that way. Ms. Swanson says that "they are just plain slow," and everything must be repeated over and over. The teachers decide to begin their co-teaching journey slowly by having Ms. Tac observe the class for a few days.

At their second planning meeting, Ms. Tac shares her observations as well as assessment data she has gathered. Together, they review the information in Table 2.7. Ms. Tac suggests that the two of them apply a retrofit approach to address the mismatch between the facts about Tina and the content, process, and product demands of the classroom.

- What mismatches do you identify between Tina's characteristics and the class demands in science? Please feel free to record your own observations of mismatches in the third column of Table 2.7.
- In what ways might Ms. Swanson and Ms. Tac address each mismatch? Please feel free to record your ideas for resolving each mismatch in the fourth column of Table 2.7.

Although skeptical, Ms. Swanson agrees to try a retrofit approach to differentiate instruction for Tina. They agree to meet with Tina, her father, and one of the instructional assistants with whom Tina has had a long-term relationship. Tina's father explains, and the instructional assistant verifies, that Tina is a student who grasps information quickly. However, it can take her ten minutes or more to generate two to three sentences on her computer. She does not type unless her dad or an assistant with whom she is familiar and comfortable is seated next to her with a hand placed on her shoulder. Her father explains that, in the past, many educators made unwarranted assumptions about Tina's capabilities because she is nonverbal, does not make eye contact, wrings her hands, and rocks her body.

Tina's father describes previous unsuccessful attempts to provide Tina with a communication system (e.g., sign language, communication books and boards). But when Facilitated Communication[1] was implemented, Tina began to type words, at first only with her father and then with a trusted teacher or paraprofessional. The method that initially worked was for the supporting adult to provide resistance at her wrist as Tina typed. When Tina typed that she wanted to learn to type without that support, the IEP team added that to her IEP goals. At this point in time, Tina is not yet typing independently, but has made progress. Instead of needing resistance at her wrist when typing, she now only needs the facilitating person to place a hand on her shoulder.

After the meeting, Ms. Swanson acknowledges that perhaps Tina could successfully participate in her class. Ms. Swanson and Ms. Tac add a number of new ideas to their initial list for addressing the mismatches between Tina and the classroom demands. After examining these ideas, Ms. Swanson agrees to start with four changes listed in Table 2.8 that she thinks would benefit and provide alternative access options to all students (e.g., requiring wait time after asking their students questions). She is so encouraged by the positive outcomes that, after three weeks, she agrees to work with Ms. Tac to figure out how to implement the remaining seven changes.

Table 2.7 Student and Class Summary for Tina

Facts About the Student Name: _Tina_	Facts About the Class/Lesson Class: _Science_	Mismatches Between Student Facts and Class/Lesson Facts	Potential Solutions to Mismatches Between Facts
Strengths Background Knowledge and Experiences: Previously assigned to self-contained classrooms with limited access to the general education curriculum Prior attempts to develop a communication system (e.g., communication board, sign language) have not worked Interests: Enjoys Internet research Likes music and poetry Learning Style(s): Auditory and multisensory learner Uses Facilitated Communication Uses a computer with portable printer Slow response time Multiple Intelligences: Verbal/linguistic Logical/mathematical Musical/Rhythmic	**Content Demands** Teacher lecture Reading from the textbook **Process Demands** Lecture Student note taking of lecture Extensive use of worksheets Students assigned 7- to 10-step tasks without written reminders or questioning for understanding No hands-on activities No projects No group work **Product Demands** Rapid fire questions with no think time Frequent use of tests and quizzes Competitive goal structure (i.e., grading on a curve) Other: Frequent behavioral disruptions in class		

(Continued)

Table 2.7 (Continued)

Facts About the Student Name: _Tina_	Facts About the Class/Lesson Class: _Science_	Mismatches Between Student Facts and Class/Lesson Facts	Potential Solutions to Mismatches Between Facts
Important Relationships: Father and two instructional assistants with whom she has had long-term trusting relationships **Other:** Grasps material quickly Nonverbal Tactilely defensive, does not like to be touched Engages in hand-wringing and body-rocking behavior Limited eye contact with others Frightened of tests Dislikes homework **Goals/Concerns** Provide increased opportunities to establish peer relationships Enhance communication via assistive technology (e.g., voice to speech) Tantrums when bored, frustrated, or stressed Low tolerance for misbehavior of fellow classmates	Repeated explanation of content in response to students saying they don't understand the content or assigned tasks. Teacher loses patience and blows up (i.e., yells) when students continue to ask for clarification. Students seem to enjoy the teacher's losing patience. It is not clear if they do not understand the task or are purposefully frustrating the teacher.		

Table 2.8   Brainstormed Solutions to Address Mismatches Between Tina and Facts About Demands of the Middle Level Science Classroom

1. Get an LCD projector for the classroom. Scan worksheets, quizzes, tests, and so forth into Tina's computer and hook it up to the projector.

2. For homework, provide Tina with a minimum of two questions that she will be asked during class the next day; have her type her responses so when she is asked the questions during class, she can project her typed answer on a screen for everyone to read.

3. Ask some questions that students, including Tina, can respond to quickly through a signal to indicate whether something is true or false.

4. Institute a 3- to 5-second wait/think period between the time when a question is asked and when students are called on to answer.

5. Reduce the amount of class work and homework that Tina is expected to complete, but be sure to give her the more sophisticated questions to address.

6. If the volume of the class is too loud for Tina, allow her to move to an auditory learning station where she can listen to enrichment activities on headphones.

7. Be mindful of traffic patterns and be strategic about where Tina is assigned to sit and which students are seated next to her.

8. Reduce the amount of worksheet activities.

9. Increase the frequency of hands-on activities and partner and group work.

10. Change from grading on a curve (norm-referenced) to grading for mastery of preset criteria (criterion-referenced). Create grading rubrics with the class. Determine at a later time if Tina will need a different rubric and, if so, include it within her IEP.

11. Develop classroom rules and set consequences for breaking the rules with the students. Assign Tina the role of monitoring students' adherence, including her own, to classroom rules.

After six weeks of implementing all eleven strategies, Ms. Swanson has stopped referring to this class as "just plain slow." She even made a special trip to her principal's office to report, "Having Tina in my class has been the best thing that has ever happened to me for my own professional growth. It is so exciting to see how Tina's classmates know how to communicate with her. Now we all know how smart she really is. By becoming a better teacher for Tina, I am becoming a better teacher for all of my students."

SCENARIO #4: HIGH SCHOOL LANGUAGE ARTS ■

Ms. Griffith is a veteran high school language arts teacher who is passionate about her content. She welcomes Ms. Lang into her class as a co-teacher but wonders how Ms. Lang, who does not have the content mastery that she does, will help her and the students. Ms. Griffith is fluent in both English and Spanish. She has taught English language learners but they have always been Spanish speakers.

Ms. Lang, an experienced teacher of English language learners, is entering her first year working at the high school level. She has worked at both the elementary and middle school levels. In the past, she has taught students through both "pull-out" and inclusive approaches such as consultation and co-teaching.

Chang is a 16-year-old immigrant from a war-torn country in Southeast Asia who has recently arrived in the United States and is living with a foster family. He is slowly acquiring English, and his foster family does not want him placed in a pullout program. Chang has just enrolled in the school and is assigned to Ms. Griffith's Language Arts class. After observing Chang for a week, both Ms. Lang and Ms. Griffith conclude that Chang might not understand the information being presented in class.

The principal of the school has instituted a practice at faculty meetings where 10 to 15 minutes are devoted to problem solving about students. At each meeting, educators present information about a student of theirs whom they find challenging and how that student compares to the classroom demands. This allows the faculty to hear what their colleagues might suggest to differentiate their instruction for that particular student. Both Ms. Griffith and Ms. Lang think that this is a great opportunity for them to put their concerns about Chang before the entire faculty. So, they assemble and present the information in Table 2.9 to their colleagues at a faculty meeting.

At the faculty meeting, the principal thanks Ms. Griffith and Ms. Lang for volunteering to present a challenging scenario to their colleagues. Everyone is given a copy of the information just as it is presented in Table 2.9, including the columns for identifying mismatches and brainstorming solutions. After the information is quickly reviewed, the faculty is divided into teams of three or four members. Teams spend two minutes reading and discussing the perceived mismatches and they record their own ideas about the mismatches in the third column of the form.

- What mismatches do you identify? Please feel free to record your own observations of mismatches in the third column of Table 2.9.
  Team members then spend an additional five minutes brainstorming ways to address the mismatches, recording the solutions in the fourth column.
- In what ways might they address each of the mismatches? Please feel free to record your ideas for resolving mismatches in the fourth column of Table 2.9.

At the end of the allotted time, the brainstormed lists are presented to Ms. Griffith and Ms. Lang. Following a review of the more than 100 different ideas generated by their colleagues, Ms. Lang and Ms. Griffith select 10 ways to change the content, process, and product demands of their instruction (shown in Table 2.10).

■ WHAT DO YOU KNOW ABOUT RETROFITTING AS A WAY TO DIFFERENTIATE INSTRUCTION?

Now that you have spent time studying four co-teaching teams who have wrestled with tough issues regarding mismatches between student characteristics

Table 2.9 Student and Class Summary for Chang

Facts About the Learner Name: Chang	Facts About Class/Lesson Class: Language Arts	Mismatches Between Student Facts and Class and Lesson Facts	Potential Solutions to Mismatches Between Facts
Strengths Background Knowledge and Experiences: Recently arrived from a war-torn country in Southeast Asia Interests: Soccer & volleyball Playing cards & artistic painting Learning Style(s): Relies on phonetic structure to decode Multiple Intelligences: Naturalist Logical/Mathematical Interpersonal Visual/Spatial Bodily/Kinesthetic Important Relationships: Two fellow students who are from the same country Mr. Johnson, guidance counselor His foster family Other: Auditory processing difficulty English language learner Very athletic Sense of humor Great personality, so appears more academically competent than he really is Popular with faculty and students Goals/Concerns: Increase English language acquisition, reading & writing	**Content Demands** Students independently read classic novels (e.g., *Animal Farm*) for homework Teacher and authors use idioms and figurative language Conceptual demands: understanding symbolism, generalize themes to real life, abstract vocabulary **Process Demands** Teacher begins class with rapid fire questions to students based upon the previous night's homework reading Lecture and whole class discussion Students assigned select passages to read to the class **Product Demands** Answer teacher-directed questions Essay tests Participation in whole-class discussions		

31

Table 2.10   Brainstormed Solutions to Address Mismatches Between Chang and Facts About Demands of the High School Language Arts Classroom

1. Allow Chang to view videos and cartoon depictions of *Animal Farm*.

2. Acquire and use a version of *Animal Farm* with a lower readability level.

3. Employ cooperative group learning structures to review content and reinforce learning.

4. After each question, give think time, then have partners discuss their answers with a peer, and then select someone from the class to answer the question.

5. Use more visuals to supplement the book.

6. Allow Chang to illustrate the content of the book.

7. Preteach idioms, figurative language, and difficult vocabulary.

8. Create a word wall.

9. Use Chang's knowledge of animals as a resource when discussing the content of the book.

10. Encourage Chang to relate his own life experiences to the totalitarian form of government represented in the book.

and the content standards, the curriculum, instruction, and assessment procedures, we invite you to ponder and respond to four questions.

Question #1:

Do you think that each of the four co-teaching teams successfully developed strategies through a retrofit approach that would address the mismatch between the learners and the content, process, and product demands of the classroom?

Question #2:

In your opinion, did each team list ideas that could support these diverse learners not just in one specific class or activity, but also in future activities and in other classes?

Question #3:

Do you feel that by working collaboratively, each team came up with ideas that one individual working alone would not?

Question #4:

In terms of the bottom line, did each team think of ideas and strategies that do not have to be limited to just these individual learners—that the solutions generated could enhance the learning of other learners in their classes as well?

As other educators who have used the retrofit approach to address student needs, we hope you, too, answered yes to each of the four questions. If so, you have acknowledged your mastery of the following essential lessons about using a retrofit approach to facilitating access to the general education curriculum:

- It is possible to correct mismatches between a student and the content, process, and product demands of a classroom through a retrofit approach to differentiate instruction.
- It gets easier over time as the solutions you generate can be used to support students in future activities.
- The keys to successfully retrofit a mismatch between students and content, process, and product demands are creativity and collaboration.
- Students who are different are a gift because they force us to collaborate and invent new solutions that are beneficial to a wide range of learners in general education classrooms, not just the students of immediate concern.

In closing this chapter, we pose a final question. As you reviewed the four scenarios, did you find yourself thinking: "But this is just one student and I have many other students in my class who are struggling to learn"? Or were you thinking: "This would be great if we had all the time in the world"?

Many educators have acknowledged the power of a retrofitting approach and expressed their concern about finding the time to apply this approach for every learner for whom there is a mismatch. We share this concern. Therefore, the remainder of this book shows you how to use an alternative approach to facilitating access to the general education curriculum and differentiation of instruction for *all* students without having to identify and deal with mismatches for each individual student. This approach, known as Universal Design for Learning (UDL), enables educators to address the needs of an entire classroom of diverse students in the most collaborative and time efficient manner.

Note

1. See www.tash.org/communication/fcreadings.htm.

3

Access to Curriculum Through Universal Design for Learning

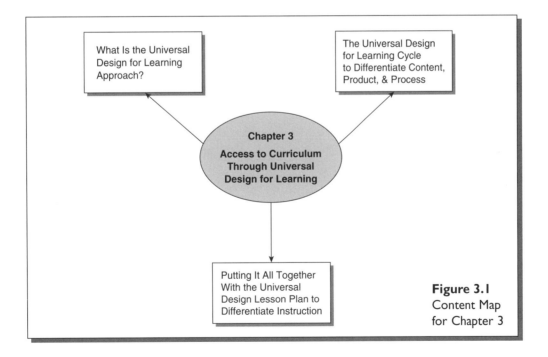

What Is the Universal Design for Learning Approach?

The Universal Design for Learning Cycle to Differentiate Content, Product, & Process

Chapter 3
Access to Curriculum Through Universal Design for Learning

Putting It All Together With the Universal Design Lesson Plan to Differentiate Instruction

Figure 3.1
Content Map for Chapter 3

The most important attitude that can be formed is that of the desire to go on learning.

—John Dewey

n this chapter, you will find the answers to the following questions:

- Why is universal design for learning (UDL) a good alternative to the retrofit approach to differentiated instruction?
- What are the design points in UDL?
- How can teachers design lesson plans by using UDL?

Collectively, we have extensive experience working with teachers doing their best to *retrofit* or alter pre-existing curriculum and instructional methods to help students to access the curriculum. As the scenarios in Chapter 2 illustrate, in a retrofit scenario, educators find themselves spending valuable time and creative energy developing individualized accommodations and modifications after the fact for any number of students. This expensive (in time and energy) retrofit approach is analogous to the earthquake retrofitting of buildings on or near fault lines or those erected before federal wheelchair access requirements. As in those situations, teachers find solutions after the fact in an attempt to fit a student into the structure that already exists.

Given state and district curriculum standards and the demands of an increasingly diverse learner population, how can teachers most efficiently design meaningful learning activities that address both the classroom standards and the educational needs of all of the students in the class without the need to retrofit lessons and units?

An alternative to retrofitting is a design approach known as *universal design.* "Universal design is a concept that refers to the creation and design of products and environments in such a way that they can be used without the need for modifications or specialized designs for particular circumstances" (Fortini & Fitzpatrick, 2000, p. 581). Curb cuts on sidewalk corners are an example of universal design. They are expensive to add after the sidewalk has already been built, but cost virtually nothing if designed in from the start. Curb cuts were originally designed to allow wheelchair access to sidewalks, but they now also ease stroller and skateboard access, and reduce faulty footing for runners and all sidewalk users.

UDL is the application of these universal design concepts to education so that the curriculum can be accessed without the need for specialized modifications and adaptations for particular students. UDL provides a way for educators to view diversity in students as a strength instead of as a problem. We have experience working with teachers who are using principles of universal design to increase access to the curriculum for all of their learners.

The rest of this chapter introduces a lesson planning cycle for applying UDL principles and also introduces the universal design lesson plan format for co-teachers to use to shift from retrofit to universal design so that students can better access the curriculum. This is not to say that curriculum retrofitting never will be needed. The authors acknowledge that sometimes a student-curriculum mismatch will not have been encountered before, so co-teachers will need to invent unique adaptations after the fact.

THE UDL CYCLE FOR DIFFERENTIATING ■ CONTENT, PRODUCT, AND PROCESS

The starting point for educators who apply a UDL framework is to gather facts about the diverse learners in their classroom. With that information in mind, materials, methods, and assessment options are considered and created in advance. Figure 3.2 represents the four primary design points of the UDL Lesson Plan Cycle to Differentiate Instruction—student facts, content, product, and process.

This cycle helps teachers think about their work in a different way. After gathering information about the learners, educators think about three additional distinct "access design points"—content, product, and process (Tomlinson, 2001a).

- The *content* access design point is focused on what is taught and what we want students to learn.
- The *product* access design point is focused on how students might demonstrate what is learned and how it is assessed.
- The *process* access design point is focused on how teachers might structure classroom-learning activities in ways that match how their students go about making sense of what they are learning.

Using a Universal Design Lesson Plan template will automatically lead to differentiation of instruction because the template suggests multiple representations of content, multiple ways for students to express or represent what they have learned, and varied ways to facilitate student learning. Table 3.1 shows these four design points translated into an easy-to-use lesson plan template to guide the planning, implementation, evaluation, and design of effective differentiated lessons.

Figure 3.2   UDL Lesson Plan Cycle

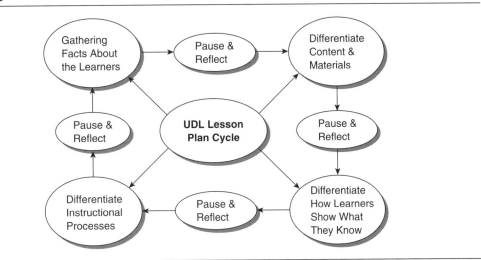

Table 3.1 Co-teaching Universal Design Lesson Plan Template

PLANNING PHASE		
Lesson Topic and Name: _____	Content Area(s) Focus: _____	
Step #1: Facts About the Student Learners		
Who are our students and how do they learn?		
What are our students' various strengths, languages, cultural backgrounds, learning styles, and interests?		
What are our students' various multiple intelligences (i.e., verbal/linguistic, logical/mathematical, visual/spatial, musical/rhythmic, bodily/kinesthetic, interpersonal, intrapersonal, naturalist)		
What forms of communication (e.g., assistive technology) do our students use?		
<u>Pause and Reflect About Specific Students</u>		
Are there any students with characteristics that might require differentiation in the content, product, or process of learning?		
Step #2: Content *(What will students learn?)*	*Step #3: Products Showing Student Success* *(How will students convey their learning?)*	
What are the academic and/or social goals? What content standards are addressed?	In what ways will the learning outcomes be demonstrated?	
Differentiation Considerations: In what order will concepts and content be taught?	Differentiation Considerations: What are multiple ways students can demonstrate their understandings (e.g., Multiple Intelligences, multilevel and/or multisensory performances)?	
What multilevel and/or multisensory materials do the co-teachers need to facilitate access to the content?	What authentic products do students create?	
What multilevel goals are needed for all students to meaningfully access the content?	What are the criteria teachers use to evaluate the products?	

Step #2: Content (What will students learn?)			Step #3: Products Showing Student Success (How will students convey their learning?)	
Pause and Reflect About Specific Students: Are there any students who require unique or multilevel objectives or materials?			Pause and Reflect About Specific Students: Are there any students who require unique ways of showing what they know?	
Step #4: Process of Instruction: (How students engage in learning)				
Instructional Formats	Instructional Arrangements	Instructional Strategies	Social and Physical Environment	Co-teaching Approach(es)
Considerations	Considerations	Considerations	Considerations	Options
Adapting lectures?	Cooperative learning structures?	Choose research-based strategies?	Room arrangement?	Supportive?
Activity-based?	Same or cross-age peer tutors?	Apply concepts from Multiple Intelligences Theory?	Use of spaces outside of class?	Parallel?
Experiential?	Independent?	Integration of the arts?	Social norms?	Complementary?
Simulations/role play?	Whole group?	Use taxonomies?	Teach responsibility?	Team teaching?
Group investigation?	Other? (Tutorial, teacher-directed small group)		Positive behavior supports?	Students as co-teachers?
Discovery learning?			Environmental alterations?	(e.g., peer tutors and cooperative learning structures under instructional arrangements)
Computer/web-based?				
Self-directed?				
Stations?				
Integrated cross-curricular thematic unit/lesson?				
Service learning?				

(Continued)

Table 3.1 (Continued)

<u>Pause and Reflect About Specific Students</u>

What student-specific teaching strategies do select students need? What specific systems of supports (e.g., assistive technology), aids (e.g., personal assistance, cues, contracts), or services (e.g., counseling) do select students need?

IMPLEMENTATION PHASE:

Who are the Co-teachers? _____

What is/are the date(s) of the lesson? _____

What does each co-teacher do before, during, and after implementing the lesson?

Co-teacher Name: →				
What are the specific tasks that I do BEFORE the lesson?				
What are the specific tasks that I do DURING the lesson?				
What are the specific tasks that I do AFTER the lesson?				

REFLECTION PHASE:

Where, when, and how do co-teachers debrief and evaluate the outcomes of the lesson?

How did students do? Were needs of the learners met?

What are recommendations for the design of the next lesson(s)?

DESIGN POINT #1: GATHERING FACTS ■ ABOUT THE LEARNERS

For every educator, the process of differentiating curriculum and instruction begins by getting to know the students. Developing positive profiles of students' social and academic abilities, strengths, learning preferences, interests, cultural backgrounds, and languages is an essential first step; such facts about students can reveal pertinent strategies for effective teaching. Learning preferences provide helpful frameworks for understanding and finding strengths in all students. (Chapter 4 describes how concepts from the Multiple Intelligences Theory [Gardner, 1983, 1997] and other strategies can be used to uncover the various strengths and learning characteristics of students.)

Gathering facts about the students involves considering the form of communication through which each student best accesses information. For example, students with speech, hearing, or movement difficulties may need to use assistive technology, such as Braille or an augmentative communication device, to assist them to access and produce learning. Other students who are learning English as a second language may require scaffolding of content via multiple visual, auditory, or kinesthetic representations in their native language as well as English.

In the UDL Lesson Plan Cycle to Differentiate Instruction shown in Figure 3.2, gathering facts about the learner is shown in the top left corner as the first of the considerations and actions of co-teachers. It also appears as the first step of the planning phase of the Co-teaching Universal Design Lesson Plan template shown in Table 3.1. As shown in both the lesson plan cycle and the lesson plan template, teachers are prompted to *pause and reflect* about all of the students and consider whether specific students may need additional individualized unique supports. (Chapter 4 offers more information on how to gather facts about your learners.)

DESIGN POINT #2: CONTENT ■

Content, the second design point, has two aspects. The first aspect focuses on *what to teach*—the standards that will be addressed in a lesson or unit. As the lesson plan template in Table 3.1 suggests, these standards or goals may be social as well as academic in nature. Goals, of course, are influenced by public policy and national and state standards; every state has adopted goals in the form of curriculum standards, frameworks, or assessment systems that provide teachers with broad parameters for the *content* of a lesson or unit.

Given these parameters, students' academic and social needs then are considered in order to create meaningful lessons from the broad guidelines. Facts about students (e.g., learning styles profiles, past learning experiences, prior knowledge, and current interests and talents) are invaluable in designing multilevel goals for members of a class.

Once the "what to teach" aspect of content is determined, then content differentiation considerations become a priority. One *differentiation consideration* is focused on instructional *materials.* Materials are the means by which students access information and demonstrate their comprehension of content. Traditional materials, such as textbooks, offer a narrow range of access. Consequently, in order to reach and teach a wider range of students, materials may need to be *multilevel* in terms of difficulty and complexity, varied in form, and *multisensory* (e.g., magazines, web-based information sources, interactive computer programs, interviews of community experts). The more varied and rich the materials, the more likely the teacher will be able to spark student engagement.

Another important *content differentiation consideration* is the scope and degree of content mastery that we expect of students. This may vary considerably from one student to the next; that is, within any lesson, unit, or classroom, there likely will be *multilevel goals.* For example, all students in a class may engage in the same curricular content, but the focus may be more or less complex for individual students. The teacher may require increased or decreased rate of completion or pacing of the content. A teacher may also require differentiated expectations in the level of mastery, degree of quality, or quantity of the curricular requirements. All students may be held accountable for a core set of learning outcomes, while some are held responsible for additional learning outcomes or more sophisticated applications of content. Finally, students may focus on similar content, but some students may have more functional applications (Udvari-Solner, 1996, 1998).

To illustrate differentiation of both materials and goals, consider the example of a fourth grade class in which most students have as a curricular goal the analysis and synthesis of daily experiences by writing two paragraphs that summarize their learning outcomes and feelings about the day.

For example, Joel, a student with moderate intellectual and physical disabilities, uses picture symbols to communicate rather than writing, and does not yet construct complex sentences. His goals are to use a name and date stamp to preface his journal entry, select one picture symbol, and glue it in his journal to represent an activity that occurred during the day. He uses his journal entry to initiate a conversation with a classmate. Notice that Joel's goals relate to the same content (journal writing) but are less complex and have been adjusted to advance the use of his primary mode of communication. (Chapter 5 offers more information on the dimensions of content and ways in which to differentiate at the content design point.)

It is important to note at this point that after selecting the curricular goals and weighing the differentiation considerations, as shown in Figure 3.2 and Table 3.1, teachers are prompted to *pause and reflect* and determine if any student needs further personalization of goals or materials.

■ DESIGN POINT #3: PRODUCT

Connected to the *content design point* of what students learn is the *product design point* of how students demonstrate and convey their learning. *Product access* and the assessment of learning outcomes require co-teachers to develop and provide multiple means for students to express their understanding of the curriculum. Here, learning preferences information (e.g., Multiple Intelligences Theory) provides an important guide to thinking about the assessment and the products of learning in new ways. Gardner (1983, 1997), in his theory of multiple intelligences, suggests that we should be asking, "How is this student smart?" This question presumes that all students are smart, but each is smart in different ways. (Chapter 6 highlights methods teachers can use to define the products of learning as well as the assessment methods for students to demonstrate their knowledge in the best and most accurate ways.)

At the product design point, co-teachers consider the learning outcomes and arrange for multilevel, authentic, performance assessments. Authentic assessment occurs when students are expected to perform, produce, or otherwise demonstrate skills that represent realistic learning demands. Curriculum-based assessment, artifact collections and portfolios, individual learning contracts, and demonstrations are other examples of authentic assessments. Performance assessments are open ended, real-world applications that allow for a variety of methods or approaches for a student to achieve a "correct" response, and can reflect a student's unique experiences and interests. An example of an authentic performance assessment is when students are expected to demonstrate the scientific method while performing an experiment about the principles of flotation, in contrast to completing a true-or-false test on the scientific method.

We would like to point out here that, as with all design points, after differentiating ways in which students can show what they know, teachers are prompted to *pause and reflect* so that they can determine if any student still needs a personalized way to demonstrate learning.

DESIGN POINT #4: PROCESS ■

Process, the fourth design point in the UDL cycle, is focused on the instructional process so as to provide students with multiple means of engaging with the curriculum. Most teachers are familiar with a wide range of instructional processes. In this book, we will highlight selected processes to illustrate the power of the teacher's choice on the learning and achievement of the learners.

We have clustered the organizational and instructional approaches for increasing student access to engage in learning into five categories as shown in Table 3.1 in the *Process of Instruction* section of the Co-teaching Universal Design Lesson Plan template:

- instructional formats
- instructional arrangements
- instructional strategies
- social and physical environment (or classroom climate)
- co-teaching approaches

For each of the five categories, considerations to guide your decision making for selecting instructional processes are discussed. (Refer to Chapter 7 for more details.)

Instructional Formats

Instructional format refers to how teachers impart information to students and how students take part in learning. The most frequently used lesson format is the expository mode, also known as lecture or demonstration or guided practice, where the teacher is *the teller.* Teachers have at their disposal a wide range of instructional formats from which to choose, including: interdisciplinary or thematic approaches, self-directed study, inquiry-based learning, learning by discovery, center or station learning, computer-based learning, student conferencing, Socratic dialogue, games, simulations, role plays, activity-based experiential or community-referenced learning, the use of constructivist principles to have students discover and construct their own knowledge, integrated cross-curricular thematic units, hands-on methods using *realia* (i.e., real objects), accessing the World Wide Web, connecting school and community through service learning, and community-based projects.

Because the instructional formats listed above naturally allow for multisensory experiences and are more active and interactive, students who do not respond well to the traditional lecture or demonstration or guided practice approach have more options for participating successfully.

Instructional Arrangements

A related consideration at this decision point in the cycle focuses on the configurations for structuring a lesson or the methods of grouping students. *Instructional arrangements* dictate whether a student will be working alone or with a partner, operating in coordination with a small number of classmates, or functioning as part of a large group. The instructional groupings in most classrooms continue to be whole class and independent seat work—arrangements that often pose problems for students with learning and language differences. Small-group or peer-mediated learning, such as cooperative learning and peer tutoring, are two of the most effective instructional arrangements for increasing student access to the curriculum (Fuchs, Fuchs, Mathes, & Martinez, 2002; Fuchs et al., 2000; Johnson & Johnson, 1989).

Teachers structure a calculated balance of a variety of instructional arrangements across the day and week. These arrangements include: cooperative learning groups; partner learning, peer tutors or cross-age tutors; independent or individual work; teacher-directed small or large group or whole class instruction; and one-to-one, teacher-student instruction (e.g., reading conferences). Cooperative group learning structures and partner-learning and peer-tutoring arrangements also can be considered in relation to co-teaching approaches and are described in more detail in Chapter 9.

Instructional Strategies

Considerations that might influence your selection of instructional strategies include availability of research to document the effectiveness of the strategy. As mandated by the No Child Left Behind Act (NCLB, 2002), teachers and administrators must, whenever possible, use research-based strategies. Ask yourself in what ways might you use research-based strategies in this lesson? How might you apply concepts from learning preferences theories to ensure active learning from students with a variety of interests? How could we integrate the arts so as to appeal to various talents of our students? How can we enfold taxonomies for cognitive, affective, and psychomotor learning objectives?

Social/Physical Environment or Classroom Climate

From a social-ecological perspective, *the social climate and physical environmental conditions* of a classroom greatly influence the behavior, interactions, and learning of its members. Important environmental design decisions include where the lesson takes place, the physical arrangement of the room, and factors such as lighting, noise level, seating, physical location, and accessibility to learning materials. The social rules governing the classroom comprise an integral part of the environmental conditions that set the learning and activity level, and guide acceptable interactions.

An example of a typical social rule is to require students to raise a hand and wait to be called upon to answer a question. Some students may have difficulty conforming to the usual conditions of a classroom. For these students, lighting, noise level, visual and auditory distractions, the seating and room arrangement, and accessibility to materials can be barriers to learning and may need to be adjusted. Making changes in the social climate or social rules can have powerful effects on comfort level and student involvement.

For example, students who have a need to move (e.g., kinesthetic learners, students with ADHD) or socialize (e.g., verbal and linguistic learners) could benefit from flexibility in rules regarding movement and socialization in the classroom. Explicitly teaching students to be accountable and responsible as well as flexible and "response-able" are other ways to improve classroom climate.

Co-teaching Approaches

Emerging research suggests co-teaching promotes the differentiation of instruction and the provision of curriculum access to all students. It does this by increasing the teacher-student ratios, providing students with access to the diverse and specialized knowledge and instructional approaches of co-teachers, and enabling co-teachers to more readily use research-proven teaching strategies mandated by the NCLB Act (Villa, Thousand, & Nevin, 2004).

Co-teaching to differentiate instruction involves at least four approaches:

Supportive teaching is when one teacher takes the lead instructional role while other teachers rotate among students and provide support. For example, the supportive co-teachers watch and listen as students work, stepping in to provide assistance as needed, while the lead teacher continues to direct the overall lesson.

Parallel teaching is when two or more people work with different groups of students in different sections of the classroom. Station teaching and monitoring of cooperative groups are examples of this approach.

Complementary teaching is when co-teachers enhance the instruction provided by the other co-teachers. For example, one co-teacher might paraphrase the other's statements or model note-taking skills on a transparency.

Team teaching is when two or more people do what the traditional teacher has done alone—plan, teach, assess, and assume responsibility for all of the students in the class. (See Chapter 9 for more details.)

Involving students in co-teaching roles can provide instructional differentiation in the process of learning through cooperative group learning and peer-tutoring instructional arrangements. There is a rich research base that documents the benefits to students of cooperative group learning and peer-tutoring arrangements (Fuchs et al., 2002; Fuchs et al., 2000; Johnson & Johnson, 1989).

For instance, in cooperative groups, students experience more frequent and open communication, deeper understanding of other perspectives, and clearer differentiated views of both content and one another. Peer tutoring helps to individualize learning and offers more opportunities for tutees to respond to and practice academic content than in conventional teacher-led lessons. Both peer-tutor and cooperative learning are especially beneficial to the achievement of English language learners (Faltis, 1993; Walter, 1998).

■ PAUSE AND REFLECT ABOUT STUDENT-SPECIFIC TEACHING STRATEGIES AND SUPPORTS

Please note, as shown in Figure 3.2 and Table 3.1, that after you have selected the instructional formats, instructional arrangements, instructional strategies, social and physical environments, and co-teaching approaches, you are then prompted to *pause and reflect*.

At this decision point, return to the facts about your learners and decide whether specific students may need unique teaching or support strategies not already built into the instructional options. This is the last time before implementing the UDL plan that designers are asked to reflect upon their entire class to ensure personalization for select students.

Additional teaching strategies are the explicit and implicit ways an educator (a) gives directions, cues, prompts, and corrective feedback; (b) checks for understanding; (c) asks questions; (d) manages behavior; or (e) provides physical assistance. Student-specific teaching strategies include techniques that go beyond the already structured technical aspects of delivering instruction and may include strategies to meaningfully connect the content of a lesson to a particular student's culture, home, and community life (Udvari-Solner, 1996).

Some students may need *support strategies*—higher levels of assistance, intervention, or supervision—than are typically provided to other students. Rarely does a student need continuous, one-to-one supervision. When additional support is warranted, *natural supports*—assistance that can be provided by the general education teacher and classmates—are preferable. Additional instructional staff (e.g., a paraprofessional) may be needed at times, but only with clear goals to increase independence and fade the additional adult support when possible, teach students self-management, or model strategies to transfer the support back to the natural support system of the classroom.

PUTTING IT ALL TOGETHER WITH ■ THE CO-TEACHING UNIVERSAL DESIGN LESSON PLAN

Like a retrofit approach, UDL requires co-teachers to exhibit collaborative and creative dispositions and actions in order to invent new ways to facilitate curriculum access for all students. We have found the Co-teaching Universal Design Lesson Plan template (Table 3.1), referred to throughout this chapter, is an effective tool for facilitating collaborative and creative thinking among co-teachers as they go through the decision-making steps of the UDL Lesson Planning Cycle (Figure 3.2).

The template for the lesson plan provides suggestions for how co-teachers might think about essential questions at each of the four design points (i.e., students, content, product, process) as well as to *pause and reflect* about individual students who may need unique supports at each design point.

Because this is a lesson plan template that would ideally be crafted and executed by two or more co-teachers, one of the four *Process of Instruction* columns includes the four types of co-teaching arrangements that a teaching team can use.

Additionally, the lesson plan format leads you to an *implementation phase* where co-teachers are asked to make decisions about what each co-teacher will do before, during, and after the lesson to ensure that the delivery and assessment of content occurs as planned. Collaboratively deciding on how to answer these questions ensures that all partners in the co-teaching venture are clear about their own and each other's instructional roles and responsibilities.

The lesson plan template ends with a *reflection phase* that includes questions for co-teachers to consider when they meet to reflect upon and evaluate the effectiveness of their efforts to differentiate instruction. They can reflect on to what extent they each engaged fully and systematically in a recurring *planning-analysis-reflection cycle* that promotes co-teachers' communication with one another. They can also evaluate the overall effectiveness of their instruction.

Of course, the implementation of any lesson gives co-teachers new facts about their students as they observe student performance during the lesson and examine their products and performances. This information, then, enables co-teachers to make even better differentiation decisions as they embark on their next lesson. (Suggestions for collaborative planning to differentiate instruction can be found in Chapter 8.) The informative, recursive nature of the lesson planning cycle is represented in Figure 3.2, with the lesson planning steps feeding back into the "Gathering Facts About the Learners" step of the cycle.

Table 3.2 Blank Co-teaching Universal Design Lesson Plan Template

PLANNING PHASE:

Lesson Topic and Name: _____ Content Area(s) Focus: _____

Step #1: Facts About the Student Learners

Step #2: Content (What will students learn?) *Step #3: Products (How will students show success?)*

Step #4: Process of Instruction (How will students be instructed?)

Instructional Formats	Instructional Arrangements	Instructional Strategies	Social and Physical Environment	Co-teaching Approach(es)

IMPLEMENTATION PHASE: Date(s) of the lesson? _____

Who are the co-teachers? _____

What does each co-teacher do before, during, and after implementing the lesson?

Co-teacher Name:			
What are the specific tasks that I do BEFORE the lesson?			
What are the specific tasks that I do DURING the lesson?			
What are the specific tasks that I do AFTER the lesson?			

REFLECTION PHASE:

48

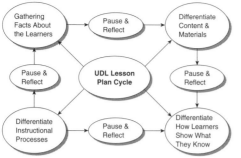

Gathering Facts About the Learners

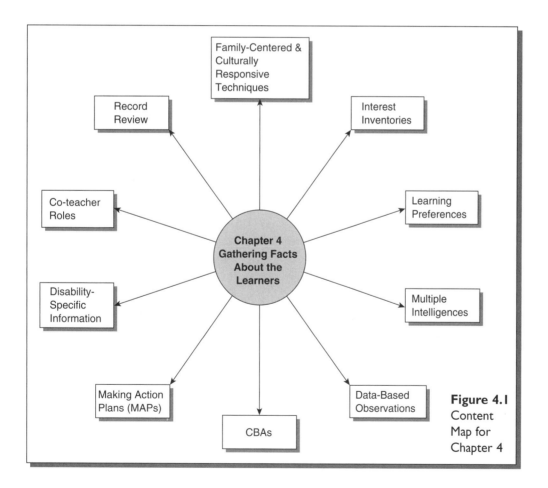

Figure 4.1 Content Map for Chapter 4

The gift of a great teacher is creating an awareness of greatness in others.

—The Tao of Teaching

The process of differentiating curriculum, instruction, and assessment begins by knowing your students. As required by a retrofit approach, teachers applying a universal design approach must gather information about their students' strengths, interests, learning styles, preferences, and intelligences. This information helps the teacher(s) establish a shared vision of their students' active involvement and can reveal pertinent strategies for effective teaching, motivation, and differentiation.

What strategies can teachers use to gather information about their students?

There are many, but the strategies for gathering facts about learners that will be described and illustrated in this chapter are record review, family-centered and culturally responsive fact gathering, interest inventories, assessment based on concepts from Multiple Intelligences Theory, and observations that include functional behavioral assessments. Additional strategies are the monitoring of students working in cooperative groups, curriculum-based assessment, the Making Action Plans (MAPs) process (Falvey, Forest, Rosenberg, & Pearpoint, 2002), and the gathering of disability-specific information. This chapter ends by exploring the role of co-teachers in gathering facts about students.

■ RECORD REVIEW

Perhaps the most common way in which teachers get to know their students is through an examination of the students' cumulative records. Records may include past report cards, incident reports regarding referrals for rule violations, Individual Education Program (IEP) documents for students with identified special education needs, level of language proficiency for English language learners, high stakes assessment results from statewide or districtwide standardized assessments, and exemplary works drawn from students' authentic portfolios.

A review of student records can offer teachers a snapshot of the range of past performances of the student with whom they are not yet acquainted and also provide an overall idea of what more they may need to learn about individual students (e.g., ways in which a student uses an augmentative communication device such as a speaking computer).

In reviewing records, it is critical that teachers remember that records do not tell the whole story about a student and the factors that might have influenced that student's past performances in school. Furthermore, teachers need to resist allowing records to set biases or preconceived expectations of how a student will behave or perform when that student enters a new learning environment with a new receiving teacher.

■ FAMILY-CENTERED AND CULTURALLY RESPONSIVE FACT GATHERING

Neal, McCray, Webb-Johnson, and Bridgest (2003) and Webb-Johnson (2003) recommend that teachers observe their multicultural and multiethnic learners in their community settings as well as within the school setting. When this is done, some remarkable findings can emerge regarding culturally relevant learning preferences. For instance, Dill and Boykin (2005) found that African American students had significantly greater recall of text when engaged in a culturally aligned learning structure—a communal (cooperative) learning structure—rather than being tutored by a peer or working alone.

When teachers visit settings with which they may be unfamiliar (students' homes, churches, barbershops, etc.), they become more culturally competent so they can understand and more positively interact with their multicultural learners. Similarly, Duda and Utley (2006) encourage all school personnel to consider interviews with cultural ambassadors (e.g., parents, family members, and other individuals in the community who can inform the school about the culture). In addition, they can interview successfully performing students from the culture so they can become familiar with cultural norms. Information gathered in this way enables teachers to connect the curriculum to the students' heritages. Buswell and Schaffner (2002), both of whom are parents of young adults with significant disabilities who were fully included in general education when in public school, reinforce the importance of deliberately seeking and really listening to the family perspective in order to understand how a student can best be engaged, motivated, understood, and valued. As they emphasize, personal contact offers the student specific, family specific, and culturally specific information that enables educators (as well as students and parents) to "step across the subcultural fragmentation fault line and break down subcultural stereotypes of one another" (p. 17).

INTEREST INVENTORIES ■

Teachers can create interest inventories to learn about their students' cognitive abilities, interests, the language spoken at home, as well as their students' preferred learning styles. This method helps teachers understand their students so as to increase students' access to and interaction with the material.

Specifically, interest inventories are used to determine the unique and shared interests of students. Teachers then follow up by using these interests as the bases for differentiating the content and materials used in lessons, motivating students to learn, differentiating instructional activities, and differentiating how students express what they have learned.

For example, Ritter and Morris (2005) described how teachers have implemented the interest inventory shown in Table 4.1 as one way to discover facts about their learners. They described how a middle school math teacher in her second year of teaching began her curriculum with an instructional unit on data analysis and graphing. She capitalized on the innate curiosity of middle-school-age students by using information relevant to them, especially information they had provided through the inventory, as shown in Table 4.1. The teacher provided them various sets of data pulled from interest inventories, removed any mode of identification, taught them to create a spreadsheet in Excel, and taught them to create their own graphs as shown in Figure 4.2. In this way, she developed keener insights about the learners and at the same time taught them skills related to the math standards.

Table 4.1   A Sample Student Interest Inventory

Name _____   Today's Date _____
Gender _____   Birth date _____
Race _____   Religion _____
Languages I can speak _____
I was born in _____
               City   State   Country

Sports:
My favorite to watch is _____
My favorite to play is _____
At my school, I play _____

Arts:
My favorite type of art to create is _____
I play this instrument _____

Free Time:
My favorite things to do on the weekends are _____
My favorite things to do after school are _____

Entertainment:
My favorite television show is _____
My favorite movie is _____
My favorite celebrity is _____
My favorite song is _____
My favorite type of music is _____

General:
The thing I like most about myself is _____
The thing I like least about myself is _____
The thing I do best is _____
The thing I do the worst is _____

Family and Home:
I have these types of pets _____
I have this many brothers and sisters _____ # of brothers _____ # of sisters
I am the oldest, middle, or youngest child *(circle one)*.
I usually speak this language at home with my family _____
I get everything I need at home   Yes   No
There is usually someone at home when I come home from school   Yes   No
I usually go to bed at this time _____
I have these chores to do at home _____
I know my neighbors   Yes   No

Homework:
I like to do homework   Yes   No
I like to eat when I study   Yes   No
I like to listen to this type of music when I study _____
Background noise bothers me when I study   Yes   No
This is where I like to do my homework _____

School:

I like to read on my own	Yes	No
My favorite book is _____		
My favorite subject is _____		
My least favorite subject is _____		
My favorite teacher from any grade level is _____		
I need to be told to stay on task often, sometimes, or never *(circle one)*		
I prefer working with a partner, in small groups, or by myself *(circle one)*		
I always do my best on my work	Yes	No
I work harder when I know my work will be graded	Yes	No
I am comfortable asking for help when I need it	Yes	No
I learn best by hearing information, seeing information, or doing activities with my hands *(circle one)*		
I pay attention in class best when I sit up front, sit in the back, or it doesn't matter where I sit *(circle one)*		
This is what I want to be when I grow up _____		
Overall, I like school	Yes	No

SOURCE: Ritter, S., & Morris, S. (2005, August). Meeting the needs of diverse learners in the general education class. Paper presented at the Inclusive and Supportive Education Congress International Special Education Conference—Inclusion: Celebrating Diversity? Glasgow, Scotland. Retrieved June 5, 2006: http://www.isec2005.org.uk/isec/abstracts/papers_r/ritter_s.shtml

Figure 4.2   Student-Generated Graphs Representing Whole Class Interests

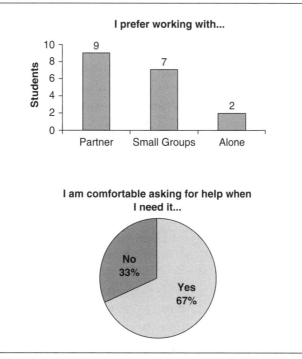

SOURCE: Ritter, S., & Morris, S. (2005, August). Meeting the needs of diverse learners in the general education class. Paper presented at the Inclusive and Supportive Education Congress International Special Education Conference—Inclusion: Celebrating Diversity? Glasgow, Scotland. Retrieved June 5, 2006: http://www.isec2005.org.uk/isec/abstracts/papers_r/ritter_s.shtml.

■ LEARNING PREFERENCES INFORMATION

Learning and Thinking Styles

Gregory and Chapman (2002) nicely summarize and compare various taxonomies of learning and thinking styles that have been proposed to assist teachers to get to know their students. A learning style model proposed by Dunn and Dunn (1987) suggests that teachers think about students in terms of auditory, visual, and tactile and kinesthetic modalities as well as other factors that affect learning such as noise and light, motivation, and task structure (e.g., independent, self-directed, or cooperative).

Kolb (1984) conceptualizes students as experiencing learning in one of four ways—as accommodators, convergers, assimilators, or divergers.

Gregorc's (1982) thinking style taxonomy classifies students as concrete-random, concrete-sequential, abstract-random, or abstract-sequential based upon two dimensions—how students *perceive* the world (i.e., concrete or abstract) and how they *order* the world (i.e., sequential or random).

McCarthy's (1990) 4Mat Model categorizes learning (and teaching) styles into four types—imaginative (experiencing), analytic (conceptualizing), common sense (applying), and dynamic (creating).

All of these approaches to assessing and classifying students' way of learning have the same overarching goal, namely, to prompt educators to "design the learning so that the diverse clientele in the classroom have their needs satisfied" (Gregory & Chapman, 2002, p. 28).

Sternberg (1997b) proposed a theory of mental self-government, which is a theory of thinking styles that emphasizes learning styles that are not abilities in themselves, but rather preferences in how people choose to use their abilities. Mental self-government involves such preferences as legislative functions, executive functions, and judicial functions.

In this theory, people typically show specific preferences; for example, people with a legislative preference enjoy generating ideas and doing things their own way. People with an executive style prefer to follow guidelines established by others and to use other people's ideas to do their work. People with a judicial preference like to evaluate the ideas of others. People are not wholly one or another of these styles, but rather some blend of them. The mental self-government theory contains 11 styles in all.

■ MULTIPLE INTELLIGENCES

Concepts from Howard Gardner's Multiple Intelligences (MI) Theory (Armstrong, 2000; Gardner, 1983, 1997) provide yet another helpful framework for gathering, understanding, motivating, and finding strengths in all students. MI theory assumes that all students possess an array of at least eight intelligences, which is pictorially represented as an MI Pizza in Figure 4.3 and described in Table 4.2.

In contrast to the theories of learning and thinking styles which classify students into separate categories, MI theory suggests that each person has all eight intelligences in different proportions or profiles that function in unique

Figure 4.3   MI Pizza

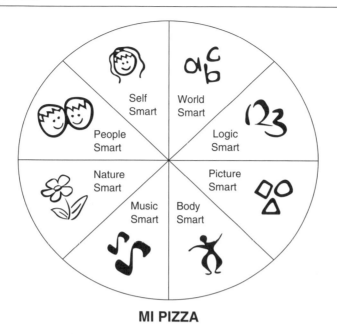

MI PIZZA

SOURCE: From Armstrong, *Multiple Intelligence 2/e*, copyright © 2000. Reprinted by Permission. The Association for supervision and Curriculum Development is a worldwide community of educators advocating sound policies and sharing best practices to achieve the success of each learner. To learn more, visit ASCD at www. ascd.org.

Table 4.2   The Eight Multiple Intelligences Defined

1. **Verbal/Linguistic**–is word oriented; is sensitive to the sounds, structures, meanings, and functions of words; may show an affinity to storytelling, writing, reading, and verbal play (e.g., jokes, puns, riddles)

2. **Logical/Mathematical**–is concept oriented; has capacity to perceive logical or numerical patterns; has a scientific or numerical nature to discover or test hypotheses

3. **Visual/Spatial**–is image and picture oriented; is able to perceive the world visually and to perform transformations on those perceptions; may daydream and demonstrate artistic, designer, or inventive qualities

4. **Musical/Rhythmic**–is rhythm- and melody-oriented; can produce and appreciate rhythm, pitch, timbre, and multiple forms of musical expression; may be animated or calmed by music

5. **Bodily/Kinesthetic**–is physically oriented; uses one's body movements for self-expression (e.g., acting, dancing, mime); excels in athletics, uses touch to interpret the environment, can skillfully handle or produce objects requiring fine-motor abilities

6. **Interpersonal**–is socially oriented, has strong mediation and leadership skills, can teach others and discern moods, temperaments, and motivations of other people

7. **Intrapersonal**–is intuitively oriented, can access and interpret one's own feelings, may be strong willed or self-motivated, may prefer solitary activities

8. **Naturalist**–has capacity to classify nature; has outstanding knowledge of or sensitivity to things that exist in the natural world; has ability to discern patterns in nature

ways for each person. What MI theory has done in education is to remind educators that intelligence is not fixed or static. Any one of a person's "weak" intelligence areas may become a strength when exercised and given an opportunity to develop. Identifying a student's strength intelligences allows educators to use those strengths to capture a student's attention and assist the student in the learning of new information.

Among the strategies teachers can employ to gather facts about the multiple intelligences of a student are record reviews, observation, and examinations of work samples. For example, teachers can observe student performance in activities that require the use of various intelligences, and they also can interview students, parents, or previous teachers.

MI surveys also have been constructed (Armstrong, 2000). A web-based instrument (www.ldrc.ca/projects/miinventory/mitest.html), although not validated with research-based procedures, does provide an intuitively congruent method for self-assessing one's own multiple intelligences. The Multiple Intelligences Developmental Assessment Scales (MIDAS) are endorsed by the MI theory originator, Howard Gardner, because of their development in accordance with valid research procedures and their track record of producing a valid and reliable profile (see www.miresearch.org/). MIDAS has both teen and adult versions. Armstrong (2000) provides MI inventories and assessment checklists for adults and students. There are other less formal ways of gathering MI assessment information about students. These methods include observations; record review; talking with students, parents, and other teachers; anecdotal records; and setting up special activities and centers for observing how students express their multiple intelligences.

■ DATA-BASED OBSERVATIONS INCLUDING FUNCTIONAL BEHAVIORAL ASSESSMENTS AND COOPERATIVE GROUP MONITORING

Data-Based Observations

Teachers often make judgments based on what they observe while their students are engaged (or disengaged) in classroom activities, recess, and other school-based interactions.

There are several guidelines for teachers to follow when developing observation procedures:

1. The target behaviors must be defined in such a way that they can be observed; this implies overt actions from the students.

2. The teacher identifies the materials that will be used to collect the observation data (e.g., check sheets, mechanical counters, timers, etc.).

3. The teacher decides the method to use to collect the data: frequency recording (e.g., tallying each time the behavior is observed to occur), sampling (e.g., recording once every 10 minutes whether or not the behavior occurred), or duration (e.g., activating a stopwatch when the behavior occurs and stopping it when the behavior ceases).

4. The teacher describes how data were collected (e.g., who, when, how long, how often) and arranges for another observer to simultaneously observe the activity so as to decrease observer bias.

For example, Shuflitowski (2005) was a school psychology intern who worked with a teacher who was concerned about attention-getting behaviors of a student they refer to as "R." Together, they decided to assess the frequency of R's "calling out" behavior during reading and language arts lessons that involved the entire class. They clearly defined the behavior in observable terms (using action verbs) and chose a time of recording when the behavior was most likely to occur. They defined "calling out" as an oral/ verbal expression directed toward the teacher during a whole group lesson (specifying that it did not include talking to classmates during a lesson). Ms. Shuflitowski used a clock, pen and pencil, and a chart to keep track of the data (see Figure 4.4) and then displayed the data in graph form as shown in Table 4.3.

Based on the data collected over ten days, the team confirmed that R's "calling out" behavior occurred an average of 9 times during a 30-minute period, ranging from 8 to 10 occurrences. During the fourth observation session, the classroom teacher intervened by publicly recording the "call outs" on the whiteboard. On this day, only 6 "call outs" were recorded, suggesting that R might be responsive to feedback on his behavior. A rate of 6 per 30 minutes was still considered a disruption (about one disruption every 5 minutes). Ms. Shuflitowski used the results of the data collection to collaborate with the teacher to develop a systematic intervention procedure to decrease R's "call outs."

Teachers can gain a rich array of information when they conduct direct observations of their students as they implement various procedures. For example, observing students as they solve mathematics problems using the division algorithm can help teachers identify what their students know and what they don't know about the process. Teachers who observe their students as they follow written directions to complete a classroom Treasure Hunt can gain an informal authentic assessment of functional reading ability.

Figure 4.4   Ms. S's Graph for R's "Calling Out" Behaviors

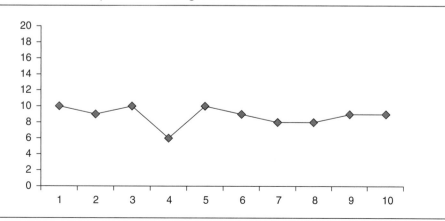

SOURCE: By Rebecca Shuflitowski; used with permission.

Table 4.3   Chart of R's Frequency of "Call Outs" During 30-Minute Sessions

Session #	Time: 30-minute sessions	Number of Events		Interobserver Agreement		
				Session #	**Time**	**Number of Events Observed by Interobserver**
1	9:00-9:30	10		7	9:00-9:30	8
2	9:00-9:30	9				
3	9:00-9:30	10		**IOA = 100%**		
4	9:30-10:00	6				
5	9:30-10:00	10				
6	9:00-9:30	9				
7	9:00-9:30	8				
8	9:30-10:00	8				
9	9:00-9:30	9				
10	9:30-10:00	9				

SOURCE: Shuflitowski, 2005. Used by permission.

■ FUNCTIONAL BEHAVIORAL ASSESSMENT

Thomas Armstrong (2000) states, "I've often humorously suggested to teachers that one good way to identify students' most highly developed intelligences is to observe how they *misbehave in class* [italics added]" (p. 21). In other words, students who violate rules can be considered to be communicating about what learning, social and emotional, or multiple intelligences needs are not being met in the classroom or in the larger world.

When a student violates rules, a type of data-based assessment known as a functional behavioral assessment (FBA) helps to determine the communicative intent, function, or purpose that a behavior serves a student. For instance, observations of a student repeatedly kicking classmates may reveal that he has few other behaviors for initiating interactions with peers and that perhaps one function of kicking is to gain attention and interpersonal contact with others.

Of course, a single observation does not provide adequate information to determine if this is the function of the kicking. To determine the relationship between a behavior and the situation in which the behavior occurs, assessment information must be gathered across time and environments from various sources (e.g., student interview, student observation, interviews with family members and past and current teachers). The assessment process includes an examination of the antecedents—the conditions (e.g., time of day, location, persons in proximity, task demands, stressors) under which the behavior occurred and what happens following the behavior, including the consequences (O'Neil, Homer, Albin, Sprague, Storey, & Newton, 1997). Given adequate information from the functional assessment, it then is possible to hypothesize the likely function, purpose, or communicative intent of the behavior and develop a positive support plan for reducing the undesired behavior and teach and reinforce a socially acceptable replacement behavior (e.g., teaching the student how to ask a classmate to play instead of the student using kicking as a way to initiate social contact).

By using both a functional assessment and a functional analysis approach to understanding student behavior, teachers are more inclined to view undesirable student behavior as just that—a behavior—and not a permanent characteristic of the student. They are also more inclined to view a behavior as a cry for help regarding unmet student needs and, in turn, to use positive teaching responses rather than punishment approaches, which have been demonstrated by research to have only temporary effects (Kagan, Kyle, & Scott, 2004; Villa, Udis, & Thousand, 2002).

MONITORING COOPERATIVE ■ GROUP LEARNING

Cooperative group learning procedures include formative and summative methods to gather information about students as they are engaged in learning activities. As Johnson and Johnson (1996) note, cooperative group learning provides an opportunity for formative student assessment processes (i.e., gathering facts about students) to become an ongoing part of classroom life. The advantages of monitoring cooperative group learning as a way to collect information are summarized in Table 4.4.

For example, Moffat (2002), after teaching a cooperative group lesson on methods to express nonverbal encouragement, asked her students to complete a self-evaluation form during the next day's activities (see Table 4.5). The information helped her decide what aspects of nonverbal encouragement needed to be further emphasized.

CURRICULUM-BASED ASSESSMENTS ■

Curriculum-based assessments (CBAs) provide a structured form of observation of students as they progress through a specified curriculum. CBAs are criterion-referenced tests that are teacher constructed and designed to reflect curriculum content. Such assessment systems have gained more and more respect as alternatives to traditional psycho-educational diagnostic techniques, which do not empower teachers to make educational decisions for students with exceptional needs.

CBAs determine the student's functioning level in the district's curriculum, determine the student's specific strengths, and provide data to monitor a

Table 4.4 Cooperative Learning and Gathering Facts About the Learners

---

Use multiple modalities. Learning in cooperative groups allows for assessment procedures that cannot be used when students work alone, individualistically, or competitively.

Discover more diverse outcomes. Cooperative learning groups enable teachers to assess critical thinking and level of reasoning, the performance of taught skills (such as conducting a science experiment), the ability to communicate knowledge, interpersonal and small group skills, self-esteem and self-efficacy, and commitment to producing quality work.

Add sources of information. Cooperative learning provides self and peer assessments, along with the teacher's assessments.

A setting in which students may best learn (and create) the rubrics used to assess and communicate about their work. This helps students produce higher quality work, understand feedback, and assess classmates' work.

Increase the possibility for students to learn from the assessment and reporting experiences. Learning is enhanced when the assessment requires group members to discuss the accuracy, quality, and quantity of their own and each other's work.

Decrease possibility of teacher bias affecting the assessment and evaluation process. Frequent sampling and evaluation by a variety of others in addition to the teacher provides a broader base of data for evaluation, a wider range of perspectives in applying criteria, and the potential for consistent patterns of interpretation to occur.

Assess group as well as individual outcomes. There are times when the scientific, dramatic, or creative project of a group will need to be assessed.

Make assessment procedures congruent with ideal instructional methods. Instruction and assessment procedures need to be aligned so they work for, not against, each other. Cooperative learning tends to result in higher achievement and a variety of important outcomes that are aims in education.

SOURCE: Adapted from Johnson & Johnson (2002).

student's progress. Research is clear that CBAs (and Curriculum-Based Measurement) can be used at the individual child level, the classroom level, school- and districtwide level (Gansle et al., 2004; Hall & Mengel, 2002; Idol, Nevin, & Paolucci-Whitcomb, 1999; VanDerHayden & Burns, 2005; see Chapter 6 for more details about CBAs).

■ MAKING ACTION PLANS (MAPs)

MAPs is a methodology for engaging a group of people who have various relationships with a particular student (e.g., parents, siblings, neighbors, friends, teachers, classmates, administrators) to highlight what they know about that student's strengths, interests, and other learning, social, and emotional characteristics in order to creatively plan for that student's future (Falvey et al., 2002).

Table 4.5   An Example of an Informal Assessment of Social Skills

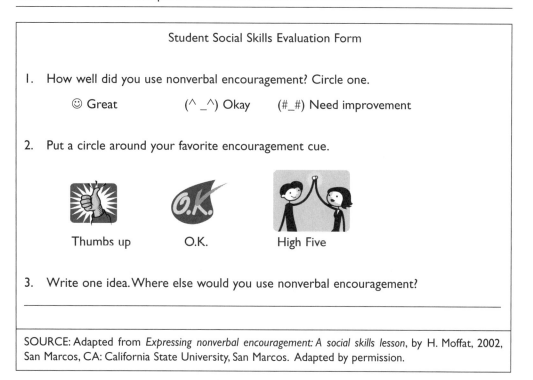

SOURCE: Adapted from *Expressing nonverbal encouragement: A social skills lesson*, by H. Moffat, 2002, San Marcos, CA: California State University, San Marcos. Adapted by permission.

A MAPs session can be as brief as an hour. The person on whom that meeting is focused determines the guest list for the MAPs session. A neutral facilitator welcomes attendees, explains the process, guides the group through a series of eight questions shown in Table 4.5, and guides the pacing of the session.

A public record of the process is created and displayed for all in attendance to see (e.g., on newsprint, on an overhead transparency, or projected from a computer hooked up to an LCD projector). At each step, the focus person and those closest to that person, such as parents and siblings, speak before the professionals who are attending the meeting.

The MAPs process helps to establish trust among families and educators by ensuring that both student and family voices are heard and provides educators with valuable information about a student that cannot be obtained by standardized assessments or any of the other methods described in this chapter. MAPs can be used with any student in a class. Many teachers have developed a mini-version of a MAPs for every child in their classroom as part of student-parent-teacher conferences. Some states have incorporated components of MAPS as part of the Individual Education Program (IEP) planning process.

DISABILITY-SPECIFIC INFORMATION ■

Although teachers often have learned about different aspects of disabilities, it is important for them to acquire up-to-date information so as to make the best use

Table 4.6   The Eight Key MAPs Questions

1. **What is MAPs?**
   MAPs (Making Action Plans) is designed to assist people to get from where they are to where they want to be (goals). At a MAPs meeting, participants are asked what a MAP means to them.

2. **What is the person's history or story?**
   The person and the family are asked to describe their history or story.

3. **What is the dream?**
   This is in many ways the most important step of the process because it identifies the goal(s) for which you will develop a plan of action. Again, the person and family members speak first and then others in attendance may add to the list of goals. The facilitator must be nonjudgmental in both words and body language.

4. **What is the nightmare?**
   This question helps those in attendance to understand the fears and concerns of the target student and family—the things they want to avoid. At times, this step elicits emotions and reactions that are strong or sad. The information is critical because the entire point of the process is to achieve the dream while avoiding the nightmare.

5. **Who is the person?**
   At this step, participants brainstorm and generate a list of words that describe the person for whom the MAPs is being held. The facilitator oftentimes groups descriptors into themes. The focus person is asked to describe himself or herself and pick out three favorite words from the list.

6. **What are the person's gifts, strengths, and talents?**
   Here particular emphasis is placed upon the learner's "giftedness." The focus is not solely academic but designed to acknowledge the learner's strengths and interests.

7. **What does the person need?**
   Participants consider what resources and supports will be needed to assist the learner to reach the dream and avoid the nightmare. Those assembled may need to consider academic, communication, behavioral, biological, health, safety, and security needs of the person.

8. **What is the plan of action?**
   The final step is the development of a plan that includes the who, the what, and the when of actualizing the dreams and avoiding the nightmares.

SOURCE: From M. A. Falvey, M. S. Forest, J. Pearpoint, & R. L. Rosenberg's Building Connections, in *Creativity and Collaborative Learning: The Practical Guide to Empowering Students, Teachers, and Familes, Second Edition*, edited by J. S. Thousand, R. A. Villa, & A. I. Nevin, copyright © 2002. Reprinted by permission of Paul H. Brookes Publishing Co.

of disability-specific data. Many general educators report they have not been exposed to any information about what students with disabilities can actually be expected to do. Special educators often have in-depth knowledge about disabilities, but they may not have been exposed to strengths-based perspectives in designing lessons that allow students access to the general education curriculum.

In addition, educators far too often focus on a student's disability label rather than learning about that individual. Teachers new to inclusion and differentiation may ask, "What is this child's disability or IQ?" In contrast, teachers with experience in meeting the diverse needs of students in heterogeneous classrooms tend to ask for information about the individual learner.

Experienced co-teachers acknowledge that homogeneity within a category of disability is impossible and that specific information about a child will be more beneficial to teaching and learning.

When gathering disability-specific information, remember that multiple perspectives can provide important facts about what the learner can and cannot do. For example, interviews with parents and family members can reveal anecdotes that explain how the child functions in the home and community environments.

Disability-specific information can be gathered from advocacy web sites such as the Educational Resources Information Clearinghouse (ERIC) and the National Information Clearinghouse for Handicapped Children and Youth (NICHCY). Both organizations explain the educational implications for specific disabilities. NICHCY has created fourteen fact sheets and three briefing papers on specific disabilities (e.g., Asperger's syndrome, autism, traumatic brain injury). Each publication defines the disability, describes its characteristics, and offers tips for parents and teachers. These publications explain the disability category in nonpejorative terms so that children and youth, as well as their parents and teachers, can better understand the impact of the condition. They also provide a list of print and video resources and disability organizations that offer more information and assistance.

The authors caution teachers and parents not to lose sight of the humanity and personal strengths and characteristics of students with diverse needs. We can often get caught up in focusing on the medical conditions, the challenging aspects of a disability, or the alphabet soup of eligibility categories (e.g., ED, LD, MR, LEP). Using a label to refer to students objectifies and dehumanizes them. Kunc, a family therapist and world-renowned advocate for disability rights—who also has cerebral palsy—refers to this dehumanizing phenomenon of seeing the person as the disability rather than the disability as a small part of a whole and complex person as "disability spread" (Kunc & Van der Klift, 1994). Figure 4.5 provides a visual representation of this phenomenon.

The pejorative dehumanizing impact of labeling is so problematic, that the Individuals with Disabilities Education Improvement Act of 2004 includes specific guidelines for using *person first language*—referring to an individual by name first and then adding a disability or other characteristic as a subsequent descriptor. For example, the co-teachers you met in Chapter 2, Mr. Gleason and Ms. Villalobos, refer to Kevin as "Kevin, a fourth grader with a learning disability" rather than the "learning disabled fourth grader, Kevin."

Figure 4.5   A Visual Representation of the Phenomenon of Disability Spread

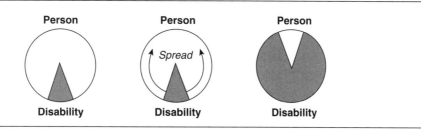

SOURCE: From Kunc, N., & Van der Klift, E., Beyond Benevolence: Supporting Genuine Friendship un Inclusive *Schools, in Creativity and Collaborative Learning: The Practical Guide to Empowering Students, Teachers, and Familes, Second Edition,* edited by J. S. Thousand, R. A. Villa, & A. I. Nevin, copyright © 2002. Reprinted by permission of Paul H. Brookes Publishing Co.

■ CO-TEACHER ROLES IN GATHERING FACTS ABOUT THE LEARNERS

Morrocco and Aguilar (2002) described the co-teaching activities between content area teachers and special educators in an investigation of a schoolwide co-teaching model in an urban middle school where students with disabilities were included in heterogeneous classrooms. In addition to interviews with school leaders, the investigation involved direct observations of co-teachers as they taught. Comparatively, the general education content teachers conducted more of the instruction while the special educators provided more individualized assistance. However, both engaged in the full range of instructional activities including assessing learner characteristics.

Co-teachers may agree to collect different types of student information based upon professional expertise. For example, some general educators are explicitly trained to administer, score, and record statewide, high stakes assessments, whereas some special educators have explicit preparation in administering, scoring, and reporting individualized criterion-referenced tests.

The division of labor for gathering facts about learners may have many dimensions. For example, both co-teachers may choose to administer informal reading, interest, and learning preference inventories where each co-teacher assesses half of the class. Other school personnel can become involved. For example, the school social worker or guidance counselor might assist co-teachers to assess the social skill competence of students either by observing classroom interactions or by using more formal protocols. A speech and language therapist might observe and record communication patterns among students during class discussions and subsequently provide guidance to enhance students' oral and written language within classroom routines. The bottom line is that co-teachers share with other personnel how they collectively will gather information about the students they serve so that functional decisions for differentiating content, products, and processes of learning can occur.

■ PAUSE AND REFLECT

Now that you have learned about the various ways in which teachers can get to know about their students, please return to the Co-teaching Universal Design Lesson Plan template shown in Table 3.1 in Chapter 3. Focus on the section titled, "Facts About the Student Learners." Once you have gathered facts about your specific students, you then can ask yourself, "Are there any students with characteristics that might require differentiation at the content, product, or process design points of instruction?" Are you thinking about and preparing to propose to your planning and teaching partners ways to make adjustments to match your students' characteristics as you move through the next step of the UDL cycle? When you have answered these questions satisfactorily, then it is time to proceed to the next step in the UDL cycle. Chapter 5 examines the dimensions of content and ways in which content can be made accessible to a diverse body of students.

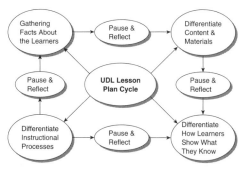

Differentiating Access to the Content of Learning

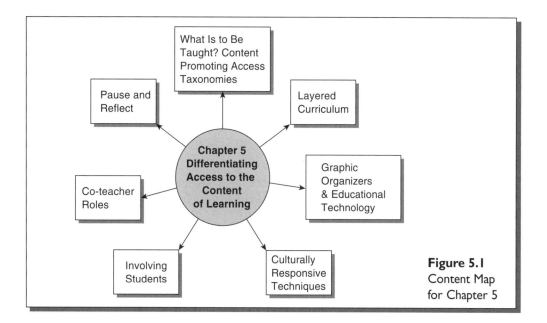

Figure 5.1
Content Map for Chapter 5

We do things backwards. We think in terms of getting a skill first, and then finding useful and interesting things to do with it. The sensible way, the best way, is to start with something worth doing, and then, moved by a strong desire to do it, get whatever skills are needed.

—John Holt

T his quote reflects the philosophy and process of Universal Design for Learning (UDL) as well as the philosophy of Wiggins and McTighe (2005), the originators of the backward design approach to curriculum and unit development—namely, curricular and instructional planning begins with the identification of worthwhile, desired results—things worth knowing and doing and understandings that are likely to endure and transfer to other tasks and settings. In this chapter, you will find answers to questions like the following:

- In what ways might teachers arrange access to the curriculum standards and content of their lessons?
- What are teachers' roles in differentiating content?

What methods do you currently use to allow your students to access the curriculum standards and the content of your lessons? Do you tell your students about the content? Do you ask them to open the grade-level textbook and turn to a specific page to begin reading the assignment?

You have already discovered from the facts that you have gathered about your learners in Chapter 4 that it is highly unlikely that all of your students will respond in the desired manner when asked to follow these approaches. That is why you are interested in the UDL lesson planning cycle and the content of this chapter. In this chapter, you will learn to expand your ways of thinking about content and ways of creating student access to the content of your lessons.

■ WHAT IS CONTENT?

Content, the second access design point, has multiple dimensions. Content includes what is to be taught; what level of understanding, knowledge, and proficiency students are to demonstrate; and what context, materials, and differentiation are necessary to allow all students a point of entry to learning. Although state and district standards provide broad parameters for the content of a lesson or unit, students' academic or social needs must be considered to create meaningful learning experiences from the broad guidelines. That is why you gather facts about learners using some of the approaches discussed in Chapter 4.

Content is often defined by the standards that are set by state departments of education and school districts and, in addition, standards are influenced by professional organizations such as the National Council for Teachers of Mathematics, National Council for the Social Studies, National Council of Teachers of English, and the National Science Teachers Association. Most teachers define these standards as the scope and sequence of the curriculum for each grade level. The scope and sequence of a curriculum is based on the assumption that there are pre-definable bodies of knowledge or information that, when achieved, result in success in post-school life (Poplin & Stone, 1992).

The standardized scope and sequence of a particular curriculum often is delivered through such means as lectures from the teacher, students reading the textbooks, and guided or independent practice (such as homework) to learn the terms, key concepts and understandings, and skills associated with the curriculum. Historically, under these methods of content delivery, when students did not learn the curriculum, they were given a failing grade and, in many cases, would be subsequently excluded from the general education classroom (Stainback & Stainback, 1996).

WAYS TO PROMOTE ACCESS TO CONTENT ■

Fortunately, school restructuring and curricular reforms have made it possible to think about content in ways that allow students multiple means to access the content. For instance, as we learned in the previous chapter, facts about students' learning preferences provide a valuable context for designing access to the content. Table 5.1 illustrates some of the ways in which teachers can facilitate access to the content for learners by using the theory of multiple intelligences (MI) as a framework.

Content differentiation also can be facilitated through the use of taxonomies, graphic organizers and technology, layered curriculum and differential levels of student participation, culturally responsive techniques, and students' interests in the curriculum. The remainder of this chapter explores these ways of providing content access and ends with an examination of co-teachers' roles in creating equitable access to content.

TAXONOMIES AND OBJECTIVES: ■
USING AND NOT ABUSING THEM

What is a taxonomy?

A taxonomy is a classification scheme for developing objectives that involves categories that are arranged in hierarchical order. Psychologists who specialized in traditional testing developed taxonomies because of their concern with the vagueness of many educational goals.

The most widely recognized taxonomy is Bloom's taxonomy of educational objectives in the cognitive domain of learning (Bloom, Englehart, Furst, Hill, & Krathwohl, 1956). Recently, Marzano (2000) proposed a revised cognitive taxonomy for educational objectives. Taxonomies also have been developed for affective and psychomotor outcomes. The taxonomy for the affective domain focuses upon values and attitudes (Krathwohl, Bloom, & Masia, 1964). The taxonomy for the psychomotor domain focuses upon physical abilities and skills (Simpson, 1972). Tomlinson (2002) suggests that Taba's (1962) Knowledge Categories, an example of which is shown in Table 5.2, can be used as a taxonomy to clarify as well as differentiate the type and amount of curriculum knowledge that is expected of diverse learners.

Educators often use taxonomies when developing objectives for lessons, units of study, and even the individual educational programs (IEPs) of students identified as eligible for special education. Reviews of the research on the

Table 5.1   Differentiating Content Using Multiple Intelligences (MI) Theory

Intelligence	Sample Ways to Access Content
Verbal/Linguistic	Oral Presentations Speeches Books Newspapers Internet Research Tape Recorders Reports Books on Tape
Logical/Mathematical	Calculators and Other Technology Math Manipulatives Outlines Timelines Lab Experiments Puzzles Formulas Math Games
Visual/Spatial	Graphs Concept Maps Graphic Organizers Videos PowerPoint Presentations Cameras Lego Blocks Posters Charts Cartoons
Bodily/Kinesthetic	Field Trips Building Tools Hands-on Tactile Learning Multisensory Learning Manipulatives Role Playing Acting Cooperative Learning Experiments Sports/Games Sports Equipment
Musical/Rhythmic	Songs About People, Books, Countries, Historic Events Raps Jingles Rhymes Mnemonic Devices

Intelligence	Sample Ways to Access Content
	Poetry Musical Instruments Tape Recorder
Naturalist	Plants Animals Field Trips Identifying Elements of and/or Relationship to Nature Gardening Tools Naturalists' Tools (e.g., Binoculars)
Interpersonal/People Smart	Think-Pair-Share Activities Cooperative Group Learning Role Play Debate Co-teaching Board Games Props for Role Plays Party Supplies
Intrapersonal/Self Smart	Journals Diaries Self-Monitoring Materials Materials for Projects

educational benefit of educational objectives (Marzano, Pickering, & Pollock, 2001) indicate that students learn more when their teachers provide them with clearly written objectives and when the objective is at the correct level of difficulty. Average-achieving students seem to gain more from being provided with written objectives than their high- or low-achieving classmates who seem to gain more when written objectives are augmented with visual and auditory exemplars.

Clearly, the use of taxonomies to select and communicate expected content outcomes could be of value to learners. With that said, we offer two cautions in using taxonomies to differentiate student access to the content of learning.

First, when using taxonomies to develop objectives, emphasis must be placed on developing a range of objectives rather than a single objective for the entire class. For decades, teachers in preparation have been taught how to write objectives based upon taxonomies such as Bloom's. Yet, this instruction has led to few teachers differentiating objectives for various learners within a lesson or unit. This may be due to the way in which teachers were taught to formulate lessons or school district requirements regarding lesson plan formats that set a single objective per lesson. A universal design perspective to differentiate

Table 5.2 Taba's Knowledge Categories

Knowledge Category	Definition	Example(s)
Fact	A specific detail; verifiable information	The president is the head of the executive branch.
Concept	A category with common elements	Executive, legislative, judicial branches of government
Principle	A fundamental truth, law, or doctrine that explains the relationship between two or more concepts	The legislative branch develops the laws. The judicial branch determines if the laws are consistent with the U.S. Constitution.
Skill	Proficient ability in using a technique, formula, method, or tool	Describe how a bill becomes a law.
Attitude	A belief, disposition, or value	Develop an appreciation for the system of checks and balances between the three branches of government.
Problem Solving, Transfer, and Application	The ability to use knowledge to address a goal that may not be immediately understandable	Examine the issues that must be addressed when there is a conflict between the executive and judicial branches of government.

objectives encourages teachers to match the complexity and diversity of the ways in which students access content.

A second caution relates to the finding that presenting students with more than one objective appears to lead to an increase in intentional learning and a decrease in incidental learning (Melton, 1978). Emphasizing single objectives for students, then, may limit student thinking by communicating that questioning, hypothesizing, and divergent thinking are not desired processes or outcomes of education. Gronlund (1995) and others have proposed that specific instructional objectives (Mager, 1997) may facilitate the learning of factual information but not advanced and complex kinds of learning. In fact, in 1984, Bloom lamented that after more than a quarter century of the use of his taxonomy, instructional and assessment materials and methods "rarely rise above the lowest category of the Taxonomy—knowledge" (p. 13).

Of particular concern to the authors is that this phenomenon endures for students identified as special education eligible or English language learners. In contrast, higher-level, real-life applications are what are needed to make learning meaningful and useful.

In summary, educators must avoid using taxonomies to pigeonhole students so that students with disabilities get only the knowledge and comprehension objectives while the gifted and talented students get the synthesis and evaluation objectives. Instead, educators can and should use taxonomies to have all students experience content at the various levels of the cognitive, affective, and psychomotor taxonomies.

Although taxonomies (and knowledge categories) are most often associated with content and the development of goals and objectives, the authors have found taxonomies beneficial for differentiating the products and processes of learning. Thus, we will revisit effective uses of taxonomies in Chapter 6, which describes methods to differentiate products and methods to assess products, and Chapter 7, which describes methods to differentiate instructional processes.

LAYERED CURRICULUM AND ■
LEVELS OF PARTICIPATION

Layered curriculum (Nunley, 1998) allows teachers to structure the content so that students with diverse abilities can focus on essential concepts and skills while performing at different levels of complexity. Although the focus of the activity is the same for all students, students can be meaningfully challenged to perform at their respective levels.

An example of layered curriculum is when teachers and students develop a contract that specifies at a minimum what content the learners will learn, how they will demonstrate the learning, and in what time period the learning will occur.

Another example of differentiated access to curriculum content is when students in a science class are offered a variety of text materials that have different readability indices or different languages (e.g., science textbooks written in Spanish). Another view of a layered curriculum can be seen when teachers set up learning centers that contain different learning materials with which to interact. One learning center might be a listening center where students follow the printed text while listening to the audio version. Another might be a hands-on activity center where various objects are provided for students to manipulate (i.e., students assemble a puzzle that contains information they need to solve a problem).

Schumm, Vaughn, and Harris (1997) have conceptualized the layering of curriculum in a somewhat different way. Their concept involves a three-tiered pyramid design with a core set of understandings and knowledge for *all* students, additional understandings and knowledge for *most* students, and yet other understandings and knowledge for *some* students.

As with taxonomies, the authors caution against using layered curriculum approaches to relegate some students (e.g., English language learners, students with IEPs) to lower-level cognitive tasks. As the examples within this book illustrate, many, if not most, students, if provided with high expectations and support, can achieve at the highest levels of thinking.

Giangreco, Cloninger, and Iverson (1993) suggest four levels of student participation—same, multilevel, curriculum overlapping, and alternative—for accessing curricular content. (See Table 5.3 for a description of each level.) They urge teachers to first gather facts about the learners before choosing a level of participation, so as to avoid an underestimation of a student's ability to participate. They further advise teachers to begin with the "doing the same as everyone else" level of participation and only proceed down the list of options as far as is needed to afford a student access to the content.

■ DIFFERENTIATING CONTENT USING GRAPHIC ORGANIZERS AND EDUCATIONAL TECHNOLOGY

Graphic organizers are one way to meet the needs for learners with a visual learning style. Graphic organizers can be used as a way to alert students to the content of a lecture or as a way to summarize what the lecture has covered. Graphic organizers also can be used to show learners various ways that the content is interrelated. The most frequently used graphic organizers include flow charts to show procedures or processes, Venn diagrams to emphasize similarities and differences, and concept maps to show relationships among concepts.

In general, educational technology provides access to visual images and graphic organizers. For example, consider *Inspiration,* a software program that students as well as teachers can use to transform outlines into various diagrams and diagrams into outlines.

But what do we mean by technology? As Udvari-Solner, Thousand, Villa, Quiocho, and Kelly (2005) note, technology is more than computers and software packages. (In fact, technology reinvents itself almost daily.) Technology in education includes calculators, video cameras, and VCRs; computers that come

Table 5.3   Levels of Participation in the Content

Level of Participation	Description
Same	Access to basically the same content as other students in the class, perhaps with minor modifications (e.g., amount or time)
Multilevel	Students are involved in the same curriculum area but pursue different objectives at multiple levels based on their individual needs. For example, the majority of students are learning about division while some students learn and practice subtraction.
Curriculum Overlapping	Students are engaged in the same lesson but pursue goals from different curricular areas. For example, a student works on range of motion, communication, and socialization goals in a science class with other students who are pursuing science goals.
Alternative	Students work on goals unrelated to what their classmates are pursuing. This may occur in a general education classroom or an alternative environment (e.g., Learning Center).

as laptops, desktops, and portable data assistants (PDAs); peripheral devices such as printers, scanners, and probeware; general software tools such as word processors, databases, spreadsheets, presentation tools, and computer-assisted instruction for drill and practice. There are also telecommunication networks that are used for electronic mail, distance education, and interactive multimedia; add to these such commonplace applications such as word prediction and spelling and grammar "checks" and unique applications such as text-to-speech and speech-to-text software, semantic mapping tools, and more.

Consider the following suggestions generated by the personnel at the Center for Applied Special Technology (CAST, 2005). Students with reading difficulty gain access to grade-level material by using computers that read textbooks and core literature aloud to them. Students who exhibit delays in the development of the fine motor skills are offered the chance to use portable keyboards to type notes, stories, and their own ideas rather than write them by hand. Students who have trouble with math are assigned to work with math software that is highly effective, interactive, and engaging. Students who have trouble with writing or composition are assigned a choice of word prediction programs to assist them with formulating sentences and paragraphs.

When teachers and other school personnel consider adopting specific textbooks, they can also review the several dozen computer-assisted curricula that increase ability to differentiate access to the curriculum. For example, achievement data on students at risk for school failure show that they can improve their achievement gains through technology-enriched instructional programs such as *STAR Early Literacy* (Renaissance Learning, 2004) and *READ 180* (Hasselbring, Kinsella, & Feldman, n.d.). *Riverdeep* offers a series of technology-based programs to meet diverse instructional needs in mathematics, reading, social studies, and science, whereas *Plato Math Expeditions Program* is a web-based comprehensive program with high student interest and involvement that includes tutorials, practice, and quizzes plus online tools such as place-value blocks and calculators. On the basis of a study conducted by Morgan and Ritter (2002), the Carnegie Learning *Cognitive Tutor Programs* software instructional program for algebra and geometry has met the research evidence test required by the U.S. Office of Education Clearinghouse for Ideas That Work.

DIFFERENTIATING CONTENT WITH CULTURALLY RESPONSIVE TECHNIQUES

Many studies have shown that African American students are disproportionately placed in special education nationwide, and that Hispanic/Latino students are disproportionately placed in certain states (Artiles & Trent, 1994; Harry, 1994; Webb-Johnson, 2003). Overrepresentation is determined to exist when a particular group is represented in a program in a substantially larger percentage than their percentage in the population as a whole. The overrepresentation of culturally and linguistically diverse (CLD) students in special education has raised concerns about how to ensure culturally sensitive differentiation of content and material.

Fortunately, researchers in many areas of the country and the world are attempting to provide solutions—the University of Texas (e.g., Webb-Johnson, 2003), the University of Kansas (e.g., Grossman, Utley, & Obiakor, 2003), Colorado State University (e.g., Klingne et al., 2004), a seven-nation collaborative project in Europe (e.g., Bartolo & Ale, 2005), and the University of Florida (e.g., Daunci, Correa, & Reyes-Blanes, 2004). To illustrate, the research analyzed by Grossman et al. (2003) indicates that the learning styles of non-Anglo students are more likely to be participatory, peer-oriented, field dependent, global, and reflective, whereas their Anglo peers are more likely to be individualistic, field-independent, concrete learners.

The research of Daunci et al. (2004) identified competencies for teachers of students with cultural and linguistic differences, an essential one being "knowledge and sensitivity about cultural influences" (p. 106). Listen to what a student suggests:

> If my teacher only knew that I have never ever seen someone like me in the stories I read. If she did, she might take the time to select novels where I can read about people like me. I might like reading and school a lot better.

This comment, made by a high school student when asked what he wanted his teachers to know about him, emphasizes the importance of students seeing themselves in the literature and textbooks they read (Udvari-Solner, Thousand, Villa, Quiocho, & Kelly, 2005, p. 102). Teachers who practice culturally sensitive differentiation of the content and materials make sure that students of color, students from various cultures, and students with disabilities can see themselves in the media used in all of the content areas. Webb-Johnson (2003) reinforces this practice when she recommends that teachers instructing African American students highlight African Americans who have excelled in the content areas being studied. When science standards relate to inventions, students can be introduced to African American inventors and scientists. When examining the expansion to the midwest and western regions of the United States, teachers can arrange for students to research and learn about the roles African American pioneers played in that development.

Other culturally sensitive methods to ensure access to the content and materials of instruction include role-plays, reenactments, and simulations. Technological tools, for example, the interactive, multimodal *History Alive!* curriculum (http://www.teachtci.com/curriculum/curriculumHA.asp) engages students in simulations and interactive and cooperative learning-based experiences (e.g., interactive slide lecture dialogs, partner skill builder exercises, problem-solving group work, response groups) that result in an *experience* of history. Cooperative learning strategies such as those used with this curriculum have been shown to be culturally sensitive.

In fact, Johnson and Johnson (2002) summarize the research in this area by arguing that little information about different cultural and ethnic heritages is attained through reading books. Rather, students learn to value diversity, use it in creative problem solving, and develop ability to work effectively with diverse peers by knowing, working with, and having personal interactions with members of diverse groups.

An important set of approaches for facilitating access to the content used to support English language learners is referred to as *sheltered instruction* or Specially Designed Academic Instruction in English (SDAIE; Echevarria & Graves, 2003). In sheltered instruction, teachers use the regular core curriculum and modify their teaching to make the content understandable while at the same time promoting their students' English language development. Teachers use clear, direct, simple English and a wide range of scaffolding strategies to communicate meaningful input in the content areas. Learning activities that connect new content to students' prior knowledge, that require collaboration among students, and that also spiral through curriculum material offer English learners the same access to the content as is offered to their English-speaking peers. At the same time, these learning activities adapt lesson delivery to suit the English learners' proficiency level. (Table 5.4 offers some strategies for sheltering content instruction.) Although traditionally used to support English language learners, these strategies can facilitate access for many other learners in general education classrooms.

INVOLVING STUDENTS IN ■ DETERMINING CONTENT

We agree with the advice from Orkwis and McLane (1998), who wrote, "Access, both cognitive as well as sensorimotor, to the curriculum begins with a student being able to interact with it to learn" (p. 6). This implies that the delivery of the content and the access to the materials must result in some form of overt

Table 5.4   Sample Sheltered English Techniques

1.   Plan lessons with a focus on just a few key ideas.
2.   Build a positive, supportive environment.
3.   Display, preview, and review key concepts.
4.   Keep activities purposeful and authentic.
5.   Use active participation, with opportunities for students to practice language.
6.   Use multiple forms of input to provide a context for the key ideas. Examples include *realia* (real things), demonstrations, and manipulatives.
7.   Access and connect to the background knowledge and experience of your students.
8.   Use real-life activities.
9.   Reduce the linguistic load of your speech. Simplify sentences and use pauses. Support your message with nonverbal clues.
10.   Adapt text to make it more accessible. Examples include outlines and graphic depictions.

activity on the part of the learner. When learners are actively engaged with the content, they also increase their time on task. Increased time on task is associated with increased achievement (Gest & Gest, 2005).

Udvari-Solner, Villa, and Thousand (2005) illustrate a method where students actively identify the content they wish to know about a topic. In the scenario they present, the teacher introduces the topic and the standards that must be addressed. Then, to solicit prior knowledge and set the unit or lesson's direction, the teacher introduces a three-column graphic organizer labeled "K-W-L" that can be used to show what students currently *know* about the topic, what they *want* to learn, and how they plan to show what they have *learned*. Carr and Ogle (1987) describe how to use a K-W-L procedure to assist students to comprehend and summarize content. In individual conferences, the teacher and each student review the curriculum standards and the class-generated list of questions of interest to select a focus for each student's work.

■ CO-TEACHER ROLES IN DIFFERENTIATING CONTENT

Teachers decide to co-teach for a variety of reasons. One of the most important reasons is that each co-teacher brings to the learners a different set of knowledge, skills, and attitudes about education. For example, is your co-teacher team similar to the Jupp and Dondero co-teaching team you met in Chapter 2? If so, then you can see how the mathematics teacher is likely to be more familiar with the content and materials for teaching specific concepts in mathematics, while the special educator will be more familiar with strategies to make the material and content more accessible to students with disabilities. With co-teaching, a natural division of labor regarding content and strategies for accessing content then emerges.

Some co-teachers decide to collect information about differentiating the content and materials by crossing the role boundaries. In other words, the special educator could gather alternatives to the material and content and the mathematics teacher could gather alternative strategies for presenting the content and materials. The most important thing for collaborating educators to do is to have a conversation about *who* will do *what* by *when*. With an articulated division of labor and a due date, the co-teachers will be able to match the facts about their learners to the content and materials in a timely fashion.

■ PAUSE AND REFLECT

It is time to again examine Table 3.1, the lesson plan template provided in Chapter 3. Focus now on the section entitled, "Content (What will students learn?)" With the facts you've gathered about your students in mind, consider the questions that appear in that content section of the template. Ask yourself the following questions: "What are the academic or social goals?" "What content standards are addressed?" "In what order should concepts and content be taught?" "Are there any particular students who require unique ways of having content represented (e.g., Braille, simplified text, pictorial representation of concepts)?" "What multilevel or multisensory materials will assist students to access the content?" "Are multilevel goals needed so different students have meaningful access to the content?"

As you consider these questions, have you considered your students' diverse learning preferences? Could you and should you use taxonomies, graphic organizers, technology, layered curriculum, differentiated levels of student participation, culturally responsive techniques, and students' strengths and interests to facilitate access to the content for all of the students in the class?

Once you make the necessary adjustments and refinements, you will be ready to proceed to the next step of the UDL cycle—that of differentiating student products. Next, Chapter 6 offers a host of ideas on how to provide students different ways of showing what they have learned and how to assess that learning.

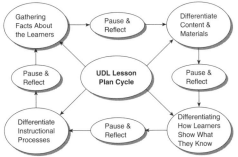

Differentiating and Assessing the Products of Learning

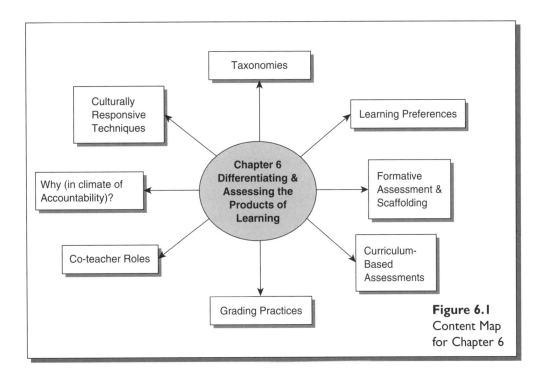

Figure 6.1
Content Map for Chapter 6

No one grew taller by being measured.

—Phillip Gammage

As illustrated in the Universal Design for Learning (UDL) lesson planning cycle, the content, products, and processes of instruction are inextricably linked to each other and to the facts about the learners. Now that you have gathered facts about your learners and identified the key content and materials needed for the lesson, it is time to focus on how students will show what they know—the products of the lesson.

In this chapter, you will discover how you might answer the following questions:

- Why should teachers differentiate the products of learning?
- In what ways might teachers differentiate and assess the products of learning?
- What are teachers' roles in differentiating and assessing products?

■ WHY DIFFERENTIATE ASSESSMENT IN A CLIMATE OF HIGH STAKES TESTING?

In this era of accountability for student achievement on high stakes tests, why should teachers consider other methods to document their students' learning? Teachers are accountable not only to administer and interpret high stakes tests, but are also accountable in ensuring that all students have access to the products of learning—*all* means *all*—including students with disabilities, students from linguistically and culturally diverse heritages, students of poverty, students eligible for gifted and talented services, and students learning English as a second language.

An important reason for considering alternative assessments of students' products is that high stakes tests are administered once a year and do not allow teachers to make changes in their instruction during the year. Additionally, affording students an opportunity to learn and demonstrate that they can learn in different formats will also strengthen their ability to perform on these once-a-year assessments.

Teachers who differentiate their assessments allow students to show what they know in a number of ways. An important reason for differentiating products and assessment procedures is to ensure that your students are learning what you are teaching. The information you gather from differentiated assessment helps you design better and better lessons that meet your students' diverse needs.

Another powerful reason to differentiate assessments is the cumulative benefits that come from adding multiple opportunities to demonstrate that learning is occurring. Students who have had frequent opportunities to speak, act out, demonstrate, and diagram their understanding of concepts may be less anxious about using another mode to show what they know (e.g., pencil and paper tests).

For example, VanDerHayden and Burns (2005) implemented a curriculum-based measurement system to track mathematics progress of K–6 students. The data, collected on a bimonthly basis, were used to track mastery at each skill level. Daily data were collected to track specific instructional interventions when needed. Their results suggested that children made significant progress within one school year and the school significantly increased Stanford-9 mathematics scores after implementing the program.

USING CULTURALLY RESPONSIVE ■ TECHNIQUES TO DIFFERENTIATE AND ASSESS THE PRODUCTS OF LEARNING

Carol Thomas, Vivian Correa, and Catherine Morsink (1995) are expert practitioners and researchers who have studied the impact of assessments on multicultural students. They suggest that educators learn to understand the purposes of various types of tests and determine whether or not the tests are culture-free, culture-specific, a translation of an English-based test, pluralistic, adaptive, or dynamic based on the following descriptions:

- *Culture-free/culture-fair* tests measure aspects of growth presumed to be unrelated to culture.
- *Culture-specific* tests assess knowledge and ability within a nondominant culture and are limited in measuring school learning, which tends to reflect the dominant culture's values.
- *Test translations* of English-language tests in the student's dominant language do not remove the inherent bias in the test items.
- *Pluralistic assessments* measure medical status, social performance, and learning potential that are normed on a diverse population (in contrast to single assessments, which are typically normed on the dominant population).
- *Adaptive behavior assessments* measure student ability to cope with social and cultural demands and do not measure academic performance.
- *Dynamic assessments* use test-teach-test procedures to provide information on what instruction may be needed for a student to acquire skills (also known as "pre-post testing" or "clinical teaching" or "data-based assessment").

Culturally sensitive assessments such as these allow students to show what they know in the style that best represents their respective cultures and also to receive immediate feedback on accuracy so that they can make corrective changes. This ensures they will practice accuracy rather than practice errors. Alternatives to pencil-and-paper expressions can often reveal a greater depth and breadth of student learning. For example, teachers might structure audiotaped interviews or instructional conversations (e.g., Echevarria & McDonough, 1995). Students can also be encouraged to show what they know by creating visuals, stories, and songs.

As described by Echevarria and McDonough (1995), instructional conversation is a method that promotes opportunities for language development, provides a thematic focus within a holistic presentation, and is easily adaptable for second language learners as well as for learners with special needs.

Compared to students who struggle to learn, students who are successful learners are more likely to construct meaningful connections among ideas, integrate what they are learning with their personal background knowledge, and constantly self-monitor what they are learning. Bilingual students and those with special needs often do not comprehend what they are learning because they do not have the underlying connections. Instructional conversations promote improvements in comprehension skills by capitalizing on what students bring to the learning situation so that they can connect, analyze, and reflect on what is being learned.

A second culturally sensitive practice is the game format with low-key competition as a form of motivation. For example, "Name that Equation," modeled after *Name That Tune-* and *Jeopardy*-formatted games (along with other methods that encourage creative problem solving), allows differential levels of difficulty or complexity. Game formats, in addition to their motivational aspects and appeal to students with a variety of movement differences, also capitalize on the Zone of Proximal Development (ZPD) that refers to an individual student's potential level of learning when helped by a teacher or peer. The ZPD measures a particular *range of ability* with and without assistance from a teacher or a more capable peer (Vygotsky, 1987).

To effectively scaffold students within their ZPDs, a teacher should also have an awareness of the different roles students and teachers assume throughout the co-teaching process; e.g., teacher or peer models behavior for the student; student imitates the teacher's or peer's behavior; teacher or peer fades out instruction; student practices reciprocal teaching (scaffolding others) until the skill is mastered. Vygotsky emphasized that what children can do with the assistance of others is even more indicative of their mental development than what they can do alone.

Duda and Utley (2006) compared the culturally influenced behaviors of children from African American, European American, Asian American, Hispanic, and Native American heritages such as their behavioral patterns, arguing style, questioning patterns, attitude toward sharing, and beliefs about leadership. Teachers are encouraged to take these into consideration when evaluating their students' performances. The importance of using evidence-based methods for assessing students from culturally and linguistically diverse populations is reinforced by Klingner and Edwards (2006). When teachers have developed culturally responsive teaching skills, they are better able to accurately assess their students' command of both language and literacy (Ortiz, 2001). Townsend (2002) argued that no teacher should be left behind with respect to knowing how to design and evaluate culturally responsive methods.

■ USING A TAXONOMY OF OBJECTIVES TO DIFFERENTIATE PRODUCTS AND ASSESSMENT

Understanding taxonomies can assist educators to differentiate the products that learners produce to demonstrate what they have learned. It is important for teachers to offer the entire range of opportunities for students to show they have the knowledge, comprehension, application, synthesis, analysis, and evaluation levels. Often teachers only offer knowledge or comprehension levels to students with disabilities or to students whose expressive language skills in English are in the process of developing.

Using taxonomies such as Bloom's, we are able to differentiate the ways students demonstrate their learning at different levels of cognition. For example, at the knowledge and comprehension level, some students will recall dates of significant events, while others enter them onto a preprepared time line, and other students illustrate the significant historical events along the time line using higher-level thinking skills.

Students can have a choice in how they represent their learning. For example, students can choose to prepare a written report, speech, PowerPoint presentation, video, demonstration, poem, or song. Table 6.1 lists a variety of products at each level of a taxonomy developed by Bloom et al. (1956) that may assist you to differentiate how your students show what they know.

How might teachers assess their students with respect to various levels of Bloom's Taxonomy?

Reciprocal teaching is an example of a teaching-learning procedure that embeds assessment of various levels of cognitive difficulty (Palinscar & Brown, 1984). This procedure is useful for any task that requires reading comprehension (such as reading to gain information from a science text, social studies text, encyclopedia text, etc.). Reciprocal teaching can be considered a study skill as well as a strategy because it requires explicit teaching of the procedures.

With reciprocal teaching, students work in pairs to complete four steps. The first step is a knowledge skill where students ask each other a question about the main idea of a selected reading. The second step is a comprehension skill where students take turns to summarize, in a brief sentence or two, the main idea and details. During the third step, which is an analysis skill, students clarify and

Table 6.1   Using Bloom's Taxonomy to Differentiate the Products of Learning

Level of Bloom's Taxonomy	A Sampling of Different Products to Demonstrate Learning
Knowledge	Flash cards, rebus story, scrapbook, drawing, puzzle, tape recording, mobile, collage, cartoon strips
Comprehension	Picture dictionary, pamphlet, news story, book report, diagram, essay, bulletin board, diary
Application	Chart, graph, model, peep show, display, interview, survey, mini-center, experiment
Analysis	PowerPoint presentation, oral report, prepare a video, scroll, collection
Synthesis	Create original poems, songs, games, plays, speeches
Evaluation	Written report, scroll, book review, photo/picture essay, advertisement, editorial, debate, project cube

identify any words or concepts that need to be defined. In the fourth step, a form of evaluation skill, students make predictions based on the information read so far, asking each other, "What will happen next?"

Carter (1997) reported that teachers who implemented reciprocal teaching as part of their reading instruction program at the elementary through high school levels found dramatic improvements on the Michigan assessment instrument in reading comprehension. At the faculty level, teachers themselves used reciprocal teaching on each other to enhance their proficiency in acquiring a second language (a goal for their staff's development).

Thus, it is possible for teachers to enfold instruction and assessment of four types of student cognitive skill levels (knowledge, comprehension, analysis, and evaluation) during a single lesson.

■ APPLYING CONCEPTS FROM LEARNING PREFERENCES FRAMEWORKS TO DIFFERENTIATE ASSESSMENT

Awareness of a student's learning styles can help teachers differentiate assessment. For example, students with an auditory learning style often perform better on assessments that require listening to directions compared to assessments that require reading the directions. Teachers can arrange for a variety of opportunities for students to show what they have learned from listening, seeing, or doing.

Sternberg (1997b) reported a framework for understanding the thinking styles or preferences of students. The study involved 199 students from high schools across the United States and some students from abroad. Students were grouped for differentiated instruction and assessment based on their preferences for activities related to memory, analysis, creativity, or practicality. Assessments included multiple-choice verbal, quantitative, and figural items, as well as analytical, creative, and practical essay items. As Sternberg wrote, "By exposing students to instruction emphasizing each type of ability, we enable them to capitalize on their strengths while developing and improving new skills" (p. 23).

Many educators report that Multiple Intelligences (MI) Theory (Armstrong, 2000; Gardner, 1983, 1997) has been helpful in their efforts to differentiate the products of learning. Students are offered opportunities to show what they have learned through their strength intelligence areas. Some students may create a rap, poem, or song while others may choose to construct models, illustrations, teach part of a lesson, write a journal about the learning, or conduct independent research. Raps, songs, and other creative expressions can capitalize on the cultural and linguistic style differences regarding movement and communal learning described by Boykin, Albury, Tyler, Hurley, Bailey, and Miller (2005) at the Center for Research on the Education of Students Placed At Risk (CRESPAR). Table 6.2 lists some examples of how concepts from MI Theory can be used to differentiate the products of learning.

Table 6.2   Using Concepts From MI Theory to Differentiate Learning Outcomes

Intelligence	Sample Products
Verbal/linguistic	Prepare a report, debate, lecture, paper-and-pencil tests, crosswords, newspaper article
Logical/Mathematical	Apply a formula, solve a problem, use the scientific method, puzzles, experiments, calculations, discover or develop a pattern
Bodily/Kinesthetic	Role-playing, sports games, acting, cooperative learning, dancing, gesturing, mime
Visual/Spatial	Artwork, photographs, posters, PowerPoint, charts, illustrations
Musical/Rhythmic	Sing, tap, create a rap, poem, or jingle
Naturalist	Care for animals or plants, gardening, investigation of nature, experiments, use the scientific method
Interpersonal/People Smart	Teach a part of a lesson, oral presentation, peer tutoring, cooperative group learning, role play, debate
Intrapersonal/Reflective	Keep a diary, journal, or learning log, independent research, reading, and writing

USING FORMATIVE ASSESSMENT ■ AND SCAFFOLDING TO DIFFERENTIATE ASSESSMENT

Scaffolding techniques are provided to the learner during both problem solving and formative assessment activities (Shepard, 2005). When using scaffolding, teachers use their knowledge of learners' current levels of understanding to alter the instruction to generate greater competence. Scaffolding and formative assessment are techniques that are part of both differentiated instruction and UDL that have a solid basis in learning theory. Vygotsky's (1987) sociocultural theory of development posits that a cognitive development occurs twice—first on the social plane in interaction with others and then on the psychological or internal plane. The ZPD framework explains how this occurs. Vygotsky describes the ZPD as the space between a child's ability to independently problem solve and the child's potential development to problem solve through guidance by, or collaboration with, more capable adults or peers.

Scaffolding is a teaching strategy wherein the teacher creates a ZPD by controlling various elements of the task so as to ensure successful completion through the use of hints, reminders, encouragement, and modeling. Shepard (2005) explains that formative assessment involves the idea that the student must hold a concept of quality similar to that of the teacher, be able to compare his current performance with the standard, and be able to take action to close that gap. Both formative assessment and scaffolding can result in increased student achievement when the teacher elicits prior knowledge, provides positive feedback during the performance of the task (not just at the end), teaches for transfer of learning, and teaches students how to self-assess. Teachers can include frequent monitoring (graphing) of progress as one way to help students develop goals to improve their best scores (competing against themselves rather than others) or their team's best score. The resulting graphic representations can be used in portfolio assessments and in student or parent conferences to show the impact of daily instruction.

■ CURRICULUM-BASED ASSESSMENTS

Curriculum-based assessments (CBAs) provide teachers with a method of scaffolding, formative assessment, and instruction within a student's ZPD. CBAs are a more structured form of observation of students as they progress through a specified curriculum. CBAs are criterion-referenced tests that are teacher-constructed and designed to reflect curriculum content. Such assessment systems have gained more and more respect as alternatives to traditional psycho-educational diagnostic techniques that do not empower teachers to make educational decisions for students with exceptional needs.

Hall and Mengel (2002) distinguish between standardized commercial achievement tests that measure broad curriculum areas or skills and curriculum-based assessment. In contrast, curriculum-based systems keep track of specific skills that are being taught in the classroom. Several approaches to curriculum-based systems share four common characteristics. First, students are assessed directly using the materials in which they are being instructed. (This involves sampling items from the curriculum.) Second, administration is generally brief in duration (typically 1–5 minutes) thus allowing teachers to collect assessment information while they are teaching. Third, frequent and repeated measures of performance allow observations to be made about student performance under conditions that might change (e.g., level of difficulty, implementation of a learning contract, and so on). Fourth, data are usually displayed graphically to allow monitoring of student performance.

Notably, CBAs have been implemented effectively for assessing and monitoring the progress of those K–12 learners with learning disabilities, gifts and talents, attention deficit disorder, emotional or behavioral problems, and speech impairments, in addition to adjudicated youth, students at risk for school failure, and students in bilingual settings. Researchers and practitioners alike have reported using CBAs for reading and language arts, science, social studies, arithmetic, and general mathematics, as well as career and vocational curriculum (Fuchs & Fuchs, 1999; Idol, Nevin, & Paolucci-Whitcomb, 1999; King-Sears, Cummings, & Hullihen, 1994).

The technical adequacy of this form of assessment has been studied by Shinn (1998), who estimated that over 150 articles were published between 1988 and 1998 on curriculum-based measurement systems. Research has been conducted on applications of CBAs in various settings, special and general education classrooms, as well as inclusive settings. Many researchers have studied computer applications, computer development of multiple measures, computer scoring, and computer graphing of student performance. Similarly, as a diagnostic tool, this type of assessment has helped teachers with error analysis and teacher decision making.

DIFFERENTIATING HOW TEACHERS ■ GRADE PRODUCTS

Overall, teachers who differentiate assessment of the products of their students' learning must overcome many traditional grading practices and procedures that are arbitrary and subjective. General and special educators alike face certain challenges and issues when grading their students in inclusive settings. In addition to meeting school district guidelines and expectations for grading, teachers must consider the impact of assessment methods (norm-referenced testing and criterion-referenced testing) as well as the impact of differentiated instruction that supports student learning. And, as shown in Table 6.3, there are several requirements that must be met if grading systems are to be considered nondiscriminatory. This means that students with disabilities and other types of unique needs are graded on their demonstration of what they know without interference from their disability or special needs.

We acknowledge that a grade per se tells nothing about what a student knows, believes, or can do primarily because of the variability within and

Table 6.3   Guidelines to Ensure Grading Practices Are Fair and Nondiscriminatory

1.	Students must be treated similarly but educators can use modified grading system if it is available to all students.
2.	For students who take a general education class for reasons other than mastery of the content, teachers can use grading procedures that differ from those used for the rest of the class.
3.	Guidelines and criteria for ranking students or granting awards cannot arbitrarily lower or exclude the grades of students with disabilities; weighting grades can occur if based on objective criteria and if the courses are open and available to all students.
4.	Report card or transcript designations that indicate participation in special education or indicate that a student received pedagogical accommodations or a modified curriculum in general education classes are not permissible unless educators treat the grades and courses of all students in the same way. Example: having a course called Practical Physics that is open to all is permissible; but having a class called Resource Room Physics that is available only to students with disabilities is not permitted.
5.	Transcripts to postsecondary institutions can contain designations of special education courses with informed written consent of families and students.

across schools regarding what a grade represents. This variability and subjectivity results in some often puzzling outcomes, such as students who are labeled gifted are awarded Cs and Ds! We agree with Nel Noddings (1992) who wrote, "We should move away from the question, 'Has Johnny learned X?' to the more revealing question, 'What has Johnny learned?'" (p. 47).

We describe the following alternatives to the traditional grading system so that you can have more choices as you develop your own system. The ultimate goal of grading practices is to shift the focus of our thinking to how a teacher might teach differently given the feedback that good grading practices yield.

■ ALTERNATIVES TO NORM-REFERENCED GRADING PROCEDURES

Many school systems use the same standards to evaluate all students. They rely on using a numeric and letter grade on the basis of a comparison with the performance of others. We acknowledge that educators working in such systems may feel constricted by the district's established A–F grading system. Even when educators work in such a system, they can remain open-minded and flexible to employing the strategies described in this section to differentiate and report on student progress. And although they may employ a variety of processes, the various grades and reports are based on clearly specified learning goals and performance standards. Tomlinson and McTighe (2006) suggest that reporting formats consider three factors: (1) achievement of goals, (2) progress toward goals, and (3) work habits. Such reporting mechanisms ensure that students are recognized for both achievement and effort.

For example, teachers can designate a level of difficulty for a specific assignment or course, computing grades on the basis of pre-established levels. Students can select assignments and receive a grade that is computed by multiplying a numerical score representing quality of the assignment by a factor that reflects difficulty level. Another option is to adapt numerical grades to reflect other factors such as achievement, effort, and level of difficulty, and average or weight the grades to produce a composite grade. Teachers can individualize norm-referenced grading by showing that a student achieved a B in the fifth grade curriculum while working in an eighth grade science class. Supplementary information can be provided to describe modifications that supported student learning. (Read about how Chang's teachers apply this concept to differentiate assessment for one of Chang's classmates, Maarten, a student with cognitive differences, in Chapter 13.)

■ ADAPTING CRITERION-REFERENCED GRADING SYSTEMS

Criterion-referenced systems grade all students on the basis of each one's mastery of a set of objectives, rather than comparing performance to that of others. Tomlinson (2001b) suggests that teachers provide some normative data to show relative standing of students and to understand the range of age-appropriate curricular expectations. Rating scales and checklists that show escalating competencies can also be used. The rating scales and checklists can also be explicit with respect to accommodations. Teachers can use contract grading where goals, learning activities, instructional accommodations, outcomes, and evaluation procedures are determined individually.

SELF-REFERENCED SYSTEMS ■

Portfolio systems are an example of self-referenced grading. Portfolios are often enhanced with rubrics that specify different levels of proficiency. The rubrics allow students to gauge their own performance on an ongoing basis. A common example of this type of grading is when the progress of a student with an individual educational program (IEP) is assessed based upon the individualized goals, instructional accommodations, performance criteria, and evaluation schedule prescribed in the IEP. According to Pickett and Dodge (2001), rubrics are authentic assessment tools that can help students understand the complex elements of the tasks that are evaluated. Three common features of rubrics include a stated objective (e.g., performance, behavior, or quality), a range with which to rate performance, and specific performance characteristics arranged in levels that indicate the degree to which a standard has been met. Using rubrics in assessment help clarify criteria in specific terms, show students how their work will be evaluated and what is expected, provide useful feedback regarding the effectiveness of the instruction, and provide benchmarks against which to measure and document progress.

It is important, however, to ensure that the rubrics have a degree of reliability and validity in order to protect students from unfair discrimination. Furthermore, rubrics should reflect culturally responsive practices. Readers are encouraged to access the many websites that provide examples of rubrics by conducting a web search. For an example of a teacher-developed rubric that Rosa and her classmates use to monitor their progress on 20 topics in an algebra class, see Rosa's lesson plan in Chapter 11.

CO-TEACHER ROLES IN DIFFERENTIATING ■ PRODUCTS OF LEARNING

Similar to the differentiated roles described for gathering facts about the learner (Chapter 4) and differentiating content and materials (Chapter 5), co-teachers who differentiate products of learning can also differentiate their roles. For example, they can differentiate their co-teaching approach by consciously selecting supportive, parallel, complementary, or team teaching arrangements. (See Chapter 9 for more detailed descriptions of the four approaches.) The approaches that are selected will dictate the type of actions co-teachers take during the process of assessing the products of learning.

For example, in the supportive co-teacher approach, one teacher circulates to monitor and correct students as they follow the directions and instruction from the other teacher. In this role, the supportive co-teacher is the grader and, in some cases, the tutor who provides extra instruction. In the parallel approach, the co-teachers can set up two learning stations where students come to one of them for the assessment interaction. This approach often is used by teachers who hold conferences with their students regarding progress on class projects, reading comprehension, and so on. In this approach, both co-teachers are equally responsible for conducting the assessments (read about how Rosa's teachers use this approach in Chapter 11).

Another role that co-teachers can take is that of advocate. In this role, co-teachers consciously accommodate their assessment of student products in such a way that the student's disability does not interfere with the assessment. This role may require co-teachers to petition district and national testing centers with respect to requests for accommodations. For example, in Florida, teachers have access to *IEP Team Guide to Florida's Comprehensive Achievement Test (FCAT) Accommodations,* written by Beech (2005) and published by the Florida Department of Education. The most important aspect of differentiating co-teacher roles is that co-teachers must have a conversation about who will collect assessment of student learning and when it will be reported to each other so that functional decisions can be made about the lesson plan itself.

■ PAUSE AND REFLECT

Please review Table 3.1, the Universal Design Lesson Plan template, to differentiate instruction described in Chapter 3. Focus on the section titled, "Products Showing Students Success (How will students show what they know?)."

Ask yourself to what extent have you considered the questions that appear in that section of the template. In what ways will the learning outcomes be demonstrated? Have you identified multiple ways your students can demonstrate their understandings (e.g., learning preferences, multilevel and/or multisensory performances)? Have you delineated authentic products your students might create to show what they know, and have you developed authentic rubrics to use when you evaluate the products? What are the criteria teachers use to evaluate the products? Are they clear and unambiguous, fair, and culturally sensitive?

Now you can review the facts you have gathered about your specific students. Ask yourself, "Are there any students who require unique ways of showing what they know?" Do you need to make any adjustments to your plans to differentiate the products and methods of assessing learning? Then make the necessary adjustments and refinements before proceeding to the next step.

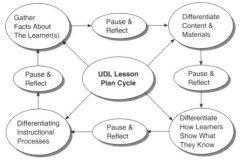

Differentiating the Instructional Processes

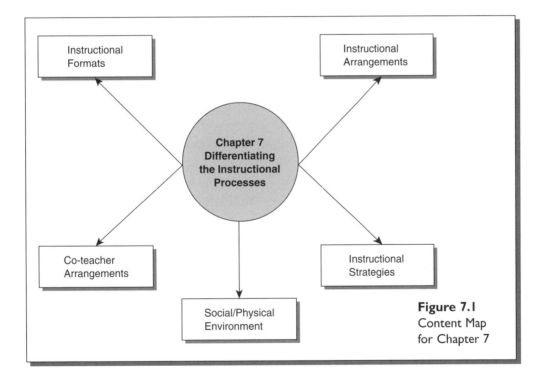

Figure 7.1
Content Map
for Chapter 7

The purpose of education is to make the choices clear to people, not to make the choices for people.

—Peter McWilliams

In this chapter, you will learn the answer to this question, "What are methods to differentiate instructional approaches so that students have multiple means of engaging with the curriculum?"

We highlight the following approaches and techniques because of the research-based evidence showing that students with a diverse array of instructional differences can gain access to the general education curriculum. We have organized the discussion of methods to differentiate instructional processes in accordance with the "Process of Instruction" section of the Universal Design Lesson Plan template to differentiate instruction found in Chapter 3 and reproduced here as Table 7.1.

■ THE COMPLEXITIES OF THE PROCESS OF INSTRUCTION (GRAPHIC ORGANIZER)

This chapter will examine some of the many options for differentiating in five areas: (1) instructional formats, (2) instructional arrangements, (3) instructional strategies, (4) social-physical environment, and (5) co-teaching approaches.

Be aware that there is a vast literature on effective instructional processes that can help you differentiate instruction. To comprehensively examine these processes would require expanding this chapter to several books. We believe that teachers have a responsibility to research and choose instructional practices that have a high probability of enhancing achievement for their students. Table 7.2 lists nine categories of instructional strategies that have been demonstrated by research to have strong effects on student achievement (Marzano, Pickering, & Pollock, 2001). We encourage you to learn more about the "do's and don'ts" of using each of these strategies as well as to think about how to more effectively incorporate these and other research-supported strategies into your teaching processes.

■ INSTRUCTIONAL FORMATS

The *instructional format* of a lesson can be defined as the way in which teachers impart information to students or the way in which students take part in learning. As the items in the "Instructional Formats" column of Table 7.1 illustrate, instructional formats vary widely from more teacher-led or controlled methods, such as the lecture, to the more student-led and interactive approaches listed in the first column of Table 7.1.

As pointed out in Chapter 3, the use of multisensory, active, and interactive formats allow students who do not respond well to lecture or demonstration formats to have more options for participating actively and successfully. To illustrate, peer-assisted computer instruction is a format that increases students' collaboration with peers, increases use of higher-order thinking skills, and improves time on task; students often continue work during recess, before school, and after school.

Table 7.1 Procedures to Differentiate the Process of Instruction

Instructional Formats	Instructional Arrangements	Process of Instruction (How students engage in learning) Instructional Strategies	Social and Physical Environment	Co-teaching Approach(es)
Considerations Adapting lectures? Activity-based? Experiential? Simulations/role play? Group investigation? Discovery learning? Computer/web-based? Self-directed? Stations? Integrated cross-curricular thematic unit/lesson? Service learning? Community referenced?	Considerations Cooperative learning structures? Same or cross-age peer tutors? Independent? Whole group? Other? (Tutorial, teacher-directed small group)	Considerations Choose research-based strategies? Use taxonomies? Apply concepts from Multiple Intelligences Theory? Integration of the arts?	Considerations Room arranged? Use of spaces outside of class? Social norms? Teach responsibility? Positive behavior supports? Environmental alterations?	Options Supportive? Parallel? Complementary? Team Teaching? Students as co-teachers? (e.g., peer tutors and cooperative learning structures under "instructional arrangements")

Pause and Reflect About Specific Students
What student-specific teaching strategies do select students need? What specific systems of supports (e.g., assistive technology), aids (e.g., personal assistance, cues, contracts), or services (e.g., counseling) do select students need?

Table 7.2   Top Nine Research-Based Strategies for Increasing Student Achievement

Strategy	We can use this strategy when...
1. Identifying similarities and differences	
2. Summarizing and note taking	
3. Reinforcing effort	
4. Homework and practice at appropriate level of difficulty	
5. Nonlinguistic representations, graphic organizers	
6. Cooperative group learning	
7. Setting objectives and providing feedback	
8. Generating and testing hypotheses	
9. Questions, cues, and advanced organizers	

As all teachers know, lecture and other didactic instructional formats are useful at times for imparting content. Fortunately, there are ways to promote active student engagement when lecture is the instructional format for part of a lesson. Table 7.3 offers several techniques for engaging students during a lecture and provides a column for you to record ideas of how and when you might use each of these techniques. Each technique is an example of a research-based strategy (e.g., similarities and differences, summarizing, nonlinguistic representation, questioning) identified by Marzano et al. (2001) that increases student achievement.

Note that several formats can be used within a single lesson and that certain formats are readily suited for certain content areas. For instance, inquiry-based learning and learning by discovery formats can naturally support the learning of science content. Service learning and other community-referenced and experiential learning formats work well in the social studies units that examine social and historical conditions.

What other techniques can you think of for "spicing up" lectures and demonstrations? One strategy that may be culturally relevant to your learners is the "Call and Response Through Affirmations" where students are encouraged to call out how they would apply the concepts explained in the lecture. Foster (2002) urges teachers not to overlook the linguistic resources of their African American students. Features of African American English might be

Table 7.3 Sample Techniques for Actively Engaging Students During a Lecture

Technique	Description	We can use this when...
Two-minute pause (Questioning and summarization)	Every 10 to 15 minutes, pause to ask students to identify key points and interesting aspects, ask questions, and/or clarify confusions.	
Think-write or draw (Summarization and nonlinguistic representation)	Pause as above, but ask students to summarize graphically or in writing reactions to content presented.	
Outcome starter sentence (Summarization)	Stop lecture at key points and ask students to finish a start phrase such as, "I was surprised to learn ...," "I am wondering..."	
Reaction diagram (Summarization and nonlinguistic representation)	Have each student use an overhead to create a visual representation of reactions (e.g., an emotional response to a story or historical event, an illustration of characters in literature or history).	
Compare/contrast diagram (Similarities and differences, summarization, and nonlinguistic representation)	Have students use a Venn diagram or other graphic organizer to show intersecting concepts or characteristics and distinct differences or unique features.	

used instructionally, especially using call-and-response where there is a rapid verbal interaction between speaker and listener. Similarly, teachers can tap the linguistic resources of their Latino and Latina students by using techniques such as instructional conversations (Tharp & Gallimore, 1991), a structured dialogue between teacher and learners where the teacher listens carefully to grasp the learners' communicative intent and uses the learners' phraseology to tailor the dialogue to meet their emerging understanding. When teachers engage learners from culturally and linguistically diverse environments, they can enrich the entire classroom with a deeper understanding of each culture's unique contributions.

■ INSTRUCTIONAL ARRANGEMENTS

Instructional arrangements or instructional groupings determine whether students will be interacting with the curriculum content as a whole group, as partners, as individuals, or as members of a structured group of classmates.

Highlights on Cooperative Learning

Marzano et al. (2001) and other researchers (e.g., Johnson & Johnson, 1989; Kagan, Kyle, & Scott, 2004) show that cooperative learning arrangements are among the most powerful methods to engage and boost the achievement of all students. It can be argued that for students with learning and language challenges, cooperative learning is a must. For students from culturally and linguistically diverse communities, cooperative or communal learning may be preferred over individualistic or competitive structures. For example, Boykin et al. (2005) found that "African American students were significantly more accepting of communal and vervistic high-achieving peers than European American students. European American students endorsed individualistic and competitive high achievers significantly more than African American students" (p. 238).

Kagan et al. (2004) make this argument:

Cooperative learning is the single most effective educational approach for meeting the needs of all students in inclusive classrooms. Attempts at inclusion without cooperative learning often backfire, resulting in students with special needs feeling isolated and segregated. . . . If we are to follow the law, if we are to create least restrictive learning environments, and if we are to integrate students with special needs into regular classrooms, it is mandatory that our instruction include frequent cooperative learning that includes teambuilding, class-building, and social skill development. Placing students in regular education classrooms is not inclusion: inclusion depends on effective cooperative learning. (chap. 17, p. 16)

Cooperative arrangements include long-term support teams known as *base teams* where students stay together for the semester or the year. Members of a base team meet regularly, even daily, to review homework assignments, help each other with classroom chores, watch out for one another on the playground or on field trips, and so forth. Teachers can construct more complex arrangements such as the jigsaw, Student Team Achievement Divisions, and group investigation arrangements presented in Table 7.4 and described in detail by Kagan (1995) and Slavin (1994). Formal lessons "ensure that students have enough time to thoroughly complete an academic assignment; therefore, they may last for several days or even weeks" (Marzano, et al., 2001, p. 90). All formal lessons require the teacher to include the basic cooperative learning components of positive interdependence, individual and group accountability, use of small group interpersonal skills, group processing of task and relationship, and face-to-face interaction decisions such as group size and member composition (Johnson & Johnson, 1989).

Cooperative learning arrangements can be informal, quick, and easily sprinkled throughout the instructional day. Table 7.5 offers a sampling of a dozen such quick cooperative structures that can be used with any content area.

Table 7.4   More Formal and Long-Term Cooperative Learning Structures

Structure Name	Description	We can use this when . . .
Jigsaw	In a simple Jigsaw, students are assigned to a cooperative group. Groups are assigned the task of learning about a specific topic. Each person in the group is assigned an area of the topic to research or is given a different set of materials to learn. Each student studies and becomes an "expert" in the assigned material and plans how to teach this information to teammates.	
Expert Group Jigsaw	In an Expert Group Jigsaw, students research and prepare their respective material individually. Then those with the same "area of expertise" from other teams on a topic meet, share information, and plan how to teach their content. The students then return to their groups and teach the material.	
Student Team Learning	In Student Team Learning (STL), students are assigned heterogeneously to groups to complete a task. Teammates study to complete the task. When the task is completed, each member is quizzed individually. Group and individual performance is monitored.	
Student Team Achievement Divisions (STAD)	In Student Team Achievement Divisions (STAD), students are quizzed and assessed before the unit for a baseline score. After studying, team members are quizzed individually. A team score is compiled by each student's "gain score" (i.e., the number of points improved over baseline) being totaled together.	
Group Investigation	Heterogeneously grouped students select or are assigned a topic to investigate. Teammates jointly plan subtopics for investigations, goals for learning, and how they will proceed with the investigation. Students work individually and regularly convene to create a culminating report or representation of the topic formulated by the team. Each team member has a role in the presentation of findings to the class. Evaluation of the project may be based upon a teacher- and/or team-generated rubric emphasizing application, analysis, and synthesis of the material.	

Table 7.5 Quick Cooperative Learning Structures for Actively Engaging Students

Structure	Description	We could use this structure in class by/when…
Think- (Optional: Write)-Pair-Share	Students think to themselves about a teacher-provided question or topic and (optional) summarize by writing or illustrating thoughts/answers. Students partner up and share thoughts. Students are called upon to share their own or partner's response.	
Formulate-Share-Listen-Create	Begin as above, and after students have shared thoughts/answers, partners formulate a new answer/idea that incorporates both members' contributions.	
Numbered Heads Together	Students in small teams count off in each team (e.g., 1, 2, 3). The teacher asks a question. Teammates consult to make sure each member knows the answer. Then a student in each group (e.g., "all number 3's") is called upon to answer.	
Mix-Freeze-Pair	The teacher asks students to stand and "mix" (walk around the room) until the music stops or the teacher signals by saying, "freeze." When the teacher says, "Freeze," or the music stops, students stop. The teacher says "Pair." Students turn to the closest person to form a pair. The teacher asks a question which pairs discuss until the music resumes or teacher says, "Mix."	
Walk-Talk	In pairs, students take a short walk together while discussing a given question, topic, or problem. Walking and talking engages physical and mental exercise, can induce a relaxed and creative state, and simultaneously promotes physiological and psychological well-being.	
Say and Switch	A student is asked to relate information or answer a question. At the end of a sentence or mid-sentence, the student is stopped and another student is asked to "pick up" where the other student left off. This process is continued for several students. This structure can effectively assist students with limited English or communication by starting with a word, picture, or idea upon which classmates then can build.	
Say Something	Given a piece of text, partners decide together how far to read silently before stopping to "say something" that can be a summary, a question, or an interesting connection. When the chosen point is reached, both partners say something. Partners repeat this process to the end of the selection. The whole class then discusses the text. Thinking out loud, supported by attentive listening, develops interpersonal relations as well as develops understanding of relationships between prior and new information.	

Structure	Description	We could use this structure in class by/when…
Round Table/Round Robin	Each student in turn writes an idea or answer as paper and pencil are passed around the group. Each idea they write down is to expand upon previous entries. With "Simultaneous Round Table," more than one pencil and paper are passed around at once.	
Graffiti or Carousel	With Graffiti or Carousel, each group is given chart paper and a different topic to write about. At a designated time (e.g., 5 minutes), groups stop and rotate sheets (e.g., clockwise). Rotations continue until all groups see each sheet and each sheet returns to the home group. Carousel is a variation of "Graffiti" in which students move among topical sheets posted on the wall or placed at tables around the room.	
Three-Step Interview	Groups of four divide up into partners and interview the partner about a question posed by the teacher. In the same partnerships, partners reverse roles so that interviewers become interviewees. Students debrief in a round robin fashion in their original group of four by taking turns sharing what they learned from interviewing.	
Toss-a-Question	Each group generates a question on a piece of paper, wads the paper into a ball and tosses it to another team which then answers the question and tosses it back to the originator to evaluate.	
Inside-Outside Circle	Students stand in two concentric circles, with the inside circle facing out and the outside circle facing inward. Inside/outside partners discuss a question/topic posed by the teacher. When signaled, the outside circle of students rotates clockwise to face a new partner and to discuss the same or a new question/topic. This is repeated for several rounds.	

Cooperative Strategies for Emerging and Struggling Readers

Progress in literacy and language curricula is a primary determinant of success in school. Students who are culturally or linguistically diverse or who have learning disabilities in reading often are at risk for underachievement in reading related activities, activities that encompass all forms of academic achievement. Collaborative Strategic Reading (Klingner, Vaughn, Arguelles, Hughes, & Leftwich, 2004) is a method based upon the research-based self-monitoring comprehension strategy of Reciprocal Teaching (Palinscar & Brown, 1987). This differentiated procedure teaches students to use four comprehension strategies—Preview, Click and Clunk, Get the Gist, and Wrap Up—before, during, and after reading a passage. Students then work in groups to apply roles they have been explicitly taught (i.e., Leader, Clunk Expert, Announcer, Encourager, Reporter, Time Keeper) to collaboratively deconstruct and analyze the text they have just read.

A Highlight on Peer Tutors and Partner Learning Arrangements

One way to differentiate the content of learning is to differentiate who teaches the content, for example, including peers as part of the delivery process. Peer tutoring, or partner learning, instructional arrangements are not new. Teachers in one-room schoolhouses relied on students as deliverers of instruction. Teachers who decide to use peer tutoring carefully select the material and content for students to use during the peer tutoring sessions. Peer tutoring can be arranged among classmates within one class or between cross-age schoolmates across classes or across an entire school.

Peer tutoring arrangements build relationships among students and offer a cost-effective way to increase learning time. The instructional as well as social and cost benefits of tutoring are abundant (McMaster, Fuchs, & Fuchs, 2002; Thousand, Villa, & Nevin, 2002). Both parties experience interpersonal communication skill development and heightened self-esteem. Not only do tutees experience learning gains, but tutors report understanding the content at a deeper level than before teaching, likely because of the metacognitive activities in which they engage as they prepare to teach.

Good and Brophy (1997) suggest that the instruction delivered through peer tutoring arrangements can be superior to that of instruction delivered by adults for at least three reasons: (1) students use more age-appropriate and meaningful language and examples; (2) peer tutors recently learned what they are to teach and are familiar with the learning roadblocks their tutees may experience; and (3) peer tutors are more direct than adults.

How might you arrange for peer tutor partnerships among some or all of the students in your class or with a partner teacher of another classroom? How might you use peer tutoring as a way to sharpen your students' math or spelling proficiency? How might you create service learning opportunities for your students so as to enhance the learning of younger students through a cross-age tutorial arrangement? However you answer these questions, it's a win-win instructional arrangement.

■ INSTRUCTIONAL STRATEGIES

McTighe and Wiggins (2004) and Tomlinson and McTighe (2006) articulately argue for understanding through the design of curriculum and instruction, where understanding is the student's ability to wisely transfer or apply knowledge and skills effectively in real tasks and settings. When we experience understanding, we have a fluent, fluid grasp rather than a tentative, formulaic grasp based on recall. *Instructional strategies* are teaching/learning techniques that help to make learners become well understood, help a skill become automatic, or help a piece of knowledge readily transfer from one person to another. We noted early in this chapter the research findings of Marzano et al. (2001) regarding techniques that have demonstrated positive effects on student achievement (see Table 7.2). All of these techniques qualify as instructional strategies, with cooperative group learning falling in both the instructional strategy and the instructional arrangement categories.

These nine categories of instructional strategies in Table 7.2 are not, however, the only instructional strategies that teachers have at their disposal to assist students to access learning. There are many more and, in the wake of the 2004 Individuals with Disabilities Educational Improvement Act and the 2001 No Child Left Behind Act with their emphasis on research-based interventions, more strategies will be invented and endorsed as research-based. Thus, in order to be armed with the most effective strategies, teachers are compelled to read and discuss the literature and attend professional development seminars and conferences on effective strategies.

As part of your consideration of instructional strategies for every lesson, we recommend that you deliberately examine your use of taxonomies. We also suggest that you consider integrating the arts and using concepts from learning preferences frameworks during instructional activities. A brief examination of how to use taxonomies, learning preferences, and the arts during instruction follows.

Use of Taxonomies

Taxonomies can assist teachers to differentiate how students make sense of content. For example, given data on the differences (e.g., population, economy, alliances, military resources) between the North and the South at the start of the U.S. Civil War, one group of students could engage at the application level of Bloom's Taxonomy by creating a diagram or other graphic representation to compare and contrast those differences. Another group of students could engage at the evaluation level by preparing for, and then engaging in, a debate about predictions regarding the outcome of the war based upon these data.

We advocate that all students have opportunities to engage in the higher-ordered thinking levels of taxonomies and that they have choice in the processes for showing thinking. Some of the different processes available at each level of Bloom's taxonomy are presented in Table 7.6.

APPLYING CONCEPTS FROM LEARNING ■
PREFERENCES FRAMEWORKS

In addition to designing instructional processes that appeal to visual, auditory, or kinesthetic learning styles, teachers can apply Sternberg's model (1997b) to differentiate instruction. In Sternberg's model, there are three functions of

Table 7.6 Differentiating the Process of Learning With Bloom's Taxonomy

Level of Bloom's Taxonomy	Different Processes to Facilitate Access to Curriculum
Knowledge	Define, draw, identify, list, label, locate, match, name, recite, select, state
Comprehension	Demonstrate, describe, define in your own words, explain, generalize, give examples, paraphrase, put in order, rewrite, show, summarize
Application	Use a formula, debate, diagram, examine, interview, construct, translate, use to solve a problem, keep records, classify, discover
Analysis	Classify, compare and contrast, deduce, determine, infer, uncover, relate two or more learning outcomes
Synthesis	Create, design, imagine, develop, prepare an original piece of work, synthesize, combine
Evaluation	Argue, award, choose, criticize, critique, defend, judge, grade, support, validate, rank, justify

thinking: legislative, executive, and judicial. People often show patterns of preference for one of these functions. If students' preferences are matched to instruction and assessment procedures, students are more likely to show how much they really know. For example, students with an executive function may respond to the lecture teaching strategy, and students with a judicial preference may appreciate small group discussions.

Many teachers with whom we have worked employ concepts from the Multiple Intelligences (MI) Theory to assist them to differentiate the instructional processes. For example, in a lesson on our solar system, students with strengths in the mathematical and logical areas might calculate and chart the time for the various planets to rotate around the sun and for a spaceship launched from earth to get to the various planets. Students with naturalist interests might conduct an inquiry into the increasing amount of space junk (e.g., used satellites) orbiting earth. Visual/spatial learners might construct models of the solar system. Bodily/kinesthetic learners could physically model with their bodies the rotation of the planets in their various orbits around the sun. Musical learners could come up with a rap, jingle, or poem to assist themselves and other students to remember the names of the planets in order of their distance from the sun. Interpersonally intelligent students could have a choice to work with a partner or a member of a cooperative group to complete an assignment. In contrast, intrapersonally intelligent students could choose to independently research and relate an experience (e.g., space travel) to themselves by creating what they believe would be a journal entry from an astronaut living for months on the International Space Station.

After they initially facilitate learning via their students' learning preferences, teachers then could assign students to mixed ("jigsaw") groups in which each student would benefit from their teammates' knowledge and ability to use their preferred strength intelligence to teach one another. Table 7.7 offers additional examples of differentiated learning processes for each of the eight multiple intelligences.

INTEGRATION OF THE ARTS ■

Thinking about integration of the arts as an instructional strategy may be a unique method of differentiating your instruction. When teachers integrate the visual and performing arts (music, theatre, dance, and visual arts) into their curriculum as an instructional strategy, there are many benefits. First, using the arts is one way for teachers to tap the multiple intelligences (e.g., visual/spatial, musical/rhythmic, bodily/kinesthetic) of their learners. Students can simultaneously expand their knowledge of content in the curriculum domains (science, social studies, language) as they *process* and *produce* their knowledge via music, theatre, dance, and the visual arts. For example, Chadwick et al. (2005) described how a group of teacher educators expanded their students' as well as their own knowledge of the arts by using it in the process of teaching. One participating teacher educator wrote:

> I have constant awareness now of the arts and how they are evident in every corner of my life. It is also evident now in my teaching—in a conscious way. I intentionally draw my students into the joy of using drama, visual arts, music, and dance in their teaching. (Chadwick et al., 2005, p. 7)

Table 7.7　Differentiation of the Learning Process Via Concepts From MI Theory

Type of Intelligence	Examples of Differentiated Learning Processes
Verbal/Linguistic	Lectures, discussions, word games, storytelling, choral reading, journal writing, debates, discussions, cooperative learning
Logical/Mathematical	Puzzles, analogies, problem solving, lab experiments, outlines, timelines, brain teasers, number games, critical thinking
Bodily/Kinesthetic	Hands-on learning, dance, drama, sports that teach, relaxation exercises, field trips
Visual/Spatial	Graphic organizers, artwork, diagrams, pictures, mind-mapping, visualization, metaphors
Musical/Rhythmic	Rhythmic learning, poetry, songs that teach, background music
Naturalist	Field trips, working outside, ecological awareness, caring for plants and animals, exploring nature
Interpersonal/People Smart	Cooperative group learning, partner learning, simulations, community gatherings, conferences
Intrapersonal/Reflective	Individualized instruction, Internet research, choice, journaling

Beecher (2006) provided a description of a writing activity for her first graders. They participated in an arts-based study of the Czech Republic and Slovakia where, through the arts, they learned about the land, food, culture, weather, music, pastimes, animals, and more. During a concurrent poetry unit, students were asked to select from a series of postcards displaying folk art from Czech and Slovak artists that depicted various works of art (e.g., paintings, ceramics, tapestries). The writing activities were scheduled in 45-minute work blocks. When they were finished writing one poem, they wrote another. Optional sharing time was included in that time frame. Computer lab was in a 30-minute block and students could return in small groups to finish their creations. The first graders were able to craft poems in response to the cue, "What do you feel when you look at this artwork?" The teacher then expanded the lesson by having the students use the computer to print their work in various fonts, colors, and spacing.

Two of the first grade students received extra tutorial services as part of the school district Title I Language Arts services and with the Reading Recovery program. Reading Recovery (Lyons, 1998), an intensive one-on-one program for at risk first grade students, included daily 30-minute lessons with the Reading Recovery teacher that focused on beginning reading and writing skills. Children also could take books home nightly to read with their family.

The students showed both sophistication and poetic understanding. Alana created her poem as a song, which she sang for the class, and performed again for the instrumental music teacher who wrote down the song. Beecher was surprised to discover this side of Alana, a shy, quiet student. Every poem Alana wrote during this unit was a new song, which she sang in a pure, beautiful voice.

Aaron, an active boy who would rather play than write, wrote poems with a style that got to the point (Figure 7.2). He also enjoyed sharing his poems with the class, demonstrating a level of seriousness not previously seen. Students enjoyed this type of writing so much that they each wrote at least four poems using Czech or Slovak art as inspiration.

In addition to the standardized methods of assessing writing skills, Beecher was able to show how these skills could be expanded to provide artistic understanding, enjoyment, and entertainment. Many of her first graders selected their works of art for inclusion in their portfolios of accomplishments

Figure 7.2   First Graders Write Poems Based on the Visual Arts

The trees are blowing	the cat sits near the pond
on the winter breeze	the crab came up
I catch one leaf	and
as they blow and blow	snapped the cat
(by Alana Golding, Beecher, 2006)	(by Aaron Fanning, Beecher, 2006)

to share during student-teacher-parent conferences, and all of them chose poems to include in their published book of poetry. Many students also chose to perform these poems during a Performance Poetry event for parents.

SOCIAL AND PHYSICAL ENVIRONMENT ■

In any classroom, and in every lesson, the *social climate and physical environment* are baseline considerations. Environmental considerations that influence the process of instruction include such things as the room arrangement, accessibility of materials, and strategic seating of individual students. The established social norms governing movement, property, and interpersonal relations set the overall climate, activity level, and interaction patterns during a lesson as well as throughout the day. When active instructional formats and interactive and cooperative instructional arrangements are used in the process of instruction, then environmental considerations such as the regulation of noise levels, visual and auditory distractions, the seating and room arrangement, and accessible pathways to jointly used materials come to the forefront as additional important instruction decisions.

The good news is that when teachers make adjustments in the social climate, or social rules, making them more flexible to accommodate best practices in teaching and learning, it can benefit students who have a need to be active (i.e., kinesthetic learners, students with ADHD) and interactive (e.g., verbal/linguistic learners). Such a shift also requires teachers to be more attentive to the teaching, rehearsing, role playing, and prompted use of (a) the prosocial communication skills needed for collaborative learning formats and arrangements, (b) self-regulatory and impulse control skills for dealing with distractions and conflict, and (c) problem-solving scripts and strategies. In other words, the teaching and practicing of responsible behavior becomes a priority curriculum domain, as it should be.

CO-TEACHING APPROACHES ■

In addition to the co-teaching approaches described in Chapter 9 (team teaching, supportive teaching, complementary teaching, and parallel teaching), co-teachers can consider having their students take on the role of co-teachers. A detailed description of students as co-teachers is found in Villa, Thousand, and Nevin (2004). Here, we briefly (a) explain methods that allow students to become co-teachers, (b) summarize what the emerging research base is for students as co-teachers, and (c) describe some of the barriers and disadvantages to students as co-teachers.

Students are more likely to become effective co-teachers when their co-teachers explicitly teach them how to tutor or work as study buddies. It is important to make sure that student co-teachers enjoy the reciprocity involved in being both teacher *and* learner. Teachers create more opportunities for students to practice co-teaching skills when they set up cooperative group learning (described above) so that each member of the group can practice communication skills involved in teaching others what each one knows.

Overall, when students have more active roles in communicating their understanding of the academic content, they increase their retention and achievement. Recent research amply documents the power of peer tutoring, partner learning, students in coaching roles in cooperative groups, and student-led conferences. In addition, there are theoretical frameworks that explain the research and practice base for students as co-teachers. For example, cognitive psychologists verified that reciprocal teaching (Palinscar & Brown, 1984) is effective in significantly raising and maintaining the reading comprehension scores of poor readers. In a reciprocal teaching exchange, students alternate being the teacher who coaches the comprehension skills. Johnson and Johnson (1989) explain the social-psychological theory that underlies cooperative group learning, indicating that students who work together and learn together in cooperative structures not only achieve better academically but also gain social competence, social acceptance, and an overall positive attraction to the subject matter.

Dialogue teaching is another instructional process that encourages and prepares students to be co-teachers. In fact, dialogue teaching may be the perfect method for students who have been silenced (e.g., students of color, those at risk, second language learners, and students with disabilities). Dialogue teaching means that students themselves help to generate the curriculum, design their own instructional methods, and report their progress within a framework of consciousness-raising group dynamics (Kluth et al., 2002). Dialogue teaching involves changing the pace of classroom speaking to allow more time to think before responding; valuing different types of contributions (e.g., laughter, gestures, typed words on a communication board); and making sure topics are important to the students (e.g., issues related to race, gender, class, ability).

Co-teachers who practice dialogue teaching develop skills in listening and differentially responding to their students' linguistic habits and verbal styles, especially for the students who are learning English as their second language or the students who are nonverbal. Student co-teachers who practice dialogue teaching can acquire powerful new awareness of their strengths and contributions.

■ PAUSE AND REFLECT

Please use Table 7.1 to guide your reflection at this point in the development of your lesson plan. Ask yourself to what extent you have thought and made decisions about the considerations regarding the five dimensions of the process of instruction presented in Table 7.1. What formats, arrangements, and strategies for instruction, social and physical environmental options, and co-teaching arrangements have you considered and decided to use?

Once you have made decisions regarding how you will engage students, take one last time to pause and reflect about specific students. Please review once again the facts about your learners to make sure that you have selected instructional processes that will allow them access to the curriculum content. Ask yourself, "Are there any unique teaching strategies needed for a particular student?" Does a student require technological support in the form of an augmentative communication system or device? Does a student need behavioral support in the form of a positive behavior support plan, a personal behavioral contract, or a token economy system for recognition of engagement? Does a student need additional adult or peer assistance to engage in learning tasks? If so, remember that when additional support is warranted, *natural supports*—assistance that can be provided by classmates and adults already in the classroom—is preferable.

Do you need to make any final adjustments to your plans to differentiate the process of learning? Also review the decisions you have made about content and product. Then make any adjustments, refinements, or additions before you implement your differentiated instruction lesson plan.

8

Collaborative Planning for Differentiated Instruction

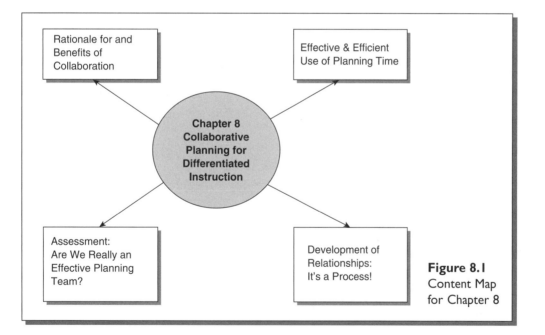

Figure 8.1
Content Map
for Chapter 8

People seldom improve when they have no other model but themselves to copy.

—Oliver Goldsmith, 1728–1774

Collaboration has become more and more of a norm in North American schools due to a number of legal, practical, and ethical reasons all related to providing all students both access to quality instruction and equity in educational experience. In this chapter, the following questions are addressed:

- What are the benefits of collaborative planning to differentiate instruction?
- What are ways to effectively and efficiently use planning time?
- How are relationships among collaborative team members developed?
- How can planning teams assess their own effectiveness?

Collaboration requires educators to think differently about their work, and it takes many forms. Co-teaching is one type of collaborative arrangement emerging as an instructional "best practice" for instructional differentiation (Villa, Thousand, & Nevin, 2004) and, therefore, it is emphasized in this book.

However, co-teaching is only one form of collaboration that supports the education of diverse learners. In some situations, the achievement of students (e.g., those with special educational needs and English language learners) often can easily be facilitated through natural peer supports where students help one another in many ways, from taking notes and role-modeling interactions to coaching each other in cooperative group and partner learning structures. In other situations, consultative or stop-in support from personnel such as special educators provides the needed assistance for a teacher to adequately differentiate instruction. In some cases, a particular student may need more individualized interactions and support from peers or even an individualized assistant. However, if a systematic approach is used to consider all student needs prior to planning for the content, product, and process of instruction, this last option should not be as necessary.

Table 8.1 describes in more detail what the levels of student support might look like at the consultative, stop-in, co-teaching, and individualized levels.

■ RATIONALE FOR, AND BENEFITS OF, COLLABORATIVE PLANNING AND TEACHING

Regardless of the level of support provided in a classroom, or how people decide to connect with one another in the classroom, to offer student support, one thing remains common and essential to all of these relationships—collaborative planning.

Why collaboratively plan? Some of the answers to this question are self-evident. For example, the probability of success in executing a lesson or unit increases when all parties are involved in the planning. As emerging data suggests, educators who collaboratively plan and teach (and include families in this process) can expect improvements in academic and social skills of students with disabilities and other learning and language differences. Federal legislation

Table 8.1 From Least to More Intense and Intrusive Support Options

---

Consultative and Stop-in Support

Consultative support occurs when one or more adults, often a special educator, meet regularly with classroom teachers to keep track of student progress, assess the need to adapt or supplement materials or instruction, and problem-solve as needed. Specialized professionals such as nurses, occupational and physical therapists, augmentative communication specialists, and guidance or career counselors often provide periodic consultation. Students also may seek assistance from consulting staff for specific assignments or general support.

Stop-in support occurs when consulting support providers stop by the classroom on a scheduled or unscheduled basis to observe student performance in the general education context, assess the need for any modifications to existing supports or curriculum, and talk face-to-face with the student, classroom teacher, and peers.

Co-teaching Support

Co-teaching support occurs when two or more people share responsibility for teaching some or all of the students assigned to a classroom. There are four predominant co-teaching approaches:

(1) *supportive*: One teacher takes the lead and others rotate among students to provide support

(2) *parallel*: Co-teachers work with different groups of students in different areas of the classroom

(3) *complementary*: Co-teachers do something to enhance the instruction provided by another co-teacher

(4) *team teaching*: Co-teachers jointly plan, teach, assess, and assume responsibility for all of the students in the classroom.

Individualized Support

Individualized support involves one or more adults, oftentimes paraprofessionals, providing support to one or more students at predetermined time periods during the day or week, or for most or all of the day. The key to successful individualized support is to ensure that designated support personnel do not become "attached at the hip" to individual students, but, instead, deliberately prompt natural peer support, support students in the class other than the focus student, facilitate small group learning with heterogeneous groups of classmates, and differentiate support as needed through planning with the classroom teacher. The ultimate goal is to fade the need for individualized support by facilitating both increased student independence and increased natural support from classmates and teachers.

acknowledges this in the findings cited in the 2004 Individuals With Disabilities Education Improvement Act (IDEIA):

> Almost 30 years of research and experience [have] demonstrated that the education of children with disabilities can be made more effective by . . . having high expectations for such children and ensuring their access to the general education curriculum in the regular classroom . . . and ensuring that families of such children have meaningful opportunities to participate in the education of their children . . . [and by] providing appropriate special education and related services and aids and supports in the regular classroom to such children, whenever possible. (P.L. 108–446, Part B, Sec. 682 [c] Findings [5])

An additional benefit of collaborative planning is that planning team members capitalize upon the unique and specialized knowledge and skills of their teammates (Hourcade & Bauwens, 2002). The "two heads are better than one" phenomenon, otherwise known as *synergy*, is activated. Planning team members experience increased higher-level thinking and generate more novel solutions (Thousand, Villa, Nevin, & Paolucci-Whitcomb, 1995). Teachers feel empowered when they jointly plan and make decisions. The basic human needs proposed by Glasser (1999) of survival, power, freedom of choice, sense of belonging, and fun can be met through the interactive interchanges that occur when teachers collaboratively plan.

Namely, each teacher's chance for *survival* and *power* in educating diverse learners increases through the exchange of resources and expertise. Teachers experience *belonging* and *freedom* from isolation as they jointly discuss and plan; and it is *fun* to engage in stimulating adult conversation and creative solution-finding.

So, if collaborative planning is so good for teachers and students, how do we get more of it going in schools? How do we do it well, so that the promise of these benefits is realized? The remainder of this chapter is devoted to describing ways to promote team effectiveness and efficiency. Two tools are introduced that have been found to be effective in assisting teams to run effective meetings and to assess where they are in the team development process.

■ EFFECTIVE AND EFFICIENT USE OF PLANNING TIME

Often we ask this question: "What is the number one resource that teachers have the least of?" The immediate answer we always receive is: "Time!" Finding time to plan is the enduring, eternal challenge for all teachers. However, when it is found, created, expanded, or rearranged, the real challenge becomes how to *effectively use* that time. Often the issue is not the amount of time that is finally set aside, added, or manipulated for planning, but rather it is changing the fundamental way that teachers use their time when they sit down to plan.

Differentiated instruction is best accomplished when those who are interested in student learning and success collaborate by literally putting their heads together in face-to-face meetings. Planning meetings are more likely to be both effective and efficient when a structured meeting format is used, such as the Co-teaching Planning Meeting Agenda Format shown in Table 8.2 (Thousand & Villa, 2000; Villa et al., 2004). This meeting format helps to make sure that team members practice the five critical elements of an effective cooperative planning process—positive interdependence, individual accountability, group processing, small group interpersonal skills, and face-to-face interaction.

Positive interdependence is structured when leadership is distributed through rotating roles. Roles may be task-related (e.g., timekeeper, recorder) or relationship-oriented (e.g., encourager, observer). As suggested in Table 8.2, roles are assigned in advance of the next meeting. This ensures that all participants have the materials needed to carry out their specific roles (e.g., the timekeeper has a watch or timer, the recorder has chart paper, markers, or a computer to record minutes). Assigning roles in advance also encourages co-teachers to rotate roles and, in this way, creates a sense of distributed responsibility and positive interdependence.

The meeting agenda format prompts planning team members' to be *individually accountable* for completing actions to which they commit by assigning Action Items to individual team members and by setting due dates in the Outcomes section of the agenda. The use of *small group interpersonal skills* is prompted and monitored by way of a pause in the agenda for *group processing* of how the group is functioning. This occurs both midway through and at the end of the meeting. *Face-to-face interaction* is prompted and recognized with the public recording of who is present, late, and absent from the meeting and with the building of the next meeting's agenda.

DEVELOPMENT OF RELATIONSHIPS ■ AMONG TEAM MEMBERS: IT'S A PROCESS!

One of the five critical elements of an effective team is conscious attention to practicing and improving planning team members' interpersonal skills and relationships. Most people develop proficiency in collaborative teaming by actually working with, and getting to know, their teammates. An initial step, then, in developing team member relations is to devote some meeting time to learning about teammates' cultural, personal, and professional backgrounds as well as each member's experiences with collaborative teaming (Webb-Johnson, 2002).

It also helps team members to know that working and planning with others is a developmental process that goes through several stages. Knowing about the skills that are expected can help teammates learn and *choose to use* specific interpersonal and communication skills that help a team accomplish goals and, at the same time, maintain and develop positive relationships.

Skills for Building Trust and Establishing Team Norms

When new teams first form, the goal is to build a mutual and reciprocal relationship. The interpersonal skills that facilitate this goal include trust-building behaviors such as arriving on time and staying for the entire meeting. Two important outcomes are to agree upon common team goals and to establish norms or ground rules such as *no put-downs* and *using each person's preferred name*.

Table 8.2   Co-teaching Planning Meeting Agenda Format

People present:	Absentees:	Others who need to know:

Roles   This meeting   Next meeting

Timekeeper   _____   _____

Recorder   _____   _____

Others   _____   _____

Agenda

Agenda Items		Time limit
1. Review agenda & positive comments		5 minutes
2.		
3.		
4. Pause for group processing of progress toward task accomplishment and use of interpersonal skills		2 minutes
5.		
6.		
7. Final group processing of task and relationship		5 minutes

Minutes of Outcomes

Action Items	Person(s) Responsible	By When?
1. Communicate outcomes to absent members and others by:		
2.		
3.		

Agenda Building for Next Meeting

Date: _____   Time: _____   Location: _____

Expected agenda items

1.

2.

3.

Norms are "a group's common beliefs regarding appropriate behavior for members; they tell, in other words, how members are expected to behave. . . . All groups have norms, set either formally or informally" (Johnson & Johnson, 1997, p. 424). By explicitly stating and committing to adhere to norms, team members create a sense of safety that allows each of them to share information with one another and "tell the truth" about concerns and needs.

Communication and Leadership Skills

Once groups have developed trust, team members can focus upon communication and leadership skills that enable efficient and organized accomplishment of goals as well as the further development of relationships. Examples of such communication and leadership skills include clarifying or explaining one's own views, coordinating tasks, paraphrasing the views of others, and checking for understanding of, and agreement with, team decisions.

Communication and leadership skills can most readily be practiced if they are well defined and assigned in a rotating fashion to different planning team members from one meeting to the next, as prompted in the agenda format of Table 8.2. To help your planning teams begin practicing these skills, we have also listed and defined in this table some leadership roles that promote task and goal achievement along with roles that promote positive interpersonal relationships. We encourage you to invent other roles as you need them.

Creative Problem-Solving Skills

Creative problem-solving skills are the third cluster of skills team members must activate to develop high-quality, innovative ways for differentiating content, instruction, and assessment. Creative problem-solving skills include generation of novel ideas, or brainstorming; seeking additional information through questioning; metacognition; asking for the underlying rationale for an argument or proposal; asking for critical feedback; taking the risk of trying unfamiliar practices in order to deepen understanding of new information, or taking risks simply in order to try something new even though you are not sure it will work.

Conflict Resolution Skills

Conflict is inevitable within all teams, especially when the goals and tasks are as important as ensuring the academic, social, and emotional success of all students. Collaborative team members who can engage in and comfortably manage controversy and conflicting opinions are more successful that those who avoid conflict. The skills and steps involved in engaging in constructive controversy include criticizing ideas, not people; differentiating different opinions; asking for more information and the underlying rationale in order to understand someone else's position; and using creative problem-solving techniques. Knowing and practicing these skills allow for the clashing of ideas to stimulate revision and refinement of the differentiated instructional methods that already have been tried. It also allows co-teacher teams to reach their highest potential and level of cohesiveness.

Table 8.3   Facilitating Task Achievement and Relationship Development

Task Roles

Timekeeper: The Timekeeper monitors the time, encourages planning team members to stop at agreed-upon times, and alerts members when it is approaching the end of the agreed-upon time period: "We have five minutes left to finish."

Recorder: The Recorder writes down the decisions made by the team and distributes copies to each present team member and absent team members within one week's time.

Summarizer: The Summarizer summarizes outcomes of a discussion before moving on to a new topic.

Checker: The Checker makes sure members understand discussion and decisions: "Can you explain how we arrived at this decision?"

Relationship Roles

Encourager: The Encourager encourages all team members to participate and carry out their roles.

Praiser: The Praiser lets members know when they are using collaborative skills that positively impact each other. The Praiser is careful to make the praise sound and feel authentic and focused (e.g., "Thanks to [co-teacher's name] for keeping us focused on our tasks!") rather than general comments (e.g., "Good job!").

Jargon Buster: The Jargon Buster lets team members know when they are using terms that not all participants may understand (acronyms, abbreviations, etc.). This is an especially important role when people from a specialty area join in: "Whoops! Does everyone know what IEP means?"

We believe that understanding and consciously practicing these four constellations of skills will improve student outcomes and your enjoyment of the planning process. And we understand that it is up to you; only you can control your own behaviors and be a model for using these interpersonal skills. The outcome is worth it—excellence in teaching and learning as well as more enjoyment from the partnership.

■ ARE WE REALLY AN EFFECTIVE PLANNING TEAM?

It is important for collaborators to craft differentiated learning experiences to know what the desired collaborative behaviors are, so that they might self-assess and reflect upon the effectiveness and efficiency with which they engage in face-to-face planning and debriefing of the practices involved in co-teaching. We have created a 25-item self-assessment checklist entitled *Are We Really a Collaborative Team?* (Table 8.4) for you to use to prompt professional

Table 8.4   "Are We Really a Collaborative Team?" Self-Assessment

Directions: Check Yes or No to each of the following statements to determine your Collaboration Score at this point in time.

Yes	No	*In our collaborative or co-teaching partnership:*

Face-to-Face Interactions

_____ _____   1. Do we meet in a comfortable environment?

_____ _____   2. When we meet, do we arrange ourselves so we can hear each other and see each other's facial expressions?

_____ _____   3. Is the size of our group manageable (six or fewer members)?

_____ _____   4. Do we have regularly scheduled meetings that are held at times and locations agreed upon in advance by teammates?

_____ _____   5. Do we use a structured agenda format that prescribes and identifies agenda items for the next meeting and setting time limits for each agenda item?

_____ _____   6. Do needed members receive a timely invitation? (Note: Needed members may change from meeting to meeting based upon agenda items.)

_____ _____   7. Do we start and end on time?

Positive Interdependence

_____ _____   8. Have we publicly discussed the group's overall purpose and goals?

_____ _____   9. Have we each stated what we individually need from the group to be able to work toward the group goals?

_____ _____ 10. Do we distribute leadership responsibility by rotating roles (e.g., Recorder, Timekeeper, Encourager, Agreement Checker)?

_____ _____ 11. Do we start each meeting with positive comments and devote time at each meeting to celebrate successes?

_____ _____ 12. Do we have fun at our meetings?

Small Group Interpersonal Skills

_____ _____ 13. Have we established norms for behavior during meetings (e.g., all members participate, active listening when others speak, no "scapegoating")?

_____ _____ 14. Do we explain the group's norms to new members?

_____ _____ 15. Do we create an atmosphere of safety for expressing genuine perspectives (negative and positive); and do we acknowledge conflict during meetings?

_____ _____ 16. Do we update tardy members at a break or after the meeting, rather than stopping the meeting midstream?

_____ _____ 17. Do we have a communication system for absent members and people who need to know about our decisions, but who are not regular team members (e.g., building or district administrators)?

_____ _____ 18. Do we consciously identify the decision-making process (e.g., majority vote, consensus, unanimous decision) we will use for making a particular decision?

(Continued)

Table 8.4 (Continued)

		Group Processing
_____	_____	19. Do we consciously attempt to improve our interpersonal skills (e.g., perspective taking, creative problem-solving, conflict resolution) by setting time aside to reflect upon and discuss our interactions and feelings?
_____	_____	20. Do we consciously attempt to improve our interpersonal skills by developing a plan to improve our interactions next time we meet?
_____	_____	21. Do we consciously attempt to improve our interpersonal skills by arranging for training to improve our skills?
_____	_____	TOTAL

growth. Co-teachers can rate the co-teaching partnership individually on the 21 items and then compare their "Yes" and "No" assessments. This allows team members to have a starting point to celebrate their strengths thus far and discuss areas in which improvement can be made. We suggest that the decision about whether a team can give an item a "Yes" rating be definitively unanimous. If any one team member is not sure about a "Yes" rating then the score must remain "No." This reduces the temptation to pressure the person with a differing perception to give up that perspective for the sake of consensus and, instead, encourages a real dialogue about differing perceptions about the team planning experience.

9

Co-teaching to Deliver Differentiated Instruction

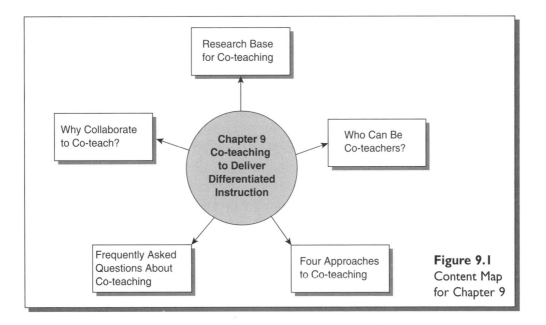

Figure 9.1
Content Map for Chapter 9

- Research Base for Co-teaching
- Why Collaborate to Co-teach?
- Chapter 9 Co-teaching to Deliver Differentiated Instruction
- Who Can Be Co-teachers?
- Frequently Asked Questions About Co-teaching
- Four Approaches to Co-teaching

Today my understanding of how we can educate all students together has broadened. I realize that my initial concerns about co-teaching were about the unknown and not being able to visualize how it might work.

—Keller and Cravedi-Cheng (2004)

In this chapter, you will discover ways to address the following questions:

- What is the rationale for collaborative teaching approaches?
- What is the research base for collaborative approaches to differentiate instruction?
- Who can collaborate?
- What are four co-teaching approaches?

Although many different kinds of co-teaching partnerships can be established among personnel who have various roles, titles, and expertise, a co-teaching team often comprises a general and a special educator who teach the general education curriculum to all students and also implement Individual Education Programs (IEPs) for students with disabilities.

All educators on a co-teaching team are responsible for differentiating the instructional planning and delivery, assessment of student achievement, and classroom management. Several collaborative teaching approaches have proven to be successful in guiding educators who partner to differentiate instruction (Villa, 2002; Villa, Thousand, & Nevin, 2004). These approaches include: (1) *consultation*, where support personnel or educators with unique expertise (e.g., literacy specialist) provide advisement to an educator; (2) *supportive co-teaching*, where one educator takes the lead and others rotate among students to provide support; (3) *parallel co-teaching*, where co-teachers instruct different heterogeneous groups of students; (4) *complementary co-teaching*, where one co-teacher does something to supplement or complement another co-teacher's instruction (e.g., models note-taking on a transparency, paraphrases the teacher's statements); and (5) *team teaching*, where partners share responsibility for planning, teaching, and assessing the progress of all students in the class.

Some co-teaching approaches (e.g., complementary and team teaching) require greater commitment to, comfort with, and skill in collaborative planning and role release (i.e., transferring one's specialized instructional responsibilities over to someone else). It is recommended that collaborative teams select among the co-teaching approaches, as needed, based on the curriculum demands of a unit or lesson and student learning characteristics, needs, and interests.

It makes good sense to collaborate in both the planning and the teaching of differentiated instruction lessons. Why? First, the 2004 Individuals With Disabilities Education Improvement Act (IDEIA) reauthorization mandated that students with disabilities have access to the general education curriculum. In addition, the act also mandated that school systems and teachers are obliged to learn and use educational practices that differentiate content, instruction, and assessment. Differentiation provides needed supports and services to enable all students to be successful in general education classrooms. Co-teaching provides a greater opportunity to capitalize upon the unique, diverse, and specialized knowledge of each instructor so as to promote effective differentiated instruction.

Second, co-teaching allows students to experience and imitate the cooperative and collaborative skills that teachers model when they co-teach. Third, with multiple instructors, there is increased flexibility in grouping and scheduling, thus making it possible for students to experience less wait time for teacher attention and increased time on task,, an important factor documented to increased academic productivity (Kneedler & Hallahan, 1981; Lloyd, 1982; Weldall & Panagopoulou-Stamatelatou, 1991).

Fourth, teachers who co-teach can structure their classes to use more effectively the research-proven strategies required of the No Child Left Behind (NCLB) Act (Miller, Valasky, & Malloy, 1998). Finally, co-teaching is a vehicle for bringing together people with diverse backgrounds and interests to share knowledge and skills to generate novel methods to individualize learning.

RESEARCH BASE FOR CO-TEACHING ■

Policy studies and reports of teacher experiences are the primary sources for the research on the benefits of collaborative teaching. In fact, we argue that collaborative teaching is an example of a policy that leads to practice that in itself leads to more research. Both the IDEIA and NCLB mandates are examples of policy that requires practitioner collaboration, which then drives further action and research by the practitioners. Thus, collaborative teaching may be an example where practitioners are leading researchers. The literature on co-teaching is at a point in its development where practice can inform theory and research while research and theory can inform practice.

In our book, *A Guide to Co-teaching: Practical Tips for Facilitating Student Learning* (Villa, Thousand, & Nevin, 2004), we provide a detailed description of the research base for co-teaching. Other research has shown that when you co-teach to differentiate instruction, you can increase your effectiveness in teaching students with a variety of instructional needs, including those students with hearing impairment (Compton, Stratton, Maier, Meyers, Scott, & Tomlinson, 1998; Luckner, 1999); learning disabilities (Klingner, Vaughn, Hughes, Schumm, & Elbaum, 1998; Rice & Zigmond, 1999; Trent, 1998; Welch, 2000); high-risk students with emotional disturbances and other at-risk characteristics (Dieker, 1998); language delays (Miller, Valasky, & Molloy, 1998); and students with and without disabilities in secondary classrooms (Mahoney, 1997; Weiss & Lloyd, 2002).

Other researchers have documented the actions taken by general and special educators as they implement co-teaching (e.g., Garrigan & Thousand, 2005; Magiera, Smith, Zigmond, & Gabauer, 2005). Recently, measurements of student achievement indicate that students with disabilities and students who are learning English as a second language in co-taught classrooms can improve their scores on standardized assessments (Cramer, Nevin, Salazar, & Landa, 2006; Garrigan & Thousand, 2005; Salazar & Nevin, 2005).

WHO CAN BE CO-TEACHERS? ■

We advocate that anyone who has an instructional role in a school can co-teach: classroom teachers, paraprofessionals, special and bilingual educators, content specialists such as reading teachers, support personnel such as speech and language therapists and school psychologists, volunteers, and students themselves. In fact, we have found that children and youth who learn and practice being student co-teachers are more likely to grow into adults who are more effective advocates for themselves (Villa et al., 2004). A common characteristic of the teaching and learning activities that promotes students in the co-teacher role (whether it is peer tutoring, cooperative group learning, dialogue teaching, or instructional conversation) is that students have more active roles in communicating their understanding of the academic content. This, in turn, leads to increased retention and achievement.

■ FOUR APPROACHES TO CO-TEACHING

In a comprehensive national survey, teachers experienced in meeting the needs of students in a diverse classroom reported that they used four predominant approaches to collaborative teaching: supportive teaching, parallel teaching, complementary teaching, and team teaching (National Center for Educational Restructuring and Inclusion, 1995). Before describing each approach, it is important to emphasize that none of these four co-teaching approaches is better than the other. All of the approaches to co-teaching bring together the masters of curriculum and the masters of access.

When deciding which approach to use in a given lesson, the goal always is to improve the educational outcomes of students through the selected co-teaching approach. Many beginning co-teachers start with supportive teaching and parallel teaching because these approaches involve less structured coordination among the co-teaching team members. As co-teaching skills and relationships strengthen, co-teachers then venture into the complementary teaching and team teaching approaches that require more time, coordination, and knowledge of, and trust in, one another's skills.

In the sections that follow, you will learn to describe, illustrate, compare, and contrast the four approaches to co-teaching. Considerations for effectively implementing each approach and avoiding the pitfalls are explained. If you like to use graphic organizers when you learn, you can use the matrix in Table 9.1 to keep your own notes about similarities, differences, and cautions. The authors model the use of this matrix to summarize the co-teaching approaches as they are introduced in this chapter.

Supportive Teaching

Supportive teaching is when one teacher takes the lead instructional role and the other rotates among the students to provide support. The co-teacher who takes the supportive role watches or listens as students work together, and steps in to provide one-to-one tutorial assistance when necessary, while the other co-teacher continues to direct the lesson.

A caution in using the supportive teaching approach is that whoever is playing the support role (e.g., special educator, paraprofessional, or bilingual translator) must not become "Velcro-ed" to individual students, or function as

Table 9.1   A Matrix for Note Taking

Similarities Among the Four Approaches			
Supportive Differences	Parallel Differences	Complementary Differences	Team Teaching Differences
Supportive Cautions	Parallel Cautions	Complementary Cautions	Team Teaching Cautions

hovercraft vehicles blocking students' interactions with other students. This can be stigmatizing for both students and the support persons, leading the other students to perceive that the support teacher and the student being supported are not genuine members of the classroom. Also beware of not using to the best advantage the skills of another educator who has been locked into the supportive role.

Parallel Teaching

Parallel teaching is when two or more people work with different groups of students in different sections of the classroom. Both teachers have shared responsibility for all the students in the classroom. As shown in Table 9.2, parallel teaching includes at least the following eight variations: split class, station teaching or learning centers, rotating co-teachers, each co-teacher teaching a different component of the lesson, cooperative group monitoring, experiment or lab monitoring, learning style focus, and supplementary instruction. Each variation is described briefly in the table.

As with supportive teaching, there are cautions in implementing parallel teaching. Primarily, there is the possibility of creating a special class within a class by routinely grouping the same students in the same group with the same

Table 9.2   Eight Ways for Co-teachers to Use the Parallel Teaching Approach

1. *Split Class*—Each co-teacher is responsible for a particular group of students. Each one monitors the students in the group to ensure students understand the lesson. They each provide guided instruction, or reteach the group, if necessary.

2. *Station Teaching or Learning Centers*—Each co-teacher is responsible for assembling, guiding, and monitoring one or more centers or stations.

3. *Co-teachers Rotate*—The co-teachers rotate among two or more groups of students, teaching the same lesson to each group.

4. *Each co-teacher teaches a different component of the lesson*—This is similar to station teaching, except that teachers rotate from group to group rather than students rotating from station to station.

5. *Cooperative Group Monitoring*—Each co-teacher takes responsibility for monitoring and providing feedback and assistance to a given number of students who are organized into cooperative learning groups.

6. *Experiment or Lab Monitoring*—Each co-teacher monitors and assists a given number of laboratory groups, providing guided instruction to those groups who might need additional support.

7. *Learning Style Focus*—One co-teacher teaches the lesson to a group of students using primarily visual strategies. Another co-teacher teaches the same lesson to a different group of students by using auditory strategies. A third co-teacher teaches another group by using kinesthetic strategies.

8. *Supplementary Instruction*—One co-teacher works with most of the class on a concept, skill, or assignment. The other co-teacher (a) instructs students to apply or generalize the skill to a relevant community environment, (b) provides extra guidance to students who are self-identified or teacher-identified as needing extra assistance in acquiring or applying the learning, or (c) provides advanced enrichment activities.

co-teacher. It is important, therefore, to deliberately keep groups heterogeneous by allowing students to learn with those students who have different approaches to learning. Beware of the negative impact on assessment measures when students of low ability are primarily grouped with other students of low ability (Marzano, Pickering, & Pollack, 2001).

It also is important to rotate students among different co-teachers so students may stretch their learning by experiencing different instructors' approaches and expertise and avoid the stigmatization that may arise if someone other than the classroom teacher (e.g., a special educator or paraprofessional) always teaches one set of students. When all co-teaching team members are familiar with all students, they are better able to problem-solve any barriers to academic, communication, and social learning that their common students encounter.

Table 9.3 shows the similarities and differences between these two approaches. Notice that there are blank spaces for you to add your own ideas.

Complementary Teaching

Complementary teaching is when a co-teacher does something to enhance the instruction provided by the other co-teacher. Both teachers have shared responsibility for all the students in the classroom. For example, the classroom co-teacher might provide a lecture on the content while the other co-teacher paraphrases statements and models note-taking of the content on chart paper or a transparency. Sometimes, one of the complementary teaching partners pre-teaches the small-group social skill roles that are required for successful cooperative group learning and then monitors the students as they practice the roles during the academic cooperative group lesson facilitated by the other co-teacher.

A common concern with complementary teaching, particularly at the secondary level, is that those co-teachers who are not the content area teachers do not have the same level of content mastery as the content teacher. This cannot be avoided and is not necessarily a drawback. Complementary teaching partners have expertise in other areas (e.g., speech and language pathologists have expertise in communication; a special educator has expertise in adapting curriculum and learning strategies; a paraprofessional speaks fluent Spanish or another language that is the primary language for many of the students in the classroom). These areas of expertise can be readily used to complement and supplement the expertise of the content area teacher. Through planning and teaching together, all members of the team have an opportunity to acquire new skills. For example, the special educator may learn new content and the classroom teacher may acquire skills to differentiate curriculum, instruction, and assessment.

Team Teaching

Team teaching is when two or more people do what the traditional teacher has always done—plan, teach, assess, and assume responsibility for all of the

Table 9.3   A Matrix to Compare-Contrast Two Co-teaching Approaches

Similarities Among Two Approaches: Supportive & Parallel
Two or more teachers in the classroom
Capitalizes on specific strengths and expertise of co-teachers
Provides greater teacher-student ratio and brings additional one-to-one support for students in the classroom
Students are heterogeneously grouped
Shared responsibility for all students

Supportive Differences	Parallel Differences
One teacher teaches whole class, other co-teachers provide tutorial supports.	One or more teachers work with separate groups of students (at least 8 different options for arranging the groups).
Other teacher is the master of content; other teacher is the master of access.	

Supportive Cautions	Parallel Cautions
Beware of the "Velcro" effect that can stigmatize the students.	Beware of creating a special class within the class by grouping all the low performers into one group.
Beware of one teacher becoming the discipline police, copier of class materials, or in-class paper grader.	Beware of the negative impact on assessment measures when students of low ability are primarily grouped with other students of low ability.
Beware of becoming "comfortable" in the supportive role based on lack of time to plan.	
Beware of not using to the best advantage the skills of another educator locked into the supportive role.	

students in the classroom. Both teachers share responsibility and leadership for all the students in the classroom. For example, the co-teachers alternate who demonstrates the steps in a science experiment and who models how to record the results of the experiment.

Co-teachers who team teach might divide a lesson in ways that allow students to experience each teacher's strengths and expertise. For example, for a lesson on inventions in science, one co-teacher whose interest is history will explain the impact on society. The other co-teacher's strengths are more focused on the mechanisms involved and can explain how the particular inventions work. In team teaching, co-teachers simultaneously deliver lessons; both teachers are alternately taking the lead and providing support. The sign of a successful team-teaching partnership is that the students view each teacher as being equal in their eyes.

Team teaching brings up its own set of issues. One issue is whether team teachers should remain together at the end of the school year or whether one co-teacher, such as the special educator, should follow students transitioning to the next grade level. There are advantages and disadvantages associated with teachers staying together or one teacher accompanying students. Starting over again every year with a new teaching team can thwart the development of co-teaching relationships and content knowledge. On the other hand, there are obvious benefits to teachers receiving new students who are at risk of failure but who are accompanied by teaching personnel who know the students. In addition, the new teacher has immediate access to resource personnel with in-depth knowledge of the students. It is up to each team to weigh the advantages and disadvantages of each option and choose what is best for students.

We suggest two other cautions. Beware of not monitoring the students who need it. Beware of too much teacher talk, repetition, and lack of student-student interaction. Table 9.4 uses the matrix to summarize the similarities and differences between the complementary and team teaching approaches.

Table 9.5 shows the similarities and differences among all four approaches to co-teaching.

QUESTIONS ABOUT CO-TEACHING ▪
TO DIFFERENTIATE INSTRUCTION

In this section of the chapter, we address questions about co-teaching to differentiate instruction. In our book, *A Guide to Co-teaching: Practical Tips to Facilitate Student Learning,* we provide more details about these and other issues such as scheduling and effective use of resources. For example, consider the questions below:

1. I have a concern about co-teaching with a paraprofessional or a volunteer who is not well trained to work with students with special needs. Isn't it a problem that people with the least amount of preparation are assigned to support children who have the most intensive needs?

Table 9.4   A Matrix to Compare-Contrast Two Co-teaching Approaches

Similarities Among Two Approaches: Complementary & Team Teaching	
Two or more teachers in the classroom	
Capitalizes on specific strengths and expertise of co-teachers	
Provides greater teacher-student ratio and brings additional one-to-one support for students in the classroom	
Students are heterogeneously grouped	
Shared responsibility for all students	
Complementary Differences	Team Teaching Differences
One teacher pre-teaches specific study skills and monitors students' use of it while other teacher teaches the content. *One teacher teaches content while the second teacher clarifies, simplifies content.*	*Both teachers coequally responsible for planning, instruction of content, study skills, assessment, and grade assignment.*
Complementary Cautions	Team Teaching Cautions
Beware "typecasting" the content teacher as the "expert" where students perceive her as the "real teacher." PLAN for role release so that all co-teachers can teach the content. *Beware of not monitoring the students who need it.* *Beware of too much teacher talk, repetition, and lack of student-student interaction.*	*Beware of not monitoring the students who need it.* *Beware of too much teacher talk, repetition, and lack of student-student interaction.*

Table 9.5 Similarities and Differences Among Four Approaches to Co-teaching

Similarities Among All Four Approaches

Two or more teachers in the classroom

Capitalizes on specific strengths and expertise of co-teachers

Provides greater teacher-student ratio and brings additional one-to-one support for students in the classroom

Students are heterogeneously grouped

Shared responsibility for all students

	Supportive Differences	Parallel Differences	Complementary Differences	Team Teaching Differences
	One teacher teaches whole class, other co-teachers provide tutorial supports. One teacher is the master of content. Other teacher is the master of access.	One or more teachers work with separate groups of students (at least eight different options for arranging the groups).	One teacher pre-teaches specific study skills and monitors students' use of it while one teacher teaches the content. Other teacher teaches content while the second teacher clarifies, simplifies content.	Both teachers coequally responsible for planning, instruction of content, study skills, assessment, and grade assignment.

	Supportive Cautions	Parallel Cautions	Complementary Cautions	Team Teaching Cautions
	Beware of the "Velcro" effect that can stigmatize the students. Beware of one teacher becoming the discipline police, copier of class materials, or in-class paper grader. Beware of becoming comfortable in the supportive role based on lack of time to plan. Beware of not using to the best advantage the skills of another educator locked into the supportive role.	Beware of creating a special class within the class by grouping all the low performers into one group. Beware of the negative impact on assessment measures when students of low ability are primarily grouped with other students of low ability.	Beware "typecasting" the content teacher as the "expert" where students perceive her as the "real teacher." PLAN for role release so that all co-teachers can teach the content. Beware of not monitoring the students who need it. Beware of too much teacher talk, repetition, and lack of student-student interaction.	Beware of not monitoring the students who need it. Beware of too much teacher talk, repetition, and lack of student-student interaction.

Paraprofessionals and volunteers alike can receive training, supervision, and coaching. This can ensure that the needs of students with special needs in the inclusive settings are being met. There are several ways to address the lack of training. For example, the paraprofessional and co-teacher could visit a paraprofessional who has received training to work with students with special needs. Or the special educator for the school district could visit the co-teaching team to show both co-teachers some strategies and techniques to use not only with the students with special needs but other students at risk for school failure. The paraprofessional could participate in training programs specially designed to differentiate instruction similar to that developed by Doyle (2002). The paraprofessional then could share the new skills with the co-teacher. The job definition for the paraprofessional must include guidelines for training and support in differentiated instruction techniques. To further avoid stigmatization, the job definition for paraprofessionals hired to work with individual children with special needs can be administratively redefined to include responsibilities for all the children in the classroom.

2. I am a professional special educator who has just been assigned to work as a co-teacher with a general educator. How do I avoid acting in a subsidiary role by just walking around and helping the students?

Are you worried that you will go into a classroom and find yourself drifting around, working with one or two students, just waiting and watching the flow of the classroom teacher's lesson? This indicates that you are concerned that not all of the skills you have acquired may be used. One way to address this concern is for co-teachers to learn to use the other approaches of co-teaching described in this chapter (and in greater detail in our book, mentioned above). Then you and your co-teacher can agree, as a goal, that your co-teaching relationship will capitalize on all four approaches of co-teaching instead of relying on only one.

The benefits of the increased awareness that all educators bring to their co-teaching partnerships far outweigh the temporary discomfort that they may experience when just beginning to use the supportive co-teacher approach. It is not uncommon to discover that many special educators and support people, when they enter a general education classroom, discover it to be a very different world than the one-on-one or small group instruction that is typically found in resource rooms or self-contained classrooms. With a supportive co-teacher arrangement, both teachers have the chance to become familiar with each other's curriculum and teaching techniques. The goal is to nurture and enrich the relationship so that both co-teachers can experience an evolution of their skills. Remember that this involves spending time to talk, establishing trust, and communicating.

3. Should students stay primarily with the same co-teachers?

In parallel co-teaching, as in other forms of co-teaching, it is most desirable for students to rotate among the different co-teaching team members. This avoids the stigmatization of students or teachers that might arise if someone other than the classroom teacher, such as the special educator or paraprofessional, always teaches one set of students. By interacting with multiple instructors, students stretch their thinking and learning approaches as they experience the differing content expertise and instructional approaches of each co-teacher. Rotating students among co-teachers ensures that all students are instructed by the professional educators as well as paraprofessionals, all of whom may have very different strengths and nonstrengths. Additionally, struggling learners can benefit from the informed problem solving in which co-teachers can engage, given those co-teachers first-hand knowledge of the students' learning characteristics.

In co-teaching, as in life, there are no perfect solutions. There are advantages and disadvantages associated with staying together as a team or accompanying the students as they move to the next grade. It is up to the team members to explore the advantages and disadvantages of each option and choose the solution that is best for the students they teach. Our observation of co-teaching teams reveals that in elementary schools, about half of the teams decide to stay together and half decide to follow the students. In the upper grades, we tend to see more of the co-teaching teams staying together; these teams cite mastery of the complex curriculum as one of the main reasons for doing so.

10

UDL Lesson Planning Cycle to Differentiate Instruction in Action

Fourth Grade Social Studies

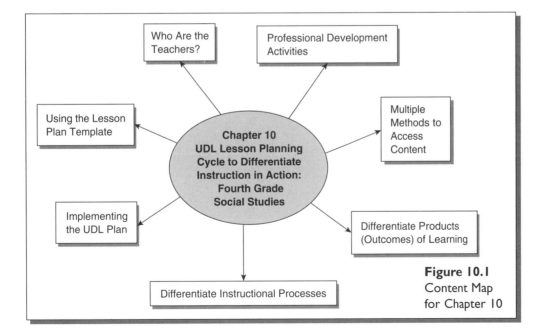

Figure 10.1 Content Map for Chapter 10

It's only an obstacle if you can't see around it.

—Anonymous

n this chapter, you will discover how Kevin's co-teachers addressed the following questions:

- How did the co-teachers use the Universal Design for Learning (UDL) lesson planning process to differentiate a history unit for a diverse group of fourth grade learners?
- What was the role of professional development activities in the process?

We join Kevin's co-teachers, whom you first met in Chapter 2. Mr. Gleason, the fourth grade science and social studies teacher, had relocated to Wisconsin and was beginning his first year of teaching in elementary school after several years of middle school teaching. Ms. Villalobos, Mr. Gleason's co-teaching partner, is a special educator who has experience with co-teaching. Together, they identified mismatches between the task demands of science and social studies and the learning characteristics of Kevin, a student with IEP goals in reading, small group social skills, and stress management who is of great concern to them.

Kevin enjoys interacting and being in a leadership role with others, but would not do homework, walked out of class when frustrated, and refused to participate in round robin reading of class texts, which were at least two grade levels above his current reading level.

For each of the mismatches between Kevin and the demands of the curriculum, the co-teachers brainstormed over three dozen ideas for resolving the mismatch (shown in Table 2.4) and generated five criteria for selecting those ideas that they would try in order to reduce the identified mismatches. One of those criteria involved bringing the student in on the decision making.

So, Mr. Gleason and Ms. Villalobos met with Kevin and his two best friends, Jose and Francisco, to share their brainstormed list and to solicit input from the boys. All three boys really liked the ideas that allowed them to work in groups or with partners, to create work in class with other students that included oral presentations (e.g., tape recorded, videoed, or theatrically presented). Kevin admitted that he walked out of class when he feared he might be put on the spot and look "dumb" in front of classmates if he could not read something or did not know the answer. Jose and Francisco, both English language learners, noted that having pictures and real objects helped them understand new information, since so much of the science and social studies vocabulary was new to them. All three boys also felt that an independently written research paper was unfair, since they did not have computers at home, transportation to the public library, or family members who could help them read research materials they did not understand.

Mr. Gleason and Ms. Villalobos, pleasantly surprised with the students' candidness, began thinking about a plan for the mandatory fourth grade Wisconsin history unit that was coming up in the next few weeks. The district had an established partnership with Sven Olsen, the local education coordinator of the Wisconsin Historical Society (WHS) Education Department, from where teachers can borrow historical artifacts and receive consultation for up to 10 hours (www.wisconsinhistory.org/teachers/). This relationship gave Mr. Gleason and Ms. Villalobos the perfect opportunity with this history unit to change how they were having students interact with the content, show their learning, and work with one another.

In addition, the district had adopted service learning as a graduation requirement and tasked social studies teachers to identify ways in which students of all ages could provide community service. An initial phone conversation with Mr. Olsen sparked the idea that, instead of assigning a research paper, students would create a history exhibit on Wisconsin frontier life for the local Children's Museum, an affiliate of the WHS.

CO-TEACHER PROFESSIONAL ■ DEVELOPMENT ACTIVITIES

The school where these co-teachers work schedules Wednesday as an early student release day. (Students leave at 1 PM rather than 3 PM.) Teachers are expected to engage in collaborative planning or participate in periodic (at least monthly) schoolwide professional development. Because co-teaching had been adopted as a schoolwide support option, in the first month of school the entire faculty received an introductory inservice on four co-teaching approaches— supportive, parallel, complementary, and team teaching (see Chapter 9).

At the end of the inservice, each co-teaching team, as well as each grade-level team, was given a copy of *A Guide to Co-teaching: Practical Tips for Facilitating Student Learning* (Villa, Thousand, & Nevin, 2004) with the instructions to skim the book, but also to carefully read the first chapter in preparation for what would be an ongoing book study over the year. This book study would be held during the first 15 minutes of each biweekly faculty meeting.

Mr. Gleason and Ms. Villalobos were really attracted to the use of parallel co-teaching, especially to station teaching and the monitoring of cooperative groups at stations. They agreed that this could work well for having students interact with artifacts in the upcoming pioneer history unit they were starting to plan.

In the next professional development event, all teachers learned about the nine research-based instructional practices that Marzano, Pickering, and Pollock (2001) identified as helping to increase student achievement (Chapter 7, Table 7.2). They also learned about ways to engage students during lectures (Chapter 7, Table 7.3). At the end of the workshop, teachers submitted a brief plan on how they would incorporate at least three of these practices into their instruction. The principal noted that she would be looking for evidence of the use of the practices in her observations and review of lesson plans and would reserve time at faculty meetings for teachers to share with one another how they were implementing their selected strategies.

Mr. Gleason and Ms. Villalobos decided to submit a joint plan and selected (1) having students show similarities and differences through compare and contrast applications, (2) pausing to have students summarize during lectures and during partner reading, and (3) using cooperative group structures.

Mr. Gleason was familiar with cooperative learning, having learned about it as part of his teacher preparation program. He admitted that in the middle school in which he had previously worked, he had developed a habit of primarily using lecture and rapid questioning, because that was what most of the other teachers did. He was grateful to learn from Ms. Villalobos that the project she had completed for her master's degree focused on cooperative learning and that she had become quite expert at infusing quick cooperative structures (Chapter 7, Table 7.5) into lessons. She offered to take the lead in thinking about ways in which to structure the social studies block to address fourth grade Wisconsin history standards via station teaching with small groups and historical artifacts and literature.

■ MULTIPLE METHODS FOR ACCESSING THE HISTORY CONTENT

As a fourth grade co-teaching team, Mr. Gleason and Ms. Villalobos examined the fourth grade Wisconsin history standards with their entire class of students in mind. For the upcoming three-week unit, the two teachers agreed that they would directly address four of the ten state standards (http://dpi.wi.gov/standards), as stated below:

B.4.1 Identify and examine various sources of information that are used for constructing an understanding of the past, such as artifacts, documents, letters, diaries, maps, textbooks, photos, paintings, architecture, oral presentations, graphs, and charts

B.4.2 Use a timeline to select, organize, and sequence information describing eras in history

B.4.3 Examine biographies, stories, narratives, and folk tales to understand the lives of ordinary and extraordinary people, place them in time and context, and explain their relationship to important historical events

B.4.4 Compare and contrast changes in contemporary life with life in the past by looking at social, economic, political, and cultural roles played by individuals and groups

Ms. Villalobos proposed, and Mr. Gleason agreed, that they would address these four standards through a three-week unit that examined pioneer life in Wisconsin, using options that would allow students to access content at different levels of difficulty. She suggested integrating literacy and social studies in a 90-minute block (including recess) for four out of five days of the week.

Each day of the week started with a brief lecture on content that was not in the other materials available to students. Mr. Gleason welcomed this because lecturing was natural for him, and he also had a wealth of knowledge on nineteenth-century life that went beyond the texts and the materials that had been gathered about the period. This was followed by 20 to 25 minutes of work by students at one of four stations. Each station focused on one of the state standards. After recess, students engaged in structured partner reading of a nineteenth-century-based piece of literature at the partners' instructional level. For Kevin, that meant the second grade level.

The 90-minute blocks closed with a class meeting where partner reading was debriefed. Small group interpersonal skills needed by students in order to cooperate with peers both in the stations and in the partner experiences were taught at this time.

Weaving social skills into the curricular content enabled the co-teachers to ensure that Kevin and others in the class could learn and practice ways in which to deal with stress and frustration. Among the social skills they modeled, practiced, and then monitored during group work were those that assisted Kevin to reduce his frustration: asking for help, asking for a break, identifying signs of distress, and using calming techniques such as deep breathing.

Because Wednesdays were early release days, and the schedule for classes was shorter, the co-teachers invited Mr. Olsen, the local WHS education coordinator, to join them for a one-hour period on Wednesday morning to guide the students in creating the history exhibit on Wisconsin frontier life for the local Children's Museum. The art room was reserved for the teams of students as a place where they could create their exhibit room, or area, using artifacts and art materials.

The co-teachers agreed that the four Wisconsin fourth grade history standards that they had selected were broad enough to enable them to differentiate both the station and partner reading materials to allow for the varied interests, literacy levels, background knowledge, and other academic and social differences among their diverse class of students without having to adapt for any particular student. See if you agree as you now read brief descriptions of the content of each of the four stations.

To address Standard B.4.1—constructing an understanding of the past— Station #1 included a variety of experiences from the 1800s (e.g., weaving on a loom, spinning on a spinning wheel, cutting cloth and hand sewing clothes from a pattern, knitting, crocheting, churning butter, making ice cream). Students received directions on how to use the materials and tools. After trying daily living activities common in the 1800s, they were asked to think, talk, and write about what they discovered about daily life in those times. The historical documents and media found at this station varied in complexity from simple photographs to dense historical biographies. At this station, as in their partner reading activity, students were given choices of "reading" materials within a range of readability.

To address Standard B.4.2, students constructed timelines to organize first information about themselves (e.g., bring in and create a timeline of their own clothes from the current year, clothes from two years ago, four years ago, six years ago, and from infancy) and to then create a timeline of items or photos or clothes worn by parents, grandparents, and great grandparents. They could then develop timelines for any set of current items (e.g., shoes, photos, toys) and compare them to the late 1800s.

At Station #3, students could learn about the lives of ordinary and extraordinary people of the late 1800s by examining photographs, letters, diaries, stories, narratives, folk tales, maps, and textbooks (e.g., McGuffey Readers) and by listening to musical recordings of the time (e.g., "Oh! Susanna," "I've Been Working on the Railroad"). The students could learn about various heritages of the early settlers including Danes, Finns, Germans, as well as African Americans (e.g., http://www.wisconsinhistory.org/oww/pleasant_ridge.asp). Students initially self-selected materials, but then they were guided by the monitoring co-teacher to analyze increasingly more challenging material at the subsequent visits to this station. This station's product was a collective wall quilt to which each student contributed items.

Station #4 directly addressed Standard B.4.4 by having students compare and contrast objects of contemporary life with objects from life in the past. The station displayed a variety of present-day items and their historical counterparts (e.g., Polaroid photo versus a tintype slide; a CD versus an early Thomas Edison recording; electric versus fire-heated irons; an electric versus a hand-operated coffee grinder). Students could explore objects and could compare and contrast those items from earlier times to those we use now and also describe what the objects tell about life in the late 1800s. As stated in this station, they had a choice to:

"Tell a partner three or more similarities and differences and something about life in the 1800s. Have your partner record."

"Write down three or more similarities and differences and something about life in the 1800s."

"Ask a partner to describe three or more similarities and differences and something about life in the 1800s. Take notes."

"Pair like items or sort the items into old and new groups. Take a digital photo of it. Be prepared to describe the photo to your teachers or classmates."

"Draw pictures of pairs of items you observed."

"Use items to act out a scene from daily life today and in the past. Videotape your performance."

In partner reading, the content was naturally differentiated as partners became familiar with past times, people, and historical events and then compared them to times, people, and events today, as they jointly read literature at their respective levels of difficulty.

Finally, the service learning project involved designing, with a team, a section of a log cabin environment complete with household features (e.g., fireplace for cooking and heating, outhouse). Preparing students for responsible citizenship can be accomplished through student involvement in community service activities. Service learning is "an educational activity, program, or curriculum that seeks to promote students' learning through experiences associated with volunteerism or community service" (Scheckley & Keeton, 1997, p. 32).

The preparation of the museum exhibit provided concrete representation of the content for students who benefit from actually seeing, touching, and experiencing events in order to construct understanding. Because such an array of reading and experiential materials was available, Mr. Gleason and Ms. Villalobos were convinced that all students would find a way to access information about the pioneer life and times. There were options for Kevin and other students for whom the traditional social studies text was beyond their current reading level.

There also were options for students considered gifted and talented for whom the traditional text was too easy, uninteresting, and unmotivating.

DIFFERENTIATING THE PRODUCTS ■ (OUTCOMES) OF LEARNING

How are Mr. Gleason and Ms. Villalobos differentiating learning outcomes and arranging for multilevel and varied ways for students to show what they know and understand? How have they developed authentic products rather than paper-and-pencil assessments? How have they asked students to perform, produce, and demonstrate understandings about late-1800s Wisconsin history?

To begin with, the co-teachers allowed students to use their strengths to express themselves. Students completed varied output tasks that allowed for (a) asking, telling, and writing products (i.e., verbal/linguistic, interpersonal); (b) matching, sorting, timeline manipulation, and acting performances (i.e., kinesthetic, logical/mathematical); as well as (c) drawing and constructing demonstrations (i.e., visual/spatial). The co-teachers also gave students choice in the design of their portion of the museum exhibit as well as in the products they wished to create at stations. At Station #1, for instance, the analysis and product of the historical media could be as simple as examining and describing a family portrait at the comprehension level of Bloom's taxonomy; it could also be as complex as reading a historical biography and completing an evaluative analysis of the impact of that particular historical figure on society.

Authentic assessment also means having multiple criteria to assess a lesson, project, or unit. Mr. Gleason and Ms. Villalobos's unit employed multiple criteria—tangible timelines, journal entries, pictorial and written responses, storytelling and role-playing, collective charting in a quilt of findings, oral responses to questions, formulation of questions, and the culminating classwide project of the museum exhibit.

This diversity of products offered ample options for Kevin and his classmates to show their knowledge. Further, by replacing the long-term project that was to be done at home with the service learning museum project that was jointly completed at school with a team, there no longer was a mismatch between Kevin and homework. Instead, the collaborative creation of a portion of the museum exhibit capitalized upon Kevin's interpersonal strengths. Likewise, by replacing quizzes and chapter tests with authentic products and performances that he created at stations and the log cabin exhibit, Kevin no longer had a string of frustrating failing grades.

DIFFERENTIATING THE ■ INSTRUCTIONAL PROCESSES

Mr. Gleason and Ms. Villalobos used a variety of lesson formats, instructional arrangements, and strategies. They adjusted the social and physical environment. They also used all four approaches to co-teaching to engage students in learning. Which of these instructional processes have you detected in the descriptions of the unit thus far?

Instructional Format

Instructional format refers to how information is imparted to students and how they will interact with that content. This teaching team took advantage of several formats during their social studies and literacy block. First, they used an adapted *lecture* format that incorporated techniques the co-teachers had learned about that involved pausing during the lecture to engage students. Remember that engaging students during lecture was one of the goals this co-teaching team set for themselves at the beginning of the year.

Each social studies block started with Mr. Gleason giving a mini-lecture of 15 to 20 minutes. About 10 minutes into the mini-lecture, Mr. Gleason stopped and Ms. Villalobos asked students to pause, reflect on what they had heard, and summarize. A favorite summarizing strategy of the students was the "think, write, or draw" strategy in which they summarized graphically, or in writing, their reactions to the content.

The daily *station teaching* allowed for activity-based and experiential as well as discovery learning. Students with interpersonal strengths were allowed freedom of interaction, while students with kinesthetic strengths had freedom to stand and move. Station teaching also allowed the co-teaching team to achieve a second goal—to use the research–based instructional practice of having students identify similarities and differences. A station task option was for students to compare and contrast experiences or items of the late 1800s with corresponding contemporary experiences or items.

The *partner reading* part of the block replaced the round robin oral reading practice. This allowed the co-teachers to use the data they had regarding their students' literacy levels to match students with choices of reading material at their instructional or independent level. Kevin no longer needed to leave the class, nor did he refuse to read in order to save face for not being able to fluently read the text that was two grade levels above his instructional level. Further, he could be partnered with a variety of classmates—ones with a similar literacy profile, ones below his level for whom he could be a model reader at his level of independence, or ones with strong reading skills who could encourage him to attempt more difficult readings of interest.

The museum project represented *service learning* and *community-referenced* learning formats. The co-teachers believed this format and experience would motivate Kevin and other students, particularly the several English language learners for whom working with *realia* (i.e., concrete, real objects) and having an obvious purpose for their lessons, made the learning more evident.

Instructional Arrangements

Instructional arrangements determine whether students work alone, with a partner, or as a member of a small or large group. The opening mini-lecture and closing class meeting circle represent *whole group* arrangements. Mr. Gleason and Ms. Villalobos consciously decided to reduce use of whole groups. When they did use whole groups, they deliberately planned how they could complement one another to differentiate support for students as needed. For example, Ms. Villalobos would pose a "think-pair-share" question after every 10 minutes of lecture. Mr. Gleason would sit next to students who needed "proximal control" as a management strategy, while Ms. Villalobos guided students through the learning about and rehearsal of a social skill in the class meeting circle.

In stations, students could work *alone,* with *partners,* or in *small groups.* On Wednesdays, when teams planned for sections of the WHS log cabin exhibit in the art room, the arrangement was in *small groups.* The daily partner reading structure represented a *cooperative grouping* and realized the third of the team's professional goals of using quick cooperative structures.

The authors would like to note that the quick cooperative structure called "Say Something" came to be a favorite. With "Say Something," partners together decided points in the reading where they would stop, pause, and "say something" that represented a summary of what they had read thus far. Each partner asked the other partner a question or made an interesting connection (in this case, to late-1800s Wisconsin life). Partners repeated this process to the end of the reading selection. Then partners shared their connections during the newly established whole group class meeting that immediately followed partner reading. The co-teachers liked "Say Something" because the act of thinking aloud combined with attentive partner listening built interpersonal relationships as well as helped students connect new and prior knowledge. This particularly benefited Kevin. As he experienced new partners, he began to develop positive relationships with classmates and also new friendships. Further, since each pair stopped at different points in the same or different piece of literature, they each contributed different information, yielding a much richer whole group discussion.

Instructional Strategies

Instructional strategies represent a broad range of techniques for engaging students. These include questioning, checking for understanding, and use of visual scaffolds such as lecture guides and graphic organizers. Mr. Gleason and Ms. Villalobos both were aware of the applications of Multiple Intelligences (MI) Theory and attempted to create learning stations that allowed students to use their strengths. They also differentiated by allowing for interaction with content and producing outcomes at different levels of Bloom's taxonomy.

They were dedicated at carrying out their plan to use research-based instructional strategies by (a) having students show *similarities and differences* through a variety of compare and contrast applications at stations, (b) structuring *student summarizations* at least every 10 minutes during lectures and partner reading, and (c) using quick cooperative group structures.

To illustrate, as a way to have reading partners both summarize and engage in a cooperative structure, the co-teachers had all of the pairs read a short, high interest passage entitled "In Sickness and in Health." The passage examined the medical challenges faced by pioneer families, especially women and children.

The readability (here at second grade level) was such that at least one of the strategically partnered reading buddies could read the passage fluently. After the pairs had read the passage, the co-teachers employed the "Toss-a-Question" quick cooperative structure. Here, each partnership was given a page with instructions to write an interesting question about the passage in a "sender" box at the top of the page, but to leave the answer box on the bottom half of the page blank. After partners formulated and wrote their questions, they crumpled up the paper and tossed it to another designated pair, who pondered the question, wrote their response in the blank space, and tossed the paper back to the original authors of the question. That pair then read the answer and were instructed to save the paper for discussion and group processing during the class meeting time. Because the class had practiced this methodology in prior class meetings, they knew the rules of "appropriate" tossing. The discussion in the class meeting was full of giggles as questions and answers were shared.

Social and Physical Environment

Social and physical environmental conditions concern such things as where instruction occurs, room arrangement, and accessibility to learning materials. Social and physical environmental conditions were important considerations for these two co-teachers, given the movement and variety of materials involved in each day's lesson block.

Let's illustrate. Staying seated is a typical social rule. However, this co-teaching team had to alter this rule at stations, and during the Wednesday service learning planning session in the art room, so that students had the choice of standing or sitting at the round tables where each group worked. This allowed students who needed opportunities for sensory stimulation to get it as part of the structure and the social rules of these activities. The decision to use the art room as a workspace on Wednesdays to prepare the exhibit under the guidance of Mr. Olsen, the Wisconsin Historical Society education coordinator, also is an example of differentiation of *environment* in order to take advantage of material resources (i.e., art supplies and a large open space in which to create exhibits).

Another example of an *environmental and social* differentiation is when students and co-teachers sat on the floor together in a circle for daily class meetings. This physical and social configuration brought all members of the learning community together in a face-to-face arrangement and symbolically represented the equity and community that the co-teachers intended to create. This learning configuration was new for both students and Mr. Gleason. However, both students and teacher quickly adapted to the environmental change. Further, as already noted, Mr. Gleason and Ms. Villalobos strategically seated themselves near certain students to ensure closer monitoring of their behavior.

Co-teaching Approaches

Mr. Gleason and Ms. Villalobos had the opportunity to use all four *co-teaching* approaches—supportive, parallel, complementary, and team teaching—through their application of UDL principals. During station teaching and partner reading, the co-teachers engaged in *parallel* co-teaching by splitting the stations and partner teams among themselves for group monitoring. They were aware of the importance of sending the message that "these are both of my teachers," so they assigned themselves to monitor different groups in a rotating fashion on an alternating basis.

In the opening mini-lectures led by Mr. Gleason, Ms. Villalobos moved in and out of the *supportive* and *complementary* co-teaching roles. She supported by monitoring, using the "management by walking around" technique. She supported by creating simple lecture guides or pulling graphic organizers and concept maps from the Internet. Ms. Villalobos used the complementary approach during Mr. Gleason's mini-lectures by modeling and guiding students through the use of the graphic organizers as note-taking tools. In contrast, they reversed their lead and supportive/complementary roles during the class meeting. Ms. Villalobos was very practiced at this structure and the social skills addressed, so Mr. Gleason put himself in the learner role, at least in the beginning. By the end of the three weeks, he felt comfortable enough to run the closing class meeting, and the co-teachers moved naturally into a *team teaching* arrangement where they shared the circle facilitation role.

On Wednesdays, when the WHS education coordinator led the exhibit construction sessions, both Mr. Gleason and Ms. Villalobos moved into *supportive* roles, joining groups and providing assistance, as needed. They also used the *complementary* co-teaching approach by paraphrasing or restating the education coordinator's directions in a language that they knew the students could understand and by writing directions on the board or checking for understanding.

Finally, students joined in as co-teachers, by engaging in partner reading and station teaching activities over the three-week period.

IMPLEMENTING THE UDL PLAN ■

Over three weeks, the co-teachers, along with Mr. Olsen, the local WHS education coordinator, collaborated to implement this unit on Wisconsin history. The culminating experience of the unit involved student teams transporting and installing their portions of their log cabin exhibit in the Children's Museum on the Wednesday morning of the fourth week. The school's principal and the WHS education coordinator led an inauguration of the exhibition, which would open that evening and run for a month. For the Wednesday evening opening, WHS sent invitations to all families in the school and members of the local Children's Museum and historical society. Photographs taken at the Wednesday morning installation plus interview comments of the students in the class were published in the local newspaper's social section, inviting the public to come to the exhibition during its one-month run. The exhibit was visited by many families, with repeat visits by its creators, the students in Mr. Gleason and Ms. Villalobos's class.

As for Kevin, the frequency with which he left the room diminished to zero within a week. He developed friendships with three of the best readers in the class, who began to shift their role in his partner reading group to more of a tutorial relationship. Given the peers' support to decode difficult words and to prompt him with decoding clues, Kevin felt comfortable to risk reading more challenging material.

Mr. Gleason and Ms. Villalobos received recognition for their community service work with the class by being granted a $500 gift from the parent-teacher association for the purchase of classroom materials, instructional programs, technology supports, and student incentives. They also were invited to develop and present a workshop for the school staff on how to incorporate service learning into the curriculum. When they conducted the inservice, they included Kevin and several of his classmates as co-teachers on the process and the impact of service learning.

As the unit was coming to an end, in a meeting of the co-teachers, Mr. Gleason commented that he had experienced an "aha" moment when he realized that he had been collaborating to set up labs for years for science classes, but had never thought to transfer collaborative work over to his social studies instruction. He laughed as he said, "I really get how difficult it can be to transfer ideas or skills. If I had such a block on transferring my teaching practices from one content area to another, imagine how difficult it must be for students to transfer interpersonal skills from our class meeting instruction to their groups. I'm glad we highlighted and required the students to use the skills."

■ USING THE LESSON PLAN TEMPLATE

Mr. Gleason and Ms. Villalobos used the Universal Design Lesson Plan template to differentiate instruction in their own way. They knew the template could be used to design single lessons, but they chose to use it as a guide for making decisions for this entire unit, noting how they wanted to differentiate at each of the design points. Note that during the implementation phase the local WHS education coordinator, Sven Olsen, is included as the third co-teacher because he joined the class on Wednesdays to guide the students in designing their portions of the exhibit. They also created quick daily lessons to be sure that materials and activities were prepared and that their actions were coordinated. See Table 10.1 for the completed UDL lesson plan.

This unit is adapted from one described by Udvari-Solner, Villa, and Thousand (2002). The authors wish to acknowledge and thank Dr. Alice Udvari-Solner for her contributions to our understanding of ways to differentiate curriculum, instruction, and assessment.

Table 10.1 Co-teaching Universal Design Lesson Plan Template: Fourth Grade Social Studies for Kevin and Classmates

PLANNING PHASE:		
Lesson Topic and Name: <u>Wisconsin History</u>	Content Area(s) Focus: <u>Wisconsin History</u>	<u>Late-1800s Wisconsin History</u>

Facts About the Student Learners

Who are our students and how do they learn? **Students are a diverse, multicultural class with a broad range of independent reading levels and prior knowledge regarding pioneer life.**

What are our students' various strengths, languages, cultural backgrounds, learning styles, and interests? **We assume our students represent all learning styles. Several students are English language learners at various levels of English proficiency and need visual and auditory scaffolding.**

What are our students' various multiple intelligences (i.e., verbal/linguistic, logical/mathematical, visual/spatial, musical/rhythmic, bodily/kinesthetic, interpersonal, intrapersonal, naturalist)? **We assume our students represent all intelligences.**

What forms of communication (e.g., assistive technology) do our students use? **Students speak and write English with various levels of proficiency as indicated by third grade end-of-year standardized assessments.**

<u>Pause and Reflect About Specific Students</u>

Are there any students with characteristics that might require differentiation in the content, product, or process of learning? **Kevin needs reading materials at his instructional level (second grade) and to learn ways for dealing with frustration (other than walking out of class).**

Content (What will students learn?)	Products Showing Student Success (How will students convey their learning?)
What are the academic and/or social goals? **Understanding of late-1800s Wisconsin life** **Understanding and use of small group interpersonal skills** What content standards are addressed? **Wisconsin History Standards B.4.1, B.4.2, B.4.3, and B.4.4**	In what ways will the learning outcomes be demonstrated? **Multiple measures:** **Differentiated outputs at each of four learning stations** **Accountability for partner reading via quick cooperative structures** **Construction and installation of each team's section of museum exhibit**

(Continued)

Table 10.1 (Continued)

Content (What will students learn?)	Products Showing Student Success (How will students convey their learning?)
Differentiation Considerations: In what order will concepts and content be taught? **Simultaneous examination of all four history standards and learning/demonstration of social skills** What multilevel and/or multisensory materials do the co-teachers need to facilitate access to content? **Modeled use of graphic organizers during mini-lectures** In learning stations, real objects, pictures, and print material about and from both the late 1800s and contemporary life. **Reading materials at various levels of difficulty** Partner reading material at partners' level of difficulty **For exhibit development, WHS historical artifacts and art materials to construct** What multilevel goals are needed for all students to meaningfully access the content? **Addressed by differentiated materials and tasks and collaborative work** Pause and Reflect About Specific Students Are there any students who require unique or multilevel objectives or materials? **Kevin has a social goal for dealing with frustration.**	**Differentiation Considerations:** What are multiple ways students can demonstrate their understandings (e.g., multiple intelligences, multilevel and/or multisensory performances)? What authentic products do students create? What are the criteria teachers use to evaluate the products? **Differentiation of product options at each learning station to allow each student to use strength intelligences and perform at differing levels of Bloom's taxonomy** Pause and Reflect About Specific Students Are there any students who require unique ways of showing what they know? **No, addressed by differentiated outputs**

Process of Instruction
(How students engage in learning)

Instructional Formats	Instructional Arrangements	Instructional Strategies	Social and Physical Environment	Co-teaching Approaches
Considerations	Considerations	Considerations	Considerations	Options
Adapting lectures?	Cooperative learning structures?	Choose research-based strategies?	Room arranged?	Supportive?
Modeled lecture guides and graphic organizers	**Informal groups at stations, quick cooperative structures in partner reading**	**Examine similarity and differences in stations**	**Station table areas; Class meeting circle area**	**Ms. Villalobos during mini-lecture**
Activity-based?	Other? (Tutorial, teacher-directed small group)	**Pause, reflect, and summarize in lectures**	**Individual seats for direct instruction and work**	**Mr. Gleason during class meeting**
Experiential?		**Partner/cooperative learning**	Use of spaces outside of class?	**Both during Wed. exhibit work**
Stations and exhibit construction		Apply concepts from Multiple Intelligences Theory?	**Art room for constructing exhibit**	Parallel?
Group investigation?		**Choices allow for use of strengths**	**Children's Museum for installation of exhibit**	**Learning Station monitoring shared and rotated.**
Yes		Use taxonomies?	Social norms?	Complementary?
Computer/web-based?		**Activity options at stations allow for differentiation of complexity**	**Allow movement and standing or sitting at stations**	**Ms. Villalobos during mini-lecture**
Yes			**Talking in "6-inch" voices during team, partner, and station work**	Team teaching?
Stations?				**Class meeting**
Yes				
Service learning?				
Community-referenced?				
Yes, museum exhibit construction				

(Continued)

Table 10.1 (Continued)

Process of Instruction (How students engage in learning)				
Instructional Formats	*Instructional Arrangements*	*Instructional Strategies*	*Social and Physical Environment*	*Co-teaching Approaches*
			Positive behavior supports? **Monitoring of Kevin** (see Pause and Reflect)	Students as co-teachers? **Partner reading** **Cooperative team exhibit builders** **Informal cooperative supports at stations**

Pause and Reflect About Specific Students

What student-specific teaching strategies do select students need? What specific systems of supports (e.g., assistive technology), aids (e.g., personal assistance, cues, contracts), or services (e.g., counseling) do select students need?

If Kevin walks out of class or refuses to participate in an activity, even with the changes in the reading task demands, data will be taken on the antecedents and consequences of the behavior, and co-teachers will meet (with the special educator, if needed) to further adjust his task demands.

IMPLEMENTATION PHASE:

Who are the Co-teachers: **Mr. Gleason** **Ms. Villalobos** **Sven Olsen, WHS Education Coordinator**

What is/are the date(s) of the lesson? **Three-week unit and Children's Museum Installation**

What does each co-teacher do before, during, and after implementing the lesson?			
Co-teacher Name →	Mr. Gleason	Ms. Villalobos	Mr. Olsen
What are the specific tasks that I do BEFORE the lesson?	Gather materials and agree on station tasks with Ms. Villalobos.	Gather materials and agree on station tasks with Mr. Gleason.	Develop lesson plans for the three one-hour exhibit planning sessions.
	With Ms. Villalobos, review students' literacy profiles and partner students strategically on rotating basis for Partner Reading.	With Mr. Gleason, review students' literacy profiles and partner students strategically on rotating basis for partner reading.	Check for agreement on lessons with co-teachers.
	Collect additional old and contemporary artifacts and reading materials.	Call museum, arrange artifact delivery, collect additional old & contemporary artifacts and reading materials.	
	Prepare mini-lecture.	Research and propose graphic organizers for mini-lecture use.	
	Agree to graphic organizer for use in each mini-lecture.	Plan Class Meeting Circle time agenda (e.g., select social skill focus, debrief questions).	
	Agree to Class Meeting agenda.		
What are the specific tasks that I do DURING the lesson?	**MINI-LECTURE** Deliver daily mini-lecture, pausing every 10 minutes.	**MINI-LECTURE** Support and complement. Explain pause and reflect exercise.	**EXHIBIT CONSTRUCTION** On Wednesdays, guide student teams through construction of log cabin environments in the art room.
	STATIONS Parallel monitoring of two of four groups; co-teachers switch stations from one day to next.	**STATIONS** Parallel monitoring of two of four groups; co-teachers switch stations from one day to next.	
	PARTNER READING Distribute reading materials and provide task instructions to all groups. Parallel monitoring while students work.	**PARTNER READING** Assign social skill to each group and explain cooperative structure. Parallel monitoring while students work.	

(Continued)

Table 10.1 (Continued)

What does each co-teacher do before, during, and after implementing the lesson?

Co-teacher Name →	Mr. Gleason	Ms. Villalobos	Mr. Olsen
What are the specific tasks that I do AFTER the lesson?	**EXHIBIT CONSTRUCTION** Supportive and complementary co-teaching support of Mr. Olsen. Check a) students' completion of mini-lecture graphic organizer, and b) student work at each station. Select reading selections for partners and reassign partners for paired reading. Determine which materials select students should examine on next day.	**EXHIBIT CONSTRUCTION** Supportive and complementary co-teaching support of Mr. Olsen Check a) students' completion of mini-lecture graphic organizer, and b) student work at each station Evaluate class meeting session re: social skills and quick cooperative structure to be targeted for next class; check for agreement with Mr. Gleason.	**EXHIBIT DISPLAY** Arrange for newspaper interview, ceremony, mailing of flyers re: exhibit opening; arrange for transportation for class to museum.

REFLECTION PHASE:

Where, when, and how do co-teachers debrief and evaluate the outcomes of the lesson?
Daily debriefing (during common prep, lunch, or early release day afternoon block) between Mr. Gleason and Ms. Villalobos on mini-lecture, stations, partner reading. Wednesday co-teacher debriefing including Mr. Olsen on exhibit construction; adjust next lesson as needed.

How did students do? Were needs of the learners met?
Daily examination of students' products and observations of students' (i.e., Kevin's) engagement.

What are recommendations for the design of the next lesson(s)?
Determined in daily debriefing.

11

UDL Lesson Planning Cycle to Differentiate Instruction in Action

Middle Level Mathematics

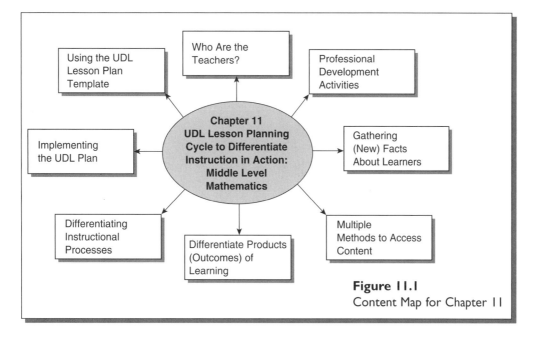

Figure 11.1
Content Map for Chapter 11

The purpose of education is to change the thoughts, feelings and actions of students.

—Benjamin Bloom, 1913–1999

n this chapter, you will revisit Rosa's teachers whom you met in Chapter 2. You will discover how they addressed the following questions:

- How did her teachers use the UDL lesson planning process to differentiate an Algebra 1 unit for a diverse group of students?
- What was the role of professional development in the process?

Mr. Jupp, a veteran teacher in his first year of co-teaching, and Mr. Dondero, a popular teacher of students with gifts and talents who is also in his first year of co-teaching, are Rosa's teachers. During the first half of the school year, the co-teachers developed a lesson using the retrofit approach to deal with the challenges they faced with respect to Rosa, who was disrupting the learning of the entire class, required a fair amount of both teachers' time, and did not achieve the class assignments.

As part of their retrofit design, they learned some helpful information about Rosa and were able to identify several strategies that seemed to help Rosa succeed. And they also identified several concerns that they could not address with the retrofit approach: (1) Rosa's difficulty with impulsivity control whenever she was frustrated with peers and teachers, (2) her ability to read in English was two years below grade level (which could account for her low achievement of class assignments), and (3) her undeveloped math skills due to frequent moves.

■ PROFESSIONAL DEVELOPMENT ACTIVITIES

The retrofit experience allowed both teachers to appreciate the need for a more proactive stance on their part in terms of designing lessons for this class. They decided to enroll in the district Universal Design for Learning (UDL) workshops together. In addition, Mr. Jupp enrolled in the district workshop on adapting cooperative learning structures to middle school classes, while Mr. Dondero enrolled in the district workshops for understanding and teaching mathematics using constructivist learning principles (an element of the National Council of Teachers of Mathematics [NCTM, 2000] recommendations for curriculum reform). In this way, both co-teachers would be tutoring each other in their respective professional development activities and simultaneously applying the concepts in the series of UDL lessons they were generating for a one-month unit in Algebra 1.

■ GATHERING (NEW) FACTS ABOUT THE LEARNERS

Mr. Jupp and Mr. Dondero attended the school celebration of Martin Luther King Day. Given their previous experiences with Rosa's disruptive and often inappropriate behavior in math class, they were stunned when they heard Rosa present King's (1963) "I Have a Dream" speech in Spanish ("Yo tengo un sueno . . ."). In English, she passionately explained why the speech was so important to her and her family who were granted asylum in the United States as political refugees during the crisis in her home country of Nicaragua.

Rosa's social studies teacher explained how he had developed assignments based on the results of an inventory that assessed the students' preferences for alternative methods of expressing their knowledge using concepts from Multiple Intelligences (MI) Theory. Because many of the students in their math class were also in the social studies class, the Jupp-Dondero team decided to organize their small group instruction activities for the UDL lessons using this information. In addition, as part of the process for designing the Algebra 1 instructional activities for the last half of the year, the co-teachers decided to conduct an academic self-assessment of the whole class using the rubric shown in Table 11.1.

Rosa was not the only one in the class who rated herself on most of the 20 topics as a "1 = *I don't have a clue what this is*" on the self-assessment (Table 11.1). In fact, the academic self-assessment revealed some surprises for the teachers. First, they were surprised that the students were remarkably honest and accurate—their self-assessments matched what the teachers' own observations and assessments had revealed. Second, about one-third of the class rated themselves as a 1 or 2 for all 20 topics, while another one-third of the class rated themselves as a 4 or 5 for the same number and the remaining one-third rated their knowledge for the 20 topics between 2 and 3. The teachers decided to use this information, along with the preferences for multiple methods of expressing knowledge, to assist them to design their instructional group activities.

Given the differences between Rosa's repertoire and interactions in the social studies class and her disruptive and antisocial behaviors in the mathematics class, the teachers asked for administrative support to develop a plan for positive behavior supports in the math class. The teachers showed the observation data that they had collected during the previous two weeks of class where Rosa's disruptive outbursts, cursing, and refusal to work had been charted similar to the procedures that Ms. Shuflitowski and her co-teacher used in Table 4.3 (Chapter 4).

The district arranged for a bilingual counselor to be present during the conference that the teachers held with Rosa and her grandmother, who had accompanied Rosa and her parents when they moved to the United States. Because the parents worked long hours, they depended on Rosa's *abuelita* ("little grandmother," a term of endearment) to look after the household and the children in their absence. Hence, she was a very important person in Rosa's life.

During this conference, they discussed the results, probed for more information, and discussed possible solutions. The counselor explained the research showing that students learning English as a second language often demonstrate reading fluency two years below grade level when compared to fluency in oral language. As a result of this meeting, Rosa agreed to monitor her own behaviors during math class and to join a counseling group to learn better ways to deal with her feelings. She stated that one of the major reasons for her frustration in class was that she could not read the math textbook. She was amazed when she was told that the teachers had located an algebra book written in

Table 11.1   Teacher-Developed Mid-Year Academic Self-Assessment for Algebra 1

Directions: You have studied these topics so far this year in Algebra 1. Please evaluate your performance in each topic. TOPIC	1 *I have no clue what this is.*	2 *I recognize the term but could not do this on my own.*	3 *With a toolkit and some guidance, I can do this.*	4 *With a toolkit, I can do this on my own.*	5 *I know this and can explain to others.*
1. Operations with integers					
2. Area, perimeter of rectangles, triangles, circles					
3. Setting up Guess and Check (Estimate) Tables					
4. Solving probability problems					
5. Using a table to graph an equation					
6. Graphing linear equations					
7. Finding the slope of a line					
8. Finding the slope between 2 points					
9. Using slope and y-intercept to graph a line					
10. Distributive property					
11. Multiplying using generic rectangles					
12. Solving equations in 2 variable					
13. Simplifying expressions by combining terms					
14. Solving systems of equations by substitution					
15. Solving proportions by cross-multiplying					
16. Solving equations using "fraction busters"					
17. Graphing quadratic equations (parabolas)					
18. Applying the Pythagorean Theorem					
19. Simplifying radicals (square roots)					
20. Factoring polynomials w/diamonds/generic rectangles					

SOURCE: By Carrie L. Kizuka; used with permission.

Spanish that she would be able to read. She agreed that she would also learn to ask her peers for support and to give support in return.

MULTIPLE METHODS FOR ACCESSING ■ THE CONTENT FOR ALGEBRA 1

The middle school curriculum was guided by both the professional requirements recommended by the National Council for Teachers of Mathematics as well as the state standards in mathematics. Table 11.2 shows the key standards related to the 20 topics that were assessed using the self-rating scale.

The co-teachers set up five learning centers that represented multiple methods of accessing the information for the standards being taught. At the Alternate Textbook Learning Center, students reviewed the concepts using algebra textbooks that were written in simplified English as well as textbooks written in Spanish (donated by the Spanish Embassy).

The Visual Arts Learning Center used the graphing tools from *Algebra 1 Explorer* (Bardwell, 2005; http://www.knowplay.com/math/algebra-explorer. html): Slope-Intercept, Line with Slope-Point, Line with Two Points, Linear Equation System, Linear Inequality System, Parabola Graphing, Quadratic Inequality, and Quadratic Absolute Value. At this center, students assessed various artworks to identify algebra concepts that the artists applied (e.g., linear versus aerial perspectives as shown on *Leonardo's Perspective*) web site (Science Learning Network, 1997; http://www.mos.org/sln/Leonardo/Leonardos Perspective.html).

The Direct Application Learning Center featured hands-on activities such as measuring, depicting, and graphing the perimeter of the classroom, the area of the cafeteria, and, using Pythagorean theorem to determine the shortest line between three points between the classroom, the cafeteria, and the outdoor recreation area. To increase student understanding that algebra concepts were relevant to their everyday lives, the teachers created an Algebra Job Jar in which students and teachers placed descriptions of various everyday tasks that could be made easier if algebra concepts were applied.

The "Famous Mathematicians" Learning Center was located in the media center where students could use the Internet to find information on mathematicians from around the world. The task was to discover what algebra concepts were evident in these mathematicians' works as well as to develop a brief skit that captured the essence of what that person added to the world of mathematics. Table 11.3 lists some of the individuals that the teachers had found. Students were encouraged to search on their own in order to expand the list of famous mathematicians.

The Teacher Learning Center was set up to make it possible for students to interact one-to-one, or in a small group of six, with one of the co-teachers at least once a week. During their time at the Teacher Learning Center, students could ask any questions that were vexing to them. They also reviewed what they had been learning at the various learning centers where they had worked during the week. Both teachers employed the elements of constructivist teaching and cognitive guided instruction when they interacted with students at the

Table 11.2 Key Mathematics Standards Guiding the UDL Lessons

Topic	Standard
1. Operations with integers	Standard 13
2. Area, perimeter of rectangles, triangles, circles	Standard 1
3. Setting up Guess and Check (Estimate) Tables	Standard 24 (reasoning)
4. Solving probability problems	Standards not available for this grade level
5. Using a table to graph an equation	Standards not available for this grade level
6. Graphing linear equations	Standard 6
7. Finding the slope of a line	Standard 7
8. Finding the slope between 2 points	Standard 7
9. Using slope and y-intercept to graph a line	Standard 6
10. Distributive property	Standards not available for this grade level
11. Multiplying using generic rectangles	Standards not available for this grade level
12. Solving equations in 2 variables	Standards not available for this grade level
13. Simplifying expressions by combining terms	Standard 4
14. Solving systems of equations by substitution	Standard 9
15. Solving proportions by cross-multiplying	Standards not available for this grade level
16. Solving equations using "fraction busters"	Standard 12
17. Graphing quadratic equations (parabolas)	Standards 14 and 21
18. Applying the Pythagorean theorem	Standard 19
19. Simplifying radicals (square roots)	Standard 20
20. Factoring polynomials w/ diamonds/generic rectangles	Standard not available for this grade level

Table 11.3 A Sampler of Mathematicians Around the World

Teresa Edwards (African American) applies mathematics concepts to study and recommend solutions to environmental problems.

Ada Lovelace, British mathematician (daughter of Lord Byron, the famous poet), is considered to be the founder of Scientific Computing.

Mary Ross (Native American-Cherokee) is a senior advanced systems staff engineer who contributed to the development of the Poseidon and Trident missiles.

Julio Rey Pastor (Spain and Argentina) invented n-dimensional geometry.

Daniel Bentil (Professor at the University of Vermont from Ghana) studies the interface of applied mathematics and the biomedical sciences.

Chinese mathematician Zhao Shuang created geometrical figures to prove the Pythagorean theorem—1700 years ago!

Teacher Learning Center. As shown in Table 11.4, the teachers primarily asked questions to probe for student understanding before offering alternative strategies for problem solving.

DIFFERENTIATING THE PRODUCTS ■
(OUTCOMES) OF LEARNING

The co-teachers decided that there would be two types of evaluation: a formative evaluation and an outcome evaluation. For each learning center, they designed a menu of possible outcomes that students could select. Students had the option for selecting individual products as well as partner or small group products. For partner or small group products, students identified the contributions of each participant.

In order to monitor student participation in the learning centers each day, the teachers designed an "Exit Slip" for the students to complete. The co-teachers reviewed this information to better address the needs of the students during subsequent lessons at the learning centers, or when they met with the students at the Teachers' Learning Center. As shown in Table 11.5, the Exit Slip included

Table 11.4 Elements of Cognitive Guided Instruction

---

1. Problem solving is the focus of instruction–teachers guide students to select and define a problem and then decide how they would solve the problem.

2. Teachers guide students to select many problem-solving strategies to solve the problem.

3. Students communicate with their instructor and peers as to how they solved the problem.

4. Teachers notice the problem-solving strategies used by students and use that knowledge to plan instruction, provide explicit feedback, and stimulate new thinking patterns.

Table 11.5   Formative Assessment for Cooperative Learning Group Activities "Exit Slip"

EXIT SLIP

Directions: Before you leave class today, please fill in the date, the name of the Learning Station, and each member of the group who participated today.

Learning Station: Date:

	S1	S2	S3	S4	S5	S6
One new thing I learned today...						
One thing I have a question about...						
One contribution I made today...						
One thing you should know is...						

SOURCE: With permission Carrie L. Kizuka.

spaces for each member of the group to identify major learning outcomes, questions, and contributions.

■ DIFFERENTIATING THE INSTRUCTIONAL PROCESSES

Given that so many of their students shared Hispanic cultural heritage or were learning English as a second language, the co-teachers decided to use two instructional processes that had been identified as especially useful in educating Hispanic students. According to Padrón, Waxman, and Rivera (2002), the following procedures are known to increase achievement for Hispanic learners:

cooperative learning, instructional conversations (via small group tutorials and cooperative learning groups), cognitively guided instruction (derived from constructivist principles), and technology-enriched instruction.

Group Investigation

The teachers used the group investigation structure described in Table 7.4 to ensure that students would have time to develop the cognitive understanding of the concepts. When attending the Famous Mathematicians Learning Center, students were scheduled for sessions to access the Internet and other printed material to research at the school media library. Similarly, for the Visual Arts Learning Center, students were scheduled to meet in the technology lab where the tech assistant had installed the necessary software for modeling various algebra functions. The students needed long-term group investigation processes in order to master the software and develop a cognitive understanding of the functions being graphed.

During Teacher Learning Center instructional time, the co-teachers rotated the use of various quick cooperative structures that increased the active responding of all students (see Chapter 7, Table 7.5 for descriptions). Given that each group consisted of up to six students and the time constraints of a typical 50-minute class period, the teachers' goal was to have each student actively contributing ideas for at least five minutes each. Activities such as "think-pair-share," "toss-a-question," and "round table/round robin" were the most popular with the students.

Cognitive Guided Instruction

Through cognitive guided instruction, as described in Table 11.4, the teachers developed student learning strategies that enhance student reasoning and understanding of mathematics. Cognitively Guided Instruction (CGI) is a researched best practice currently being implemented in many mathematics classrooms (Fenna, Carpenter, Levi, Franke, & Empson, 1977). Directly teaching and modeling cognitive learning strategies made it possible for students to practice them at the various learning centers.

English Language Learner Technique

In addition, the students and teachers created a Dictionary of Algebra Terms which translated the glossary of the textbook into everyday language that they could understand. In fact, many of the bilingual students entered translations into the dictionary in their respective languages.

■ IMPLEMENTING THE UDL PLAN

Over the next four weeks, Mr. Jupp and Mr. Dondero, along with the media/library personnel and computer technology aide, implemented their UDL plan.

They were able to monitor and adjust based on the information collected from the Exit Slips that the groups completed each day. The group monitoring techniques helped to increase the students' sense of being responsible, especially when they were out of the classroom at the library or computer lab.

In addition, Rosa was able to shine in several of the learning centers. For instance, at the Famous Mathematician Center she and her teammates created a 15-minute play to illustrate the life of Julio Rey Pastor, which included a vivid computer modeling of n-dimensional geometry. The guidance counselor reported that Rosa had made remarkable progress in understanding the source of her frustrations and in asking for help by using either Spanish or English. Both teachers also noticed these changes. Additionally, they noticed that Rosa was able to explain concepts to one of the other students in the group when she attended the Teacher Learning Center. They decided to ask her to become a peer tutor for the next round of lessons. She beamed with pride when they asked her, saying that her *abuela* (grandmother) would be proud to know she was helping others.

■ USING THE UNIVERSAL DESIGN LESSON PLAN TEMPLATE

Table 11.6 shows the UDL lesson plan for the unit that the teachers developed using the template introduced in Table 3.1 in Chapter 3. The teachers responded to each of the suggested queries when making decisions about each step in the UDL cycle—gathering facts about the learners in the class, differentiating access to the content and materials, differentiating the products, and differentiating the processes of instruction. They used the *pause and reflect* queries to ensure that they were connecting the various aspects of the lesson to their students' needs and interests.

Table 11.6 Co-teaching Universal Design Lesson Plan Template: Middle Level Mathematics for Rosa and Classmates

PLANNING PHASE:

Lesson Topic and Name: _Algebra 1_   Content Area(s) Focus: _20 topics_

Facts About the Student Learners

Who are our students and how do they learn?
Several students prefer learning in small group and partner activities, only a few prefer to work alone, and about ½ the class prefers hands-on concrete learning activities.

What are our students' various strengths, languages, cultural backgrounds, learning styles, and interests?
Students include a multicultural mix of Hispanic/Spanish speakers, Anglos, African Americans, Asian Americans.

What are our students' various multiple intelligences (i.e., verbal/linguistic, logical/mathematical, visual/spatial, musical/rhythmic, bodily/kinesthetic, interpersonal, intrapersonal, naturalist)?
About 1/5 of the learners a verbal/linguistic, 1/10 are logical/mathematical, 1/10 are musical/rhythmic, 1/5 are bodily/kinesthetic (football, basketball, and swimming teams), and so on.

What forms of communication (e.g., assistive technology) do our students use? **All students are computer-literate and have access to email and internet.**

Pause and Reflect About Specific Students

Are there any students with characteristics that might require differentiation in the content, product, or process of learning?

Rosa is an English language learner (as are at least 4 others); Rosa's ability to read in English is about 2 years below the level of difficulty for the Algebra textbook. In addition, Rosa may need support for impulsivity control (use of inappropriate language when frustrated).

Content (What will students learn?)	Products Showing Student Success (How will students convey their learning?)
What are the academic and/or social goals? **Applying algebra 1 concepts (academic) in a way that contributes to solving problems (social interaction)**	In what ways will the learning outcomes be demonstrated? **A menu of options related to preferences in learning styles**
What content standards are addressed? **California Standards: Mathematics: Algebra 1**	

(Continued)

Table 11.6 (Continued)

Content (What will students learn?)	Products Showing Student Success (How will students convey their learning?)
Differentiation Considerations:	Differentiation Considerations:
In what order will concepts and content be taught? **Simultaneous review and expansion of current skills in 20 different topics**	What are multiple ways students can demonstrate their understandings (e.g., multiple intelligences, multilevel and/or multisensory performances)? What authentic products do students create? **Skits of famous mathematicians from around the world & how they use algebra I concepts; visual graphic representations of algebraic functions; responses to constructivist question-and-answer procedures; etc.**
What multilevel and/or multisensory <u>materials</u> do the co-teachers need to facilitate access to the content? **Hands-on learning centers (e.g., computer modeling for displaying algebraic functions)**	What are the criteria teacher(s) use to evaluate the products? **Process Evaluation (Exit Slip)** **Outcome Evaluation (Post tests and authentic project outcomes)**
What multilevel goals are needed for all students to meaningfully access the content? **Rosa has social goals related to appropriate language in class, anger management, and/or impulsivity control.**	Pause and Reflect About Specific Students
Pause and Reflect About Specific Students	Are there any students who require unique ways of showing what they know? **Yes; it's apparent that Rosa can express her knowledge using drama and artistic expression better than traditional pencil-paper testing.**
Are there any students who require unique or multi-level objectives or materials? **No.**	

Process of Instruction
(How students engage in learning?)

Instructional Formats	Instructional Arrangements	Instructional Strategies	Social and Physical Environment	Co-teaching Approach(es)
Considerations	Considerations	Considerations	Considerations	Options
Adapting Lectures? **Yes**	Cooperative learning structures? **Yes**	Choose research-based strategies? **Yes—constructivist teaching in math**	Room arranged? Use of spaces outside of class? **Yes—media (library) and computer lab**	Supportive? **Media and computer lab personnel**

		Process of Instruction (How students engage in learning)		
Instructional Formats	Instructional Arrangements	Instructional Strategies	Social and Physical Environment	Co-teaching Approach(es)
<u>Considerations</u> Activity-based? **Yes** Experiential? **Yes** Group investigation? **Yes** Computer/web-based? **Yes** Stations? **Yes** Community referenced learning? **No** Service learning? **No**	<u>Considerations</u> Other? (Tutorial, teacher-directed small group) **Yes.**	<u>Considerations</u> Apply concepts from Multiple Intelligences Theory? **Yes.** Use taxonomies? **Application and synthesis of learning**	<u>Considerations</u> Room arranged? Use of spaces outside of class? **Yes—media (library) and computer lab** Social norms? **Yes—explicit instruction in how to be a partner learner** Positive behavior supports? **Yes—especially for resolving disagreements agreeably Self-monitoring appropriate remarks**	<u>Options</u> Supportive? **Media and computer lab personnel** Parallel? **Learning Station monitoring shared co-equally** Complementary? **No** Team Teaching? **No** Students as co-teachers? (e.g., peer tutors and cooperative learning structures under instructional arrangements) **Yes**

<u>Pause and Reflect About Specific Students</u>

What student-specific teaching strategies do select students need? What specific systems of supports (e.g., assistive technology), aids (e.g., personal assistance, cues, contracts), or services (e.g., counseling) do select students need?
Rosa was scheduled to see the school counselor once every other week to learn appropriate language to express frustration (and request help and assistance) as well as to express her feelings and sadness about leaving family members behind in Nicaragua when her family fled to USA (survivor guilt).

(Continued)

163

Table 11.6 (Continued)

IMPLEMENTATION PHASE:

Who are the Co-teachers:	Jupp	Dondero	Media	Computer Lab

What is/are the date(s) of the lesson? **January 20–February 20**

What does each co-teacher do before, during, and after implementing the lesson?

Co-teacher Name →	Jupp	Dondero	Media/Library	Computer Lab
What are the specific tasks that I do BEFORE the lesson?	Check availability of materials.	Check availability of materials.	Check with Jupp re suitability of materials for the Mathematicians Project.	Check with Dondero re matching textbook and state standard to software.
What are the specific tasks that I do DURING the lesson?	Use CGI and information from Exit Slips to tutor specific topics.	Use CGI and information from Exit Slips to tutor specific topics.	Monitor and assist students to access appropriate information.	Monitor and assist students' use of the software to model algebra functions.
What are the specific tasks that I do AFTER the lesson?	Collect & review Exit Skips.	Collect & review Exit Slips.	Collect Exit Slips and send to Jupp or Dondero.	Collect Exit Slips and send to Jupp or Dondero.

REFLECTION PHASE:

Where, when, and how do co-teachers debrief and evaluate the outcomes of the lesson? **Daily de-briefings**

How did students do?
End of month re-evaluation of student mastery of topics.

Were needs of the learners met?
Increased participation at every learning station; increased competence; increased positive mental attitudes about algebra

What are recommendations for the design of the next lesson(s)?
Students want to meet people in the "real world" who use Algebra I concepts. Teachers are in the process of identifying various professionals and blue collar workers who might be willing to participate with student study groups.

12

UDL Lesson Planning Cycle to Differentiate Instruction in Action

Middle Level Science

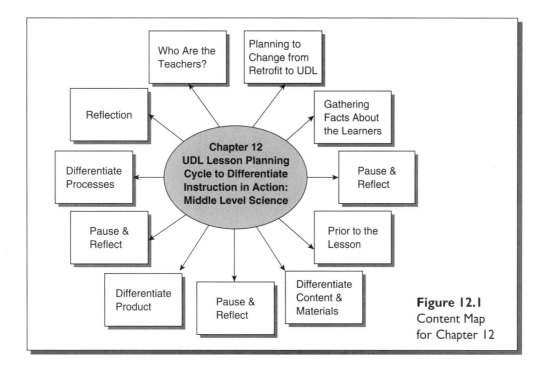

Figure 12.1 Content Map for Chapter 12

Students should succeed because of their teachers, not in spite of them!

—Anonymous

In this chapter, you will have a chance to peek in on the planning and teaching of another co-teaching team you met in Chapter 2: Ms. Swanson, a middle level science educator, and her assigned co-teaching partner, Ms. Tac, a speech and language therapist. In what ways did these co-teachers use the universal design for learning lesson planning process to differentiate a genetics lesson for a diverse group of middle school students?

As you may recall, when they started co-teaching, Ms. Swanson was experiencing great difficulty establishing discipline and facilitating her students' learning of the content. She was concerned about poor test results, daily discipline referrals to the office, parental and administrative complaints about her classroom, and the sheer exhaustion she felt at the end of the day. In addition, Ms. Swanson was particularly concerned about the placement in her classroom of a new student, Tina, who had significant disabilities, including autism.

Ms. Tac was assigned to assist Ms. Swanson with her instruction and discipline as well as to support Tina because she had experience teaching a wide range of students with communication, cognitive, academic, and behavioral difficulties.

Although Ms. Swanson was initially reticent about both Tina's placement and the assignment of a co-teacher, she and Ms. Tac were able to establish a working relationship and successfully "retrofit" Tina into the lessons that Ms. Swanson had designed. As a result, Ms. Swanson began to feel more confident in her instruction and classroom management. In fact, she reported to the principal that she had become a better teacher for all of her students as a result of having Tina in her class. Ms. Swanson had learned that many of the adaptations designed for Tina worked for other learners as well.

■ PLANNING TO CHANGE FROM A RETROFIT APPROACH TO A UNIVERSAL DESIGN APPROACH

During one of their weekly planning meetings about six weeks into their use of the retrofit approach, Ms. Swanson acknowledged to Ms. Tac that things were going fairly well in their co-taught class but wished that they did not have to spend so much time redoing everything so that Tina and some of the other students could participate in the lessons. Ms. Swanson said that she felt that she was "doing double work."

Ms. Tac thanked Ms. Swanson for all of her efforts thus far and suggested that if they tried a different approach, a universal design approach, they could be more time-efficient. Ms. Swanson said she was "game to try" anything that could save her time. Ms. Tac then explained the Universal Design for Learning (UDL) Lesson Plan Cycle to Ms. Swanson. When Ms. Tac explained that the UDL Lesson Planning Cycle could be used to design a single lesson or an entire unit of study, Ms. Swanson stated that she wanted to go slow and so they decided to start with using the UDL Lesson Planning Cycle to design an upcoming lesson on genetics.

GATHERING (ADDITIONAL) FACTS ■
ABOUT THE LEARNERS

Ms. Tac and Ms. Swanson decided to gather additional facts about all of the learners in their co-taught class through administering a multiple intelligences (MI) survey to the students. Ms. Swanson said that she felt confident that, based upon their knowledge of the students and the information they would gather from the MI survey, they would have enough information to differentiate and facilitate the learning of most students.

Pause and Reflect

However, Ms. Swanson said that she was not certain that a MI survey would provide all the information necessary to support Tina. Ms. Tac agreed and said that there was another process for gathering facts that she had wanted to discuss with Ms. Swanson. She explained that a MAPs meeting (see Chapter 4) for Tina had been scheduled and that it might provide an excellent opportunity to gather additional facts about Tina that they could use in their planning and teaching. Ms. Tac invited Ms. Swanson to the MAPs meeting at Tina's request because "she is my favorite teacher." Ms. Swanson blushed at hearing this compliment and admitted that she was flattered but unfamiliar with, and confused about, the process and purpose of a MAPs meeting.

Ms. Tac provided Ms. Swanson with an overview of the MAPs process (Falvey, Forest, Rosenberg, & Pearpoint, 2002), and Ms. Swanson agreed to attend the meeting. Ms. Tac explained that this meeting would not only provide information helpful to their planning for the co-taught class but also for revisions to Tina's current and future IEPs and transition plan.

Mr. Maloney, an instructional coach, who knew Tina and her dad and was familiar with conducting MAPs meetings, was chosen as the facilitator of the meeting. He explained the process to those in attendance (i.e., Tina, her dad, her grandparents, best friend Carla, older cousin Jamie, Ms. Swanson, Ms. Tac, the school nurse, and the two instructional assistants who had experience in supporting Tina).

Tables 12.1 and 12.2 graphically present the steps of, and the information gathered at, Tina's MAPs meeting.

At the conclusion of the MAPs meeting, it was agreed that a smaller group would meet within a week to continue work on the action plan (i.e., Mr. Maloney, Tina, Tina's dad, Ms. Tac, and Ms. Nyda, who was one of the instructional assistants who supported Tina). Following the MAPs meeting, Ms. Swanson expressed to Ms. Tac that she had felt emotionally overwhelmed at times during the meeting. She acknowledged that the MAPs process helped her "put things in perspective" and motivated her to work harder to meet Tina's needs in her science class. Ms. Swanson and Ms. Tac scheduled a time to review the information gathered during the MAPs meeting and from the MI surveys as the next step in planning their first UDL lesson.

Table 12.1 Results of Tina's MAPs Meeting

What is Tina's history?

Happy, healthy baby at birth.

Mom died of cancer—Tina was 2.

Raised alone by dad.

In Montessori daycare did not appear to attend to lessons or other children.

No verbal language development.

At 4, diagnosed as having autism.

Removed from daycare; placed in a communication disorder preschool with nonverbal classmates.

Rocking & hand wringing increase.

Interested in books at an early age, books taken away by teachers because she "could not read."

Dad challenged placement with non-verbal classmates. Professionals convinced him it is best placement.

At 9, begins protesting going to school by tantruming in the morning.

Not responsive to sign language or use of a communication board.

At 11, dad and Tina move to a new state.

New IEP focuses on developing a communication system using typing with Facilitated Communication (FC) & inclusion 50% of the day in general education, with a goal of full-time inclusion.

When Tina first typed via FC, people were in awe of how much she knew and questioned whether the words were hers or those of the facilitator.

Tina tolerates facilitation by her father & two instructional assistants she has worked with for several years.

Now only tantrums when bored, frustrated, or stressed in class.

Is on the Honor Roll.

Who is Tina? What are Tina's gifts?

Very smart

Funny, a bit sarcastic

Thoughtful

Considerate of others

Creative

What are the dreams?

To be an author of children's literature or an investigative reporter.

To go to college and continue to learn.

To write and present about her life so as to teach others about autism and encourage them to find ways to communicate with all children.

To communicate independently (type without facilitator) some day.

To marry some day and have a family.

To go sky diving.

To be a race car driver.

To have more fun.

To make friends.

What are the nightmares?

Worries what will happen to her when her father dies; conversely, her father worries what will happen to Tina when he passes.

Fears being returned to a special class.

Fears having a life without friends.

Fears others will assume a lack of competence because she does not speak and, therefore, others make choices for her she does not want.

Concerned others will be impatient and not give her the time she needs to communicate.

Being around people who will stare at her and view her as odd.

What does Tina need to realize the dreams and avoid the nightmares?

Tina needs facilitation from people she trusts to communicate (type).

Tina needs to expand the range of people who can facilitate her typing.

Tina needs assistive technology (e.g., text to speech conversion) to give her a "voice" and independence.

Tina needs a more challenging curriculum; she is bored by classes.

Tina needs a way to deal with noise.

Tina needs to develop peer relations (including understanding of autism and Facilitated Communication).

Voracious reader, especially of mystery novels and current events	Tina needs a supportive team (i.e., teachers, paraprofessionals, peers) to assist her to self-advocate now and for transition to high school.
Loves and has lots of pets (i.e., a dog, a cat, and 8 rabbits)	
Likes rapid movement	Tina needs to stay in general education classes with in-class support (i.e., ideas generated by Ms. Swanson and Ms. Tac and listed in Table 2.8 of Chapter 2).
Enjoys roller coaster rides	
Likes to gamble	
Likes to go to auto races	
Likes country music	
Enjoys school, especially science	
Intense curiosity	
Understands information quickly	
Has difficulty with high noise levels	
Intolerant of misbehavior of classmates	
Observant	
Motivated to learn	
Persistent	
Gets good grades	
A creative writer and "speaker" (via typing with adult facilitation)	

Table 12.2 Action Plan for Tina Resulting From MAPs Meeting

1. Because Tina still needs others to facilitate her typing, a paraprofessional whom she trusts is assigned to each of her classes.

2. To expand the number of potential facilitators, Ms. Tac will work with Tina to identify classmates whom she trusts for training in facilitation.

3. To explore voice output for Tina's typing, Mr. Maloney will arrange for an evaluation and consultation from the Assistive Technology consultant, Ms. Callis.

4. Because the curriculum is not challenging, Tina will be provided enrichment options in class.

5. To help Tina deal with noise, Mr. Tac will arrange in each of her classes an "auditory center" with earphones where Tina can go should she choose.

6. To facilitate relationship development with peers, Mr. Maloney will establish a "Circle of Friends" social support group of classmates.

7. A support team will be assembled and meet with Tina monthly to monitor this action plan and to assist Tina to self-advocate (e.g., challenging middle school classes; Transition Plan that includes college-prep classes at the high school level).

8. Support ideas that are generated by Ms. Swanson and Ms. Tac (listed in Table 2.6 of Chapter 2) will be shared with Tina's other teachers and used, as needed, to facilitate her involvement and access to the curriculum.

■ PRIOR TO THE LESSON

At their next planning meeting, they reviewed the information from the MI surveys, shared information from observation and experience with the students, and reflected on Tina's MAP as they developed lessons on genetics and patterns of inheritance of one and two traits. They carefully selected student pairs to avoid pairing worst enemies and best friends and to ensure diversity among the pairs.

For example, they paired academically strong students with peers who struggled, students with behavioral challenges with socially appropriate peer models, and students with complementary strengths related to their multiple intelligences. Reflecting on the recent MAPs meeting, Ms. Swanson noted that, in the past, she had often used pictures of rabbits when discussing inheritance, but now that she knew that Tina raised rabbits—perhaps Tina would like to bring the rabbits to class. Ms. Tac agreed that this was a good idea. Ms. Swanson replied that she would discuss it with Tina. Ms. Tac further suggested that they use Tina's interest in gambling as a way to link probability of winning at games of chance to probability of inheriting traits. Ms. Swanson agreed that this would be an excellent way to get many of the students excited about probability. Ms. Swanson noted that when she previously taught this content, students were assigned to study genetic disorders (e.g., Huntington disease, cystic fibrosis) and wondered if there was a way to share information about Tina's autism as a way to contrast disabilities that are inherited with those that are not. Ms. Tac agreed that this might provide an opportunity for Tina to meet one of the goals she had articulated in the MAPs meeting—to write and speak about her life and to teach others about autism so as to encourage them to find ways to communicate with all children.

They decided that they would use a fill-in-the-blank version of the Universal Design Lesson Plan template form (see Table 3.2), including on the form only the items and activities that they planned to use. Prior to the lesson, Ms. Swanson agreed to gather the lab materials and Ms. Tac offered to go to the store and purchase the beans that they would need for the lesson. Ms. Tac said that since so many of the student MI profiles indicated a strength or preference for visual/spatial learning, she wanted to increase the use of visuals and therefore would prepare some PowerPoint slides as well as word strips of the new vocabulary. Ms. Swanson agreed to create PowerPoint slides as a lecture guide with a key that correlated color combinations to straight-ear and floppy-ear phenotypes in rabbits.

Differentiate Content and Materials

Ms. Tac and Ms. Swanson decided that all students would be able to work on the same New Jersey Science Standards (i.e., Standard 2.8—Collect and organize data to support the results of an experiment; Standard 2.9—Communicate experimental findings using words, charts, graphs, pictures, and diagrams; and Science Standard 7.5—Illustrate how the sorting and recombining of genetic material results in the potential for variation among offspring; New Jersey Science Standards, 2002).

The materials they planned to use (e.g., Internet, manipulatives, science text, graphic organizers, LCD projector, newsprint, live animals, journal writing) seemed to be diverse enough to capture the interests and preferences of the students as well as allow all of them to access the content. Ms. Swanson wanted to introduce the concepts sequentially (i.e., inheritance of one trait and then inheritance of two traits) so as to establish a new concept to be learned before adding additional content. She said that, in her experience, students appeared interested in genetics but often confused terms and concepts.

Pause and Reflect

At this point in the planning process, the team checked the decisions about content with the information they had gathered about the learners in their class. They decided to scan the advance organizer and lab journal materials into Tina's computer. They decided to ask her to assist them in teaching the class by hooking up an LCD projector to her computer. No further decisions needed to be made with respect to multilevel objectives or materials.

DIFFERENTIATE PRODUCTS ■

Ms. Swanson and Ms. Tac decided that the ongoing and final summary of learning seemed to afford students an opportunity to show what they know through differentiated means of expressing their knowledge. More specifically, students would produce various products as they (1) record the data and observations in their science journals (or in Tina's case, on her computer), (2) record data on the board, (3) record data on teacher-generated model of inheritance chart, and (4) respond when randomly called upon to define new vocabulary and the questions assigned to them and their partner.

In addition, the students could develop a rap, jingle, acronym, poem, poster, or personal reflection related to what they were learning about inheritance. Finally, students would be assigned a disability or genetic disorder to study so as to determine whether or not either of them was inheritable and, if so, the probability of inheritance by offspring.

Pause and Reflect

The planning team agreed that they needed some way to ensure that Tina could express herself in a way that would communicate what she actually knows about the content. The decision was made to provide Tina with the questions she would be asked in class in advance so she would have additional time to record her answers.

■ DIFFERENTIATE THE LEARNING PROCESS

Planning to Differentiate the Process

Ms. Swanson shared with Ms. Tac a variety of resource materials to review as part of their decision making for differentiating the learning processes. They decided to modify a lesson from a science text (*BSCS Biology: A Human Approach, 1997*).

They determined that Ms. Swanson would begin the class by asking students if any of them had ever played "games of chance" and then broaden the discussion by asking the students to share experiences that they have had with gambling, card playing, dice, and other games of chance. Then Ms. Tac would connect the discussion to the laws of probability. Ms. Tac shared with Ms. Swanson that most of the students in the class had recently participated in a unit on probability in the math class that she co-taught and thought this prior knowledge would transfer into this lesson and assist the students in the new learning. Ms. Swanson was pleased to hear of this and remarked that it was valuable to her planning and teaching to learn what the students were doing in other curriculum areas and that this would not have happened if Ms. Tac had not been co-teaching in the math class.

Ms. Swanson reported that she had spoken with Tina and that she was eager to share some of her gambling experiences and the data she had been collecting about her own wins and losses in blackjack. Tina was excited about bringing her rabbits to class and thrilled to have a chance to share her experience with autism and her use of an alternate communication system.[1] Ms. Tac agreed to meet with Ms. Nyda, who would be facilitating Tina's communication, specifically providing assistance when Tina was typing her thoughts, prior to the start of the lesson to give her an overview of what they were planning and indicate the times when Ms. Nyda would be called upon to work with Tina.

To reduce hovering around Tina and over-relying on adults, they planned to assign Ms. Nyda two additional pairs of students to help with monitoring and who would be seated in close proximity to Tina and her partner. Ms. Tac asked if it would also be all right if Ms. Callis, an assistive technology consultant, observed this lesson to gather diagnostic information about Tina's current use of technology and to assist Ms. Tac in determining any additional technology that might be of benefit to Tina. Ms. Swanson was thrilled that this particular item from the action plan that was generated at Tina's MAPs meeting was being addressed so quickly and agreed to arrange for Ms. Callis observe the class.

They reviewed the lesson plan and agreed to touch base for 10 minutes on each of the next two mornings to firm up the product and process pieces of the lesson. Their mutual goal was to be "ready to go" in two days' time when they would introduce the new lesson on genetics.

■ DIFFERENTIATED PROCESSES IN THE CLASS

During the first class after the anticipatory set on probability, Ms. Swanson told the students that they were going to function as "investigative reporters" because they were going to do what good scientists always do—investigate and report on their findings. (As she said this, she could not help but notice the smile on Tina's face at the mention of a career interest that she had identified during her MAPs meeting.) Ms. Tac added that in order to be good investigative reporters, they needed to learn some new vocabulary.

Ms. Swanson introduced two new vocabulary terms (i.e., *heterozygous* and *homozygous*). Ms. Tac added these words to the word wall as she facilitated large group discussion and then partner practice on pronouncing the new terms. Students were then asked to "write" the term and its definition into their lab journal. Most students completed the task in the standard way. Instructional supports were provided for two students who had been given a page with the vocabulary terms to be introduced on the left-side of the page; with their partner's assistance, if needed, these students were prompted to match the term to the definition on the right-hand side of the page.

Another student was expected to show that he or she knew the meaning of the first root of each of the terms—that *homo* meant *same* and that *hetero* meant *different*. For two other pairs, the partners shared a lab journal with one of them doing the recording; a copy was later made of the journal entry for the other student.

Because it was understood that Tina would quickly grasp the concepts but that it would take time for her to type in the words and their definitions, the terms and definitions had been scanned into her computer. When Tina's partner read a term, Tina, with facilitation assistance from Ms. Nyda, moved the computer cursor key to indicate which term was being defined.

Next, Ms. Tac and Ms. Swanson simultaneously modeled the first part of the lab activity for the students to follow. Specifically, they wanted the students working in pairs on the following five steps:

1. Select two beans randomly from the container that their co-teachers provided.

2. Record in their journal the color of their beans (e.g., red or white) and if their pair was homozygous or heterozygous.

3. Select one bean from their pair by putting both in their fist and randomly selecting one.

4. Add that bean to the one that their partner selected.

5. Record whether the new pair was homozygous or heterozygous.

Ms. Swanson, Ms. Tac, and Ms. Nyda brought an opaque jar to each of the pairs so that the students could randomly select beans. Ms. Swanson requested the students to follow the same steps that she and Ms. Swanson had modeled (i.e., Steps 1 through 5). After the students recorded their results, Ms. Swanson explained that the bean activity was a great way to illustrate some of the principles of genetics. Just as each partner contributed only one of his or her beans to the new combination, each parent contributes only half of his or her genetic information to the new offspring.

Ms. Swanson nodded at Tina who then, through the use of her computer and the assistance of Ms. Nyda, projected a slide that illustrated a trait key for all to see via the LCD projector. The Trait Key chart and the explanation provided the students with information about how the different bean combinations represented inherited genes that determine whether or not rabbits will inherit floppy or straight ears.

Ms. Tac explained that the genetic information comes in different forms, contributes to physical traits, and can be found in different combinations. Again working in pairs, the students completed an additional part (Step 6) of the activity by determining and recording the ear trait (i.e., straight or floppy) that each of their initial pairings represented as well as the pairings that their combined pairing indicated. Ms. Tac encouraged the pairs to select one member of the team to record his or her findings on the class chart while the other member of the pair compared his or her findings with those of two or three other groups seated near by them.

Ms. Swanson facilitated a class discussion where students were (a) asked to *think* about whether or not one bean color (representing one piece of inherited information) had a greater influence in determining the ear trait (i.e., floppy or straight) than the other bean color, (b) asked to turn to the other member of their *pair* to *share*, and (c) told to be prepared to share their thoughts about the questions if called upon by either of the co-teachers.

Tina and her partner alternated recording their responses to the prompt questions. When it was Tina's turn, Ms. Nyda facilitated Tina entry of her responses on her computer. When it was her partner's turn, he also used Tina's computer to record his answer. Later, a copy of the joint responses was printed by Ms. Nyda for Tina's lab partner.

Ms. Tac and Ms. Swanson had assigned the student pairs to each other as well as with Ms. Nyda. They monitored those that were assigned to them during the discussion. Then Ms. Swanson, Ms. Tac, and Ms. Nyda called on various members of the groups they had monitored to share their answers to the two prompt questions. Ms. Tac introduced two new terms: *phenotype* and *genotype*, which were added to the word wall. Once again, she facilitated a choral rehearsal of the pronunciation of the new vocabulary terms.

The students were asked to take turns within their pairs reading an essay entitled "Phenotype and Genotype." Ms. Tac, Ms. Swanson, and Ms. Nyda each told the members of one of the pairs they were monitoring that they could choose to alternate readers like everyone else, or to select only one of the partners to read, or to engage in echo reading. Tina, who is nonverbal, listened as her partner read the essay. After the oral reading experience, Ms. Swanson randomly called on some learners to check their understanding of the new terms.

Tina, who had been given the terms in advance, had typed, with assistance from Ms. Nyda, into her computer a definition in her own words for the two terms that she now projected onto the screen. Many of the students agreed that they liked Tina's definitions better than the textbook definitions. Ms. Swanson asked the students to return to their findings for Steps 2, 5, and the last part of the lab activity (Step 6) of the activity as they labeled the combinations and conditions at each step either phenotype or genotype.

Ms. Swanson and Ms. Nyda called on learners to share their answers. The students correctly identified the fact that one type of genetic information can be more powerful or influential than another (dominant versus recessive traits). Ms. Swanson introduced the two new terms and Ms. Nyda placed the cards containing the terms *dominant* and *recessive* on the word wall. Ms. Swanson asked the students if they could think of examples from their own lives and experiences where one trait seemed to be dominant. The students did not respond.

Ms. Tac decided to provide an example. She asked if any of them had one parent with brown eyes and one with blue eyes. Several students, including Tina, indicated that they did. Ms. Tac asked a student seated near the students who had indicated they had a parent with each eye color, to share what color eyes that student's parents had. In all instances, the eyes of both that student's parents were brown. To conclude this part of the activity, Ms. Tac generated a three-sentence summary using the four genetic terms introduced thus far. She wrote the summary using Tina's computer and projected it on the screen with the LCD projector.

Following a teacher prompt, and with assistance from Ms. Nyda, Tina projected a new visual on the screen. The visual graphically displayed the results of a cross (mating) that followed two traits in rabbits: ear type (floppy ears or straight ears) and gender (female or male). The results for 100 offspring from a male with floppy ears mated with a female with floppy ears indicated that there were 52 males and 48 females, all with floppy ears. The students were asked to discuss these findings with their partner and try and draw some conclusions. Tina, with Ms. Nyda's facilitation, typed her thoughts so she could share with her partner. Ms. Tac facilitated a class discussion in which students clearly demonstrated an understanding that the inheritance of ear type is different than inheritance of gender (inheritance of all traits does not occur in a simple 1:1 ratio).

Ms. Swanson wrote the following formula on the board:

$$\% \text{ with trait} = [(\# \text{ with trait}) / (\text{total} \# \text{ of offspring})] \times 100$$

Tina projected a new visual showing the results of a cross of a male with straight ears and a female with floppy ears. The chart indicated that they had 100 offspring and that 47 were male and 53 were female and they all had straight ears. Ms. Tac asked the students to use the formula that Ms. Swanson had written on the board to determine the percentages of offspring that were female and male, and the percentages that had straight ears and floppy ears. In most partnerships, the students were directed to rotate the role of problem solver and verifier. In some partnerships, students were given a calculator to assist in either determining the answers or verifying the answers. Ms. Tac's knowledge of students from the math class assisted the teachers in determining those students who needed to use a calculator.

Once the students calculated the percentages, Ms. Swanson asked them to discuss their findings with their partner so as to draw some conclusions. Ms. Tac asked them to also consider whether or not there was any connection between ear type and gender. Tina, with Ms. Nyda's facilitation, typed her thoughts to share with her partner. Then Ms. Nyda facilitated the student sharing of their observations, Ms. Tac recorded various comments on the board, and Ms. Swanson paraphrased some of the answers. The students correctly calculated the percentages and recognized that for both males and females the percentage with straight ears was 100 percent. They also found that when one of the parents had straight ears and the other had floppy ears, all offspring had straight ears because straight ears was the dominant trait, while floppy ears was the recessive trait. They concluded that the type of ear a rabbit is born with is not affected by gender.

Tina projected a picture of rabbits on the screen. The slide was titled, "Tina's Rabbits." Ms. Swanson explained that Tina had brought six one-month-old rabbits to class. She directed one member of each pair to view the three rabbits placed in the box on the teacher's desk and the other member of the pair to view the three rabbits placed in the cardboard box that Ms. Nyda placed on Tina's desk. After viewing the rabbits, the students were to meet with their partners to discuss their observations about ear type and to use the formula to determine the percentage of rabbits with floppy ears or straight ears.

After the partner discussion and determination of the percentage of rabbits with floppy ears or straight ears, Tina projected another picture of two rabbits on the screen. The title on the picture indicated they were the parents of the six rabbits she had brought to class. The male was named Sniffles and the female was named Daisy. It was obvious from the picture that both had floppy ears. The next slide Tina projected solicited suggestions for names for the six one-month-old rabbits (three females and three males) and shared the fact that Tina was willing to give four of them away if any of the students wanted to adopt one. The slide included her e-mail address so that classmates could contact her if they wanted one of the rabbits.

Ms. Tac asked the partners to select a method that they would use to summarize what they had learned thus far. More specifically, they were asked to use the new terminology (e.g., genotype, phenotype, heterozygous, homozygous, dominant, recessive) to describe the events that occurred during the lab activities this day. The pairs had twelve minutes to develop a rap, jingle, acronym, poem, drawing, or written product that summarized the learning outcomes. Two students who were very reflective had been paired together for this activity; they were given an additional option of working alone on their summary. They each chose to write a summary in their lab journals in which they connected the new learning outcomes to their own lives.

The lesson ended when two of the pairs (one chosen by Ms. Tac and one chosen by Ms. Swanson) shared their summaries. The students were told that the remaining pairs would have a chance to share their summaries the next day, when they would be divided into three groups for the beginning of the next lesson. One-third of the class would go with Ms. Swanson to an empty classroom across the hall, one-third would work with Ms. Nyda in the front part of the science class, and another third would meet with Ms. Tac at the back of the science class.

Ms. Tac briefly introduced the new topic—genetic disorders—explaining that the students would be doing more investigative reporting on genetic and non-genetic disorders. The assignment and directions would be further explained on the following day after the partner sharing of their learning summaries.

■ REFLECTION

Ms. Swanson and Ms. Tac met at lunchtime to share their observations. They both felt that their teaching procedures for the lesson were easy to implement, and that all students appeared engaged. They agreed to think about how they might further differentiate the "report" on genetic and non-genetic disorders by e-mailing ideas to each other later that night. Ms. Tac shared that she had met with Ms. Callis, who had identified some technology that might be of assistance to Tina and that she would schedule a meeting with Tina's support team within two weeks.

The teachers' lesson plan is shown in Table 12.3.

Note

1. For more information about Tina's alternate communication system, refer to www.tash.org/communication/fcreadings.htm.

Table 12.3 UDL Lesson Plan to Differentiate Instruction: Middle Level Science

PLANNING PHASE:

Lesson Topic and Name: <u>Patterns of Inheritance</u>	Content Area(s) Focus: <u>Biology</u>

Facts About the Student Learners

MI student survey results indicate that the students are diverse and that they vary in strength intelligences and interests (i.e., verbal/linguistic, logical/mathematical, visual/spatial, musical/rhythmic, bodily/kinesthetic, interpersonal, intrapersonal, naturalist). Tina uses Facilitated Communication, a computer, portable printer, and an LCD projector.

<u>Pause and Reflect About Specific Students</u>

The use of Multiple Intelligences Theory, partner and group work, and co-teacher monitoring will work for most students. Tina and some of the other students will require additional differentiation to access content, product, and process. The data gathered at Tina's MAPs session also is a potential source for differentiation ideas.

Content *(What will students learn?)*	Products Showing Student Success *(How will students convey their learning?)*
What are the academic and/or social goals? What content standards are addressed? **New Jersey Science Standard 2.8.: Collect and organize data to support the results of an experiment.** **New Jersey Science Standard 2.9.: Communicate experimental findings using words, charts, graphs, pictures, and diagrams.** **New Jersey Science Standard 7.5: Illustrate how the sorting and recombining of genetic material results in the potential for variation among offspring.**	In what ways will the learning outcomes be demonstrated?

Table 12.3 (Continued)

Content (What will students learn?)	Products Showing Student Success (How will students convey their learning?)
Differentiation Considerations: In what order will concepts and content be taught? 1. **Introduce new vocabulary, add to word wall and enter into journals (i.e., *hetero- and homozygous, genotype and phenotype, dominant and recessive traits, monohybrid and dihybrid inheritance, independent assortment*)** 2. **Inheritance of one trait (bean activity)** 3. **Inheritance of two traits (rabbit activity)** What multilevel and/or multisensory <u>materials</u> do the co-teachers need to facilitate access to the content? **Opaque container, 50 red beans, 50 white beans, sheets of poster board, transparencies, computers, rabbits, textbook and other print resources, Internet** What multilevel goals are needed for all students to meaningfully access the content? <u>Pause and Reflect About Specific Students</u> Are there any students who require unique or multilevel objectives or materials?	Differentiation Considerations: What are multiple ways students can <u>demonstrate</u> their understandings (e.g., multiple intelligences, multilevel, and/or multisensory performances)? What authentic products do students create? What are the criteria teachers use to evaluate the products? **Match bean combinations with a trait key and record data.** **Use a model of inheritance to record how physical traits correlate with different combinations of genetic information.** **Identify genetic patterns in their bean combinations as homozygous or heterozygous.** **Identify the effect that different bean combinations had on genetic traits.** **Define new vocabulary in a lab journal.** **Develop with a partner a rap, jingle, acronym, poem, or drawing that summarizes the major learning or enter independently into a journal an entry that discusses how the information learned relates to your own life.** **Develop answers to two questions.** <u>Pause and Reflect About Specific Students</u> Are there any students who require unique ways of showing what they know?

(Continued)

Table 12.3 (Continued)

	Process of Instruction (How students engage in learning)			
Instructional Formats	Instructional Arrangements	Instructional Strategies	Social and Physical Environment	Co-teaching Approach(es)
<u>Considerations</u>	<u>Considerations</u>	<u>Considerations</u>	<u>Considerations</u>	<u>Options</u>
Activity-based **Experiential** **Group investigation** **Discovery learning** **Computer**	**Partners** **(pre-selected)** **Cooperative learning structures** **Whole group**	**Choose research-based strategies:** **Summarizing and note taking, non-linguistic representations, cooperative group learning, generating and testing hypotheses, questions, cues, and advanced organizers** **Apply concepts from Multiple Intelligences Theory**	**Room arranged for partner and group work** Environmental alterations? **Preferential seating for Tina outside of traffic pattern, near her rabbits, and where her computer could be linked to the LCD projector.**	**Supportive** **Parallel** **Complementary** **Team teaching** **Students as co-teachers**

<u>Pause and Reflect About Specific Students</u>

What student-specific teaching strategies do select students need? What specific systems of supports (e.g., assistive technology), aids (e.g., personal assistance, cues, contracts), or services (e.g., counseling) do select students need?

Assistive technology, personal assistance, cues

IMPLEMENTATION PHASE:

Who are the Co-teachers: **Ms. Swanson, Ms. Tac, & Ms. Nyda**

What is/are the date(s) of the lesson? **March 19**

What does each co-teacher do before, during, and after implementing the lesson?

Co-teacher Name: →	Ms. Swanson	Ms. Tac	Ms. Nyda
What are the specific tasks that I do BEFORE the lesson?	**Gather lab materials.** **Talk to Tina about bringing her rabbits to class and sharing information about gambling experiences.** **Prepare PowerPoint slides in advance of class.** **Prepare a key that correlates color combinations with straight-ear and floppy-ear phenotypes.** **Scan materials into Tina's computer.** **Provide Tina with questions in advance.** **Determine heterogeneous student groups of two.**	**Buy red and white beans.** **Create PowerPoint slides with new vocabulary words and their definitions.** **Create word strips for new vocabulary to add to the word wall.** **Talk to Tina about sharing about autism and Facilitated Communication with her classmates.** **Review content and activity procedures in both student and teacher texts.** **Create modified materials for some students to use when learning and defining new terms.** **Determine heterogeneous student groups of two.** **Meet with Ms. Nyda to provide overview of the lesson and information about two additional pairs she will monitor.**	**Meet with Ms. Tac to review responsibilities and learn about additional students she will monitor.**

(Continued)

181

Table 12.3 (Continued)

Co-teacher Name: →	Ms. Swanson	Ms. Tac	Ms. Nyda
What are the specific tasks that I do DURING the lesson?	Deliver anticipatory set re: gambling.	Connect gambling discussion to laws of probability taught in math class.	Have students assigned to select two beans from jar.
	Link probability to genetics.	Add terms *heterozygous* and *homozygous* to the word wall.	Monitor student pairs as they randomly create and record three new bean combinations.
	Introduce terms *heterozygous* and *homozygous*.	Facilitate partner practice of pronouncing and defining the new terms.	Facilitate Tina's communication.
	Model the activity of randomly selecting one bean from each partner with Ms. Tac.	Model the activity of randomly selecting 1 bean from each partner with Ms. Swanson.	Continue facilitating for Tina and monitoring the same groups.
	Record the color of the 2 beans in the new combination on the board.	Record whether or not the new combination is homozygous or heterozygous.	Randomly call on learners.
	Have students assigned to select 2 beans from jar.	Have students assigned to select 2 beans from jar.	Monitor pairs.
	Monitor student pairs as they randomly create and record 3 new bean combinations.	Monitor student pairs as they randomly create and record 3 new bean combinations.	Prompt Tina to project slide of rabbits.
	Introduce trait key to students.	Request students to record their data on the class chart.	Monitor students who come to Tina's desk to look at baby rabbits.
	Encourage 1 member of each pair to visit and observe findings from three other pairs.	Introduce terms *phenotype* and *genotype*.	Prompt Tina to project slide of Sniffles & Daisy.
	Facilitate class discussion.	Facilitate choral rehearsal of pronunciation of new terms.	Monitor groups as they prepare their summary of learning.
	Add new words to word wall.	Randomly call on students to explain new vocabulary introduced thus far.	
	Prompt Tina to project slide showing possible combinations for inheritance of two traits (i.e., gender and straight- or floppy-eared).		
	Assign think-pair-share activity for two prompt questions.		

182

Co-teacher Name: →	Ms. Swanson	Ms. Tac	Ms. Nyda
	Switch groups with Ms. Tac to monitor for the second part of the lesson.	Facilitate student recording of ear-type data on board.	
	Facilitate discussion for question #1.	Prompt Tina to project slide with 2 questions for partner groups to discuss.	
	Randomly call on learners.		
	Prompt students to label steps 2, 5, and 6 as either phenotype or genotype.	Switch groups to monitor with Ms. Swanson.	
		Facilitate discussion for question #2.	
	Prompt Tina to project new slide showing results for two traits.	Randomly call on learners.	
	Write formula on the board.	Model write a short paragraph with genetic terminology that describes all events so far.	
	Explain formula.		
	Monitor pairs.	Facilitate class discussion.	
	Monitor students who come to teacher's desk to look at baby rabbits.	Request students to use the formula.	
		Monitor pairs.	
	Monitor groups as they prepare summary of learning.	Request students to use formula to determine percentage of each type of ear.	
	Select 1 group to present.	Present options for group to summarize key learning.	
	Briefly explain plan for all partners to share their learning on the next day.	Monitor groups as they prepare their summary of learning.	
		Select one group to present.	
		Briefly introduce topic of genetic disorders and related assignment.	

(Continued)

Table 12.3 (Continued)

Co-teacher Name: →	Ms. Swanson	Ms. Tac	Ms. Nyda
What are the specific tasks that I do AFTER the lesson?	**Meet to share observations and brainstorm additional ways to differentiate.**	**Meet to share observations and brainstorm additional ways to differentiate.** **Meet with Ms. Callis to learn of her observations of Tina and thoughts about how Assistive Technology might assist her.**	

REFLECTION PHASE:

Where, when, and how do co-teachers debrief and evaluate the outcomes of the lesson?

The teachers agreed to meet that day at lunchtime as well as the following day at their weekly planning meeting.

How did students do?

All students met with success and demonstrated interest in the topic and activities.

Were needs of the learners met? **Yes.**

What are recommendations for the design of the next lesson(s)?

Brainstorm additional ways to differentiate the "report" on genetic and non-genetic disorders. Meet with Ms. Callis, Tina, and Tina's support team to discuss the use of voice-to-text software that Tina might be able to use when she presents to the class on autism and the use of Facilitated Communication and whether or not autism is a genetic disorder.

13

UDL Lesson Planning Cycle to Differentiate Instruction in Action

High School Language Arts

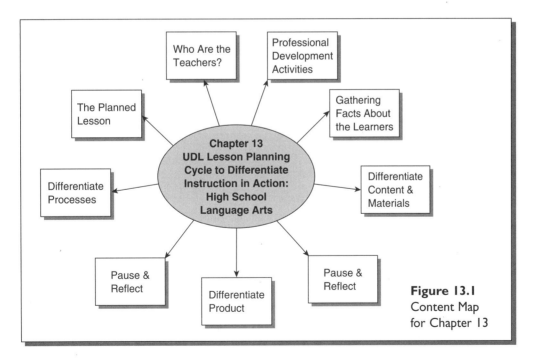

Figure 13.1 Content Map for Chapter 13

No pessimist ever discovered the secret of the stars, or sailed on uncharted land, or opened a new doorway for the human spirit.

—Helen Keller

In this chapter, you will learn how Ms. Griffith and Ms. Lang, two high school level co-teachers whom you met in Chapter 2, are planning to differentiate their instruction through the Universal Design for Learning (UDL) Planning Process to Differentiate Instruction. Ms. Griffith is a veteran high school language arts instructor and Ms. Lang is a teacher of students who are English language learners. They have completed one semester co-teaching together in a Language Arts class. They successfully differentiated for numerous students, including Chang, a young man newly arrived from a war-torn country in Southeast Asia who is also an English language learner. They applied a retrofit approach (see Chapter 2) to solving the mismatches between Chang and the content, process, and product demands of their classroom. They have been informed that they will continue co-teaching the class that Chang attends as well as an additional class during the upcoming semester.

■ CO-TEACHER PROFESSIONAL DEVELOPMENT ACTIVITIES

Both Ms. Griffith and Ms. Lang wanted to acquire greater skills in co-teaching and differentiation of instruction. They approached their school's administration to share their desire to learn. The principal was supportive and responsive. He sent them for additional training sessions on co-teaching and universal design and differentiation of instruction. He also established a professional support group on the campus to support them and other teachers interested in implementing differentiated lessons.

Ms. Griffith and Ms. Lang attended a one-day regional conference. At the conference, they were introduced to the universal design process. They were both excited about employing this process as the new semester began because they knew that the information provided would assist them to meet Chang's needs as well as those of three new students who would be in their co-taught classes. The new students were: (a) Yolanda, a student who was blind, who would be in the same class as Chang, (b) Maarten, a young man with significant disabilities, who would be in their other co-taught class, and (c) Deeandre, a student who struggled to learn, did not like working with others, and who would be in the same class as Maarten.

They were eager to attempt a universal design lesson because they wanted to teach in a way that would meet the needs of all of the students in both of their co-taught classes. They joined the professional support group established at their school where teachers who were interested in differentiation of instruction were provided with relevant resource materials such as books and videos. Members of their professional support group volunteered to meet once a week for eight weeks and then two times a month for the remainder of the semester.

Given the training and the support available from colleagues through the professional support group, both Ms. Lang and Ms. Griffith expressed optimism that they would be able to follow the Universal Design Lesson Plan template and design differentiated lessons. Ms. Griffith and Ms. Lang developed the co-taught lesson on *Romeo and Juliet* described in this chapter and shared it with their support group for feedback prior to implementation.

Now that you are reaching the end of this book, perhaps you are feeling confident to critique their lesson as well. We invite you to review their plan and identify its strengths and shortcomings. As you read this chapter and review their lesson plan, think about what additional suggestions you would make to Ms. Griffith and Ms. Lang if you were a member of their professional support group.

GATHERING FACTS ABOUT THE LEARNERS ■

Ms. Griffith and Ms. Lang felt that they had a handle on most of the students in their co-taught classes but believed that it was important to revisit the information about Chang and also gather information about the strengths, knowledge and experiences, learning preferences, interests, and challenges of the three new students: Maarten, Yolanda, and Deeandre.

Of particular concern to both Ms. Lang and Ms. Griffith was Maarten, a student with significant disabilities and numerous labels including being developmentally disabled, noncommunicative, a child with cerebral palsy, multi-handicapped, and medically fragile. They questioned how a student with significant disabilities could benefit from placement in a high school language arts class.

Ms. Ciallela, Maarten's IEP manager and an inclusion facilitator, met with them several times to share information about Maarten's strengths and his IEP goals before the start of the new semester. She developed a Program-at-a-Glance that highlighted Maarten's strengths as well as his IEP goals. The Program-at-a-Glance that she developed for Maarten and shared with the co-teachers appears below in Table 13.1.

Table 13.1 Maarten's Program-at-a-Glance

Strengths	IEP Goals-at-a-Glance
Great smile	Vocalizations
Responsive to peers	Object discrimination
Curious	Maintain range of motion
Cooperative	Use of a switch
Quiet in class	Visual tracking
Enjoys music	Respond to his name
Likes music	Develop friendships
Enjoys being outdoors	Participate in noncurricular activities

Ms. Ciallela offered to cover Ms. Griffith's third period class so that both Ms. Griffith and Ms. Lang could observe Maarten in a social studies class. Following that class, Ms. Lang and Ms. Griffith met again with Ms. Ciallela and Mr. McCoy, a paraeducator who had been supporting Maarten in the social studies class and who would be accompanying Maarten into the Language Arts class.

Ms. Griffith said that seeing Maarten in the social studies class working toward his goals had reduced her anxiety about having him in her class. Ms. Ciallela offered to assist Ms. Lang and Ms. Griffith in figuring out how to use the participation option known as curriculum overlapping (see Chapter 5; Giangreco et al., 1993) to *integrate* Maarten's diverse needs into their language arts class.

Ms. Griffith and Ms. Lang decided to make a chart (Table 13.2) where they could visually display the strengths, along with other important information, and brainstormed ideas about how to facilitate access to the content, products, and processes of learning for the four students they were concerned about (i.e., Chang, Maarten, Deeandre, and Yolanda). They planned to refer to that chart as they went through the various phases of the Universal Design for Learning Lesson Planning Process.

■ DIFFERENTIATE THE CONTENT AND MATERIALS

Ms. Lang and Ms. Griffith wanted to design a lesson that would address the following four New Mexico Language Arts Standards (2000):

1. Compare words and symbols that express a universal theme and reflect upon personal perspective and response.

2. Respond to a variety of literary works and media that offer an audience (a) understanding of a student's personal reactions; (b) a sense of how the reaction results from a careful consideration of the text; (c) an awareness of how personal and cultural influences affect the response.

3. Make thematic connections between literary works and contemporary issues.

4. Explain the effects of point of view on the reader's understanding of literary work.

Pause and Reflect

The co-teachers believed that the four standards were appropriate for all of the learners, with one exception. They believed that they would need multilevel goals for Maarten so he could address his IEP goals during the activities. Working with Ms. Ciallela, they developed a matrix (see Table 13.3) to brainstorm how they might integrate Maarten's goals into the various activities.

Table 13.2 Detailed Information From Gathering Facts About Four Learners

Student	Multiple Intelligences What are students' strengths and intelligences	Other Important Information	Content How do we best facilitate their accessing the content?	Products How might they best show you what they have learned?	Process How to afford these students a means to engage with the curriculum?
Deeandre	Intrapersonal/ self smart Verbal/Linguistic		Read about it	Traditional paper-pencil tasks, journal writing, independent research, Internet research	Read about it, write about it, relate it to himself.
Yolanda	Bodily/kinesthetic Musical/Rhythmic Verbal/Linguistic	Blind Disrupts others with tapping if she is bored.	Braille materials Auditory presentation	Create a rap, poem, song. Write about it using a Braille keyboard.	Hands-on and multisensory activities, mnemonic devices, songs, poetry
Chang	Visual/Spatial Naturalist Interpersonal	English language learner	Pictures Illustrations PowerPoint	Pictures and illustrations (e.g., cartoon strips) Software programs	Graphic organizers, concept maps Lecture guides Take his notes in words Interdisciplinary instruction (i.e., relate science and nature to math, language arts, social studies)
Maarten	Interpersonal Musical/Rhythmic Naturalist	Curious Cooperative Responds to peers Enjoys music, activity, and being outdoors. A student with significant disabilities (i.e., non-communicative, medically fragile, developmental disability, multi-handicapped, cerebral palsy)	Curriculum overlapping	Relate to mastery of his IEP goals: 1. object discrimination 2. visual tracking 3. response to his name 4. use of a switching device 5. vocalization 6. develop friendships	Peer interactions Music Field trips

Table 13.3   Matrix Meshing the Facts About Maarten and the Lesson's Goals and Activities

	Compare Notes	Use Graphic Organizer	View DVD	Act out Scenes	Draw Scenes	Clap out Iambic Pentameter	Task Sheets #1 & #2
Use of Switch			X				
Vocalize						X	
Object Discrimination		X			X		
Respond to Name							X
Range of Motion		X					
Visual Tracking		X		X	X		X
Friends	X	X	X	X	X	X	X
Co-curricular							

The co-teachers discussed the need to utilize multilevel goals and multisensory materials to facilitate access to the content for Yolanda and Chang. Yolanda, who was blind, would need access to Braille materials and a computer with a Braille keyboard. Because Chang is an English language learner, they wanted him to have access to the story of *Romeo and Juliet* in contemporary English rather than Elizabethan English.

Differentiate the Product

Ms. Griffith and Ms. Lang met to plan the lesson. They started by reviewing the chart that they had developed (Table 13.2). They became excited during their brainstorming as they thought of the various ways that the students could use their strengths to demonstrate their learning. They decided to include written responses, visual representations, role play, chanting, clapping out a beat, and oral responses among the options that students could use to demonstrate their learning.

They decided that the students would be graded based upon the percentage of accuracy of their answers on two task sheets (see Tables 13.4 and 13.5), the degree to which they could correctly sort characters into one of two sides of a graphic organizer (see Figure 13.2) to reflect whether the characters were friends or family members of the Montagues or the Capulets, and the completeness of their notes when reviewed at the end of the week by Ms. Griffith and Ms. Lang. (Chang would be allowed to draw his notes with simple sentence descriptions under the pictures.)

Table 13.4   Task Sheet #1

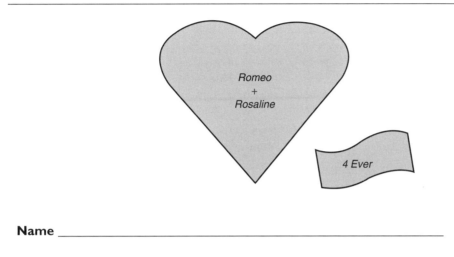

Name _____

Part 1: **Working with your partner(s), complete the column on the right.**

What Shakespeare says:	What it means to us:
Bid a sick man in sadness make his will! Ah word ill urged to one that is so ill. In sadness cousin, I do love a woman.	Romeo admits to Benvolio that he is in love.
She hath forsworn to love, and in that vow Do I live dead that live to tell it now.	He says that she does not love him back and he is in despair.
The woman who has caught Romeo's eye is ROSALINE.	
At this same ancient feast of Capulet's Sups the fair Rosaline whom thou so loves, With all the admired beauties of Verona.	Benvolio tells him that his "love," Rosaline, will be at the Capulet's party.
One fairer than my love—the all-seeing sun Ne'er saw her match, since first the world begun.	
Romeo sees JULIET at the party.	
O she doth teach the torches to burn bright.	
So shows a snowy dove trooping with crows, As yonder lady o'er her fellows shows.	
Did my heart love till now? Forswear it sight, For I ne'er saw true beauty till this night.	
Look on the board for the "Shakespeare-isms."	

SOURCE: By Frances R. Duff; used with permission.

Table 13.5   Task Sheet #2

Names _____

_____

Part 2:

What do Romeo's reactions tell you about his personality? If you were with him at the party, what would you say to him? After you and your partner have discussed your response, rewrite it in four lines imitating blank verse.

What would you say to Romeo (in your own words)?

How would you say it in blank verse?
Da DUM / da DUM/ da DUM / da DUM/ da Dum/ "Oh she / doth teach/ the tor / ches to / burn bright"/

SOURCE: By Frances R. Duff; used with permission.

Figure 13.2 Montague and Capulet Graphic Organizer

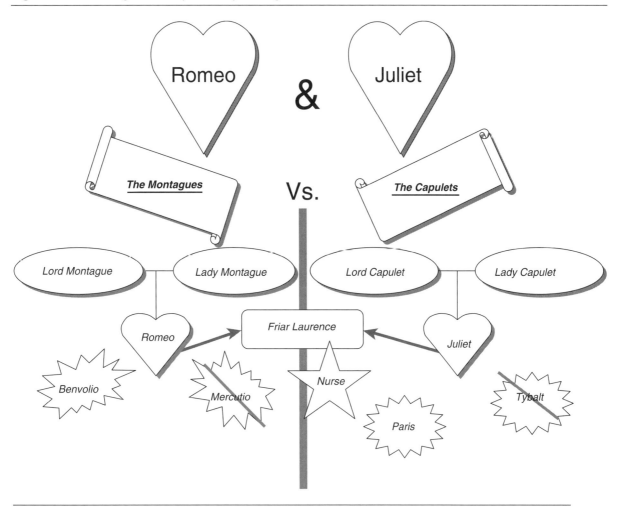

SOURCE: By Frances R. Duff; used with permission.

Pause and Reflect

After determining how most students would demonstrate their learning, Ms. Lang and Ms. Griffith turned their attention to the matrix showing where Maarten's IEP goals might be addressed within the lesson (Table 13.3). They met with Ms. Ciallela and Mr. Moreno to continue their brainstorming. They soon realized that they could overlap most of Maarten's goals into the lesson. They decided that during the lesson they would focus on range of motion, use of a switch, visual tracking, object discrimination, vocalization, response to his name, and friendship development. The co-teachers decided that Mr. Moreno would collect data on Maarten's performance as he demonstrated mastery of his IEP goals.

DIFFERENTIATE THE PROCESS ■

Co-teacher Roles

The co-teachers were committed to showing their high school students how to collaborate. They wanted to model the natural give-and-take relationships that occur when people work together to achieve mutual goals. They had completed the "Are We Really a Collaborative Team?" self-assessment (see Table 8.4 in Chapter 8). They realized that, at some time, each had felt at a loss as to what role to play when they were co-teaching.

They searched the web to find literature on how other high school co-teachers addressed this problem and discovered the "If one does this, the other can do this" tips and strategies that Murawski and Dieker (2004) had generated based upon their research with high school teachers. The tips and strategies are shown in Table 13.6 and can be detected in the roles that all three members of the co-teaching team planned to fulfill for the upcoming lesson. The co-teachers developed the detailed lesson plan shown in Table 13.7 to share with their professional support group prior to implementation.

■ THE PLANNED LESSON

Before the Lesson

Both classes. Ms. Griffith developed the two task sheets and the graphic organizer. Ms. Lang and Ms. Griffith determined which students in each class would be working together. They pre-assigned them to groups of two or three. Prior to the students entering the class, Ms. Griffith planned to draw a heart on the blackboard with the words "Romeo & Rosaline 4 Ever" written underneath the heart.

A Block. Ms. Lang planned to talk with Chang prior to the lesson to secure his willingness to share with the class his experiences in learning a new language. They wanted to use this analogy to motivate and support students as they began to study Elizabethan English. The co-teachers also decided that since Yolanda liked to drum and tap, they could use her musical intelligence during the upcoming lesson. Ms. Lang planned to meet with Yolanda prior to the class period to rehearse clapping out the beat of iambic pentameter. Ms. Lang prepared the Braille version of the materials for Yolanda.

B Block. Mr. Moreno met with Ms. Griffith and Ms. Ciallela to review Maarten's goals and how they would be met in the upcoming lesson and to clarify his own role in the classroom. He also observed both Ms. Ciallela and the occupational therapist, Ms. Jenkins, working with Maarten and other students. They demonstrated for Mr. Moreno how to facilitate peer interactions with Maarten. Ms. Jenkins modeled how to train peers to use hand-over-hand assistance to facilitate Maarten's range of motion. Ms. Lang created laminated materials for Maarten to use with his partners when sorting and placing characters into the Montague or Capulet side of the graphic organizer. Ms. Lang also planned to meet with Maarten's peers to explain the activities and how they could support Maarten prior to the class.

Ms. Griffith shared that she was concerned that Deeandre would not fare well in the class because of the amount of partner and group work. She

Table 13.6 Murawski and Dieker's Tips and Strategies for Co-teacher Role Differentiation Teacher Actions During Co-teaching

If one of you is doing this . . .	The other can be doing this...
Lecturing	Modeling note taking on the board/overhead
Taking roll	Collecting and/or reviewing last night's homework
Passing out papers	Reviewing directions
Giving instructions orally	Writing down instructions on board
Checking for understanding with large heterogeneous group of students	Checking for understanding with small heterogeneous group of students
Circulating, providing one-on-one support as needed	Providing direct instruction to whole class
Prepping half of the class for one side of a debate	Prepping the other half of the class for the opposing side of the debate
Facilitating a silent activity	Circulating, checking for comprehension
Providing large group instruction	Circulating, using proximity control for behavior management
Running last minute copies or errands	Reviewing homework
Re-teaching or pre-teaching with a small group	Monitoring large group as they work on practice materials
Facilitating sustained silent reading	Reading aloud quietly with a small group; previewing upcoming information
Reading a test aloud to a group of students	Proctoring a test silently with a group of students
Creating basic lesson plans for standards, objective, and content curriculum	Providing suggestions for modifications, accommodations, and activities for diverse learners
Facilitating stations or groups	Also facilitating stations or groups
Explaining new concept	Conducting role play or modeling concept
Considering modification needs	Considering enrichment opportunities

SOURCE: From Murawski, W., & Dieker, L. Tips and strategies for co-teaching at the secondary level, from *Teaching Exceptional Children*, 36(5), 53–58. Copyright © 2004 by The Council for Exceptional Children.

explained that he struggled to learn and did not like to work with others. They decided that he would be given the option of working alone or with a partner when it was new or difficult learning. Once they thought he understood a concept, he would be assigned a partner to work with while he firmed up his learning. The partner with whom he would be assigned would also be intrapersonal and thus not mind if Deeandre chose to work alone.

The Planned Instructional Sequence

They planned for Ms. Lang to greet the students as they entered the class. She would pass out a list of the student groupings and ask students to sit near their newly assigned partners. Both Ms. Lang and Ms. Griffith planned to ask students questions at the start of the lesson to check their understanding of the learning from the previous day's class. Ms. Griffith would refer students to their previous day's notes and Ms. Lang would prompt the students to compare their notes with classmates seated nearby. They would compare their notes to check for completeness and accuracy. While students completed these tasks, Ms. Griffith and Ms. Lang would circulate and monitor their pre-assigned groups. In the class where Maarten and Mr. Moreno joined them, Mr. Moreno would monitor Maarten's group as well as two others that were pre-assigned to him.

Ms. Griffith would pass out the graphic organizer for the Montagues and the Capulets (Figure 13.2). Ms. Lang would ensure that Yolanda received the Braille version in the A Block class and Mr. Moreno would ensure that Maarten and his peers received the laminated graphic organizer in the B Block class. Using a PowerPoint presentation, Ms. Griffith would model for the class how to add information onto the graphic organizer for what they had learned thus far. Mr. Moreno would collect data on Maarten's visual tracking when Maarten was prompted by peers to look at various objects. He would also collect data on student use of hand-over-hand assistance so that Maarten could place objects on the laminated graphic organizer.

Next, Ms. Griffith would show selected clips from a play version of *Romeo and Juliet*. In the A Block class, Mr. Moreno would prompt Maarten to start and stop the DVD through the use of a switching device. In the A and B Block classes, Ms. Griffith planned to ask for student volunteers to act out some of the other action that they had read about. Students would be given an option of drawing cartoon strips to summarize the action thus far. Chang would be given an overhead transparency and his drawing would be shared with the entire class. Ms. Lang would monitor the students preparing the visual representations and Ms. Griffith would monitor the students rehearsing the dramatic reenactment. In the B block class, Mr. Moreno would join Ms. Griffith in monitoring the students.

Ms. Griffith agreed to ask if anyone had ever tried to learn a second language. In A Block, Ms. Lang would call on Chang to share some of his frustrations at learning English. Ms. Griffith would make the connection between learning a foreign language and attempting to understand and translate Elizabethan English. Ms. Lang would next introduce iambic pentameter, using the Elizabethan English text of *Romeo and Juliet*. In Block A, Yolanda would model clapping out the beat of iambic pentameter. In B Block, Maarten's partners would model clapping out the beat in an attempt to prompt his vocalization in response to musical sounds that he liked.

Ms. Griffith and Ms. Lang planned to pass out Task Sheet #1 (Table 13.4): Romeo and Rosaline. Ms. Griffith would demonstrate the translation of Item 1 and Ms. Lang would demonstrate the translation of Item 2. Ms. Griffith would facilitate partner sharing via guided practice for Item 3. Then Ms. Griffith planned to ask students to discuss Item 4 and to attempt to translate it into contemporary English.

In Block B, Ms. Griffith and Ms. Lang planned to guide students through Items 5, 6, and 7 with Mr. Moreno's assistance. They planned to rotate the roles of facilitator of sharing and recorder of the correct answer on an overhead transparency for each of the items. Maarten's peers would continue to prompt him to visually track during activities and to use his name to see if he would respond. In addition, Maarten had responded to Ms. Griffith's strong voice when they met and the co-teachers were hoping that he would visually track her movements as she paced around the room during instruction, as was her custom.

Students working in their small groups would be given passages to read and discuss. Chang would be assigned strong readers for his two partners. The students would be asked to determine what is happening in the play. Ms. Griffith, Ms. Lang, and Mr. Moreno would monitor their respective groups.

Ms. Griffith would pass out Task Sheet #2 (Table 13.5). The students would then discuss Romeo's personality and create a response as to what they would say to Romeo at a party if they encountered him today. Ms. Lang would request that the students attempt to translate their response into four lines of blank verse. Ms. Lang would provide Yolanda with the Braille versions of the task sheets. Ms. Griffith, Ms. Lang, and Mr. Moreno would monitor their respective groups. Each would pick one of their groups to each share their response in front of the entire class. Yolanda would quietly clap the beat as each group shared.

PAUSE AND REFLECT ■

Ms. Lang and Ms. Griffith were eager to share their lesson plan with their support group. They wanted additional suggestions about how to differentiate their plan prior to implementation.

Now that you have finished this chapter and are reaching the end of this book, we think that you would be an excellent resource for the co-teaching team of Ms. Griffith, Ms. Lang, and Mr. Moreno. Please review the lesson plan in Table 13.7 to determine how else they might use the facts about the learners to differentiate the content, product, and process demands of this lesson. What feedback would you provide to them? What do you see as the strengths of their lesson? What areas can you help them improve upon? We know that they will appreciate your feedback just as you will appreciate the feedback of your colleagues as you attempt to implement the Universal Design for Learning Lesson Planning Process.

We would like to acknowledge and thank Ms. Frances Duff from Cibola High School in Albuquerque, New Mexico, for sharing her advance organizer, student task sheets, and overall lesson idea.

Table 13.7 The Completed UDL Plan for High School Language Arts

PLANNING PHASE:

Lesson Topic and Name:	Literature & Media	Content Area(s) Focus:	Romeo & Juliet

Facts About the Student Learners

Who are our students and how do they learn? **See brainstorming chart developed by Ms. Griffith and Ms. Lang (Table 13.2)**

What forms of communication (e.g., assistive technology) do our students use? **Yolanda uses Braille**

Pause and Reflect About Specific Students

Are there any students with characteristics that might require differentiation in the content, product, or process of learning?

Yes: Yolanda, Maarten, Deeandre, and Chang

Content (What will students learn?)	Products Showing Student Success (How will students convey their learning?)
What are the academic and/or social goals? What content standards are addressed? **New Mexico Language Arts Standard III-A-1:** **Compare words and symbols that express a universal theme and reflect upon personal perspective and response.** **New Mexico Language Arts Standard III-A-3:** **Respond to a variety of literary works and media that offer an audience (a) an understanding of a student's personal reactions; (b) a sense of how the reaction results from careful consideration of the text; and (c) an awareness of how personal and cultural influences affect the response.** **New Mexico language Arts Standard III-B-3:** **Make thematic connections between literary works and contemporary issues** **New Mexico language Arts Standard III-4:** **Explain the effects of point of view on the reader's understanding of literary work**	In what ways will the learning outcomes be demonstrated? Differentiation Considerations: What are multiple ways students can demonstrate their understandings (e.g., multiple intelligences, multilevel and/or multisensory performances)? **Visually, role play, written response, oral responses** What authentic products do students create? **Complete task sheets, use graphic organizer, take journal notes** What are the criteria teacher(s) use to evaluate products? **Percentage of accuracy on task sheets 1 and 2** **Percentage of accuracy of listing characters and placing them into the correct side (Romeo or Juliet) of the graphic organizer** **Completeness of notes as judged by the co-teachers**

Differentiation Considerations:

In what order will concepts and content be taught?

What multilevel and/or multisensory materials do the co-teachers need to facilitate access to the content?

Visuals, auditory, Brailed materials and computer with Braille keyboard

What multilevel goals are needed for all students to meaningfully access the content?

Maarten's goals will be overlapped/integrated into the activity

Pause and Reflect About Specific Students

Are there any students who require unique or multilevel objectives or materials?

Chang will be given a version of the story written in contemporary English rather than Elizabethan English and he will explain his understanding of the events as they unfold, using contemporary English.

Pause and Reflect About Specific Students

Are there any students who require unique ways of showing what they know?

Data on Maarten's IEP goals during this class:

(a) **use of the switch to start and stop the DVD**

(b) range of motion as he physically places items on graphic organizer

(c) any vocalizations when students clap and chant blank verse (Da DUM/ da DUM/ da DUM/ da DUM/)

(d) object discrimination response to request to gaze at various objects: (picture of a man (Romeo); woman (Juliet); Friar (looks like robes that the priest in his church wears)

(e) response to his name when spoken to by peers

(f) visual tracking when prompted by peers

(g) friendship development by working with peers in small groups

Yolanda needs access to a Braille keyboard.

Software (i.e., *Co-Writer* and *Intellitalk*) will be used to support Chang and he will be able to graphically represent his learning to support what he writes.

Deeandre will be encouraged to relate the learning to himself and record his thoughts in his journal.

Process of Instruction
(How students engage in learning)

Instructional Formats	Instructional Arrangements	Instructional Strategies	Social and Physical Environment	Co-teaching Approach(es)
Considerations	Considerations	Considerations	Considerations	Options
Adapting Lectures	**Cooperative learning structures**	Choose research-based strategies:	N/A	Supportive
Activity-based	**Same age peer tutors**	**Questioning at all levels of Bloom**		Parallel
Experiential	**Whole group**	**Graphic organizers**		Complementary
Simulations/role play				Team teaching
				Students as co-teachers

(Continued)

Table 13.7 (Continued)

Process of Instruction (How students engage in learning)				
Instructional Formats	Instructional Arrangements	Instructional Strategies	Social and Physical Environment	Co-teaching Approach(es)
		Cooperative Group Learning **In-class guided practice** **Summarizing and note taking** Apply concepts from Multiple Intelligences Theory: **Verbal/linguistic, bodily/ kinesthetic, intrapersonal, musical/rhythmic, interpersonal**		

Pause and Reflect About Specific Students

What student-specific teaching strategies do select students need? What specific systems of supports (e.g., assistive technology), aids (e.g., personal assistance, cues, contracts), or services (e.g., counseling) do select students need?

Deeandre will be given the choice of whether to work alone or with a partner when he appears to be struggling with the learning. Once we think he has it, he will begin to work with a partner for a short period of time. He will be encouraged to write in his journal about how he would feel if he were one of the characters in the play.

IMPLEMENTATION PHASE:

Who are the Co-teachers?:   Ms. Griffith   Ms. Lang   Mr. Moreno

What is/are the date(s) of the lesson?:

200

What does each co-teacher do before, during, and after implementing the lesson?

Co-Teacher Name: →	Ms. Griffith	Ms. Lang	Mr. Moreno, Educational Assistant for B Block class
What are the specific tasks that I do BEFORE the lesson?	Draw a "Valentine" heart on the board and underneath it write the words, "Romeo & Rosaline 4 Ever." Along with Ms. Lang, pre-assign students to heterogeneous groups of two or three. Prepare Task Sheets and Graphic organizer for Montagues and Capulets.	Talk with Chang prior to class to ask if he is willing to share a bit about how hard it is to learn a foreign language. Rehearse with Yolanda clapping out the beat of Iambic pentameter. Along with Ms. Griffith, pre-assign students to heterogeneous groups of two or three. Prepare Brailed graphic organizer and task sheet for Yolanda. Create laminated materials for Maarten to sort and place during graphic organizer activity for sorting characters into Romeo's family and friends or Juliet's family and friends. Meet and explain activity with Maarten's peers who will help overlap his goals into the lesson.	Meet with Ms. Griffith and the special education teacher to review goals for Maarten and clarification of role in class. Observe special educator and Occupational Therapist working with Maarten in other general education classrooms. Learn how to teach students to do a hand-over-hand assist to support Maarten.
What are the specific tasks that I do DURING the lesson?	Review the opening scene and ask questions to check students understanding of the learning from the previous day. Refer students to their notes on Shakespeare's verse. Monitor student partner sharing. Pass out graphic organizer for Montagues and Capulets. Model entering information onto the graphic organizer for what is known thus far. Show selected clips of action from a play version of Romeo and Juliet. Ask for student volunteers to act out the action in two other scenes.	Greet students at the door as they enter the class. Pass out list of student groupings. Review the opening scene and ask questions to check students understanding of the learning from the previous day. Ask students to compare their notes to a classmate's to check for accuracy and completeness. Monitor student partner sharing. Pass out graphic organizer for Montagues and Capulets, including Yolanda's Brailed version. Ask for student volunteers to draw cartoon strips on transparencies depicting the action thus far.	Monitor three partnerships assigned for this class, including Maarten's group of three. Facilitate Maarten's use of his switch to start and stop the DVD. Model instructional process to use with Maarten for the two peers working with him: Object Discrimination Prompt Maarten to look at the visual (e.g., picture of a man: Romeo) Provide hand-over-hand assist that will enable Maarten to practice range of motion while he places laminated cut outs of characters (i.e., Romeo, Juliet, Friar) onto the graphic organizer developed for his group.

(Continued)

Table 13.7 (Continued)

Co-Teacher Name: →	Ms. Griffith	Ms. Lang	Mr. Moreno, Educational Assistant for B Block class
	Monitor students not participating in acting out or visually representing the action thus far.	Monitor students participating in acting out the action thus far.	Prompt students to use Maarten's name—see if he responds.
	Ask if anyone has ever tried to learn another language? Ask them to share their experiences.	Call on Chang to share a bit about how hard it is to learn English.	Prompt students to cue him to do <u>visual tracking.</u>
	Relate Chang's experiences to trying to understand Elizabethan language.	Briefly review the pattern of iambic pentameter.	Teach students to clap out Iambic pentameter—see if Maarten <u>vocalizes.</u>
	Pass out the Romeo & Rosaline task sheet 1.	In A Block, have Yolanda model clapping out the beat of the Iambic pentameter examples. Encourage other students to join in.	Collect data on Maarten's progress in meeting IEP goals.
	Have students get into their pre-assigned heterogeneous groups of two or three.	Pass out the Romeo & Rosaline task sheet.	Monitor other student groups assigned.
	Demonstrate the translation of Shakespeare's verse for item #1 on the task sheet.	Demonstrate the translation of Shakespeare's verse for item #2 on the task sheet.	
	Facilitate partner sharing via guided practice for translating item #3 on the task sheet.	Facilitate the sharing of answers for item #4.	
	Ask students to discuss item # 4 and see if they can translate it into today's English.	Rotate role of facilitator of sharing and recorder of the answer with Ms. Lang for item #s 5, 6, & 7.	
	Rotate role of facilitator of sharing and recorder of the answer with Ms. Lang for item #s 5, 6, & 7.	Monitor students visually representing the action thus far (Maarten is assigned to one of these groups).	
	Read and re-read as is necessary several new sections of *Romeo and Juliet.*	Read and re-read as is necessary several new sections of *Romeo and Juliet.*	
	Ask students to discuss the new content and identify what is happening.	Ask students to discuss the new content and identify what is happening.	
	Pass out task sheet #2. Students talk about Romeo's personality and create a response as to what they would say personally or in a note to Romeo at a party.	Request that students attempt to translate their response into four lines imitating blank verse.	
	Monitor students working in partners and small groups.	Monitor students working in partners and small groups.	
What are the specific tasks that I do AFTER the lesson?	To be determined following feedback from the Professional Support Group.	To be determined following feedback from the Professional Support Group.	To be determined following feedback from the Professional Support Group.

REFLECTION PHASE:

Where, when, and how do co-teachers debrief and evaluate the outcomes of the lesson? How did students do? Were needs of the learners met? What are recommendations for the design of the next lesson(s)?

To be determined following feedback from the Professional Support Group

14

Epilogue

Pause and Reflect

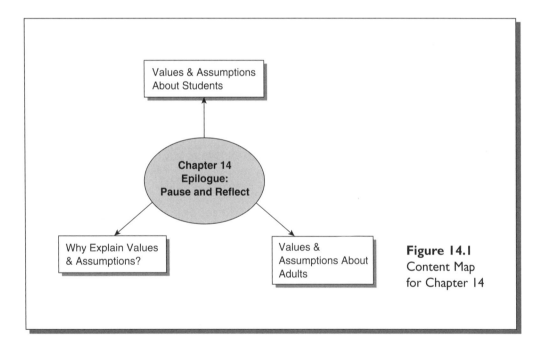

Figure 14.1
Content Map for Chapter 14

We will never successfully restructure schools to be effective until we stop seeing diversity in children as a problem.

—Grant Wiggins (1992, p. xv)

n this book, we have integrated the principles and practices of universal design, collaborative planning, and co-teaching into a Universal Design for Learning (UDL) Lesson Plan Cycle to Differentiate Instruction (represented in Figure 14.2) that bundles innovative practices together in a way that we hope will change the way teachers think about students, curriculum, instruction, and assessment. Namely, UDL provides a way for educators to view diversity in children and youth as a strength instead of as a problem and to put their students first in lesson design rather than last, as in a retrofit approach.

For example, remember how Rosa's teachers changed their perceptions of Rosa as a learner once they heard her bilingual translation of Martin Luther King, Jr.'s "I Have a Dream" speech (Chapter 11)? Recall the changes in how Kevin responded to his lessons once his teachers tapped into his strengths and interests (Chapter 10)? And, of course, the changes in Tina (Chapter 12) and Chang (Chapter 13) were dynamically associated with the differentiated lesson plans that their teachers developed using the principles of universal design. By viewing individual students' differences as strengths instead of problems, the teachers facilitated a richer learning environment for all the students!

As you finished each of the chapters of this book, did you detect any values that may have guided us in our writing? Are there any beliefs or convictions that come across as basic to undertaking the effort to try a universal design method of thinking and planning? If you had written this book, what might you have been thinking about the dispositions of teachers and administrators? What might you have been thinking about the actions teachers, administrators, and other school leaders would need to take in order to support co-planning and co-teaching to design and deliver universally accessible lessons and units?

We assert that the field of education is at a potential turning point—where values and action can converge and work together to ensure equitable access to learning for all students. What might those values and actions be? For us, the values were simple—ones we all have heard and perhaps recited many times.

Figure 14.2 Universal Design for Learning Lesson Plan Cycle to Differentiate Instruction

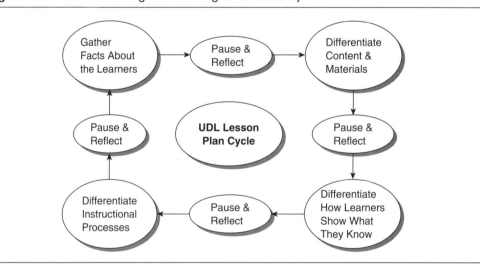

The assumptions and beliefs about children and youth that guided us throughout the journey of writing this text were:

- Each student is an individual and, no matter what we do, our foremost responsibilities are to *cause no harm* to the student.
- Each student can and will learn.
- Each student has the right to learn under effective and motivating instruction and, when necessary, with personalized accommodations.
- Each student's diversity is a gift, as it is a catalyst for inventing new ways of providing access to learning.

The assumptions and beliefs about adults that guided us were:

- All teachers can and will learn.
- All administrators can and will learn.
- All administrators have the responsibility to provide effective support and professional development and feedback to allow teachers to meet the needs of each student.

Why do we share our values with you at this point in the book? First, we believe that adopting and endorsing a collaborative and UDL approach to teaching will likely be a values-driven decision. Look at our personal histories as teachers and administrators. Neither co-teaching nor UDL was likely a part of our experience base as elementary and high school students, nor as professionally prepared educators. For most of us, UDL represents an emerging paradigm, a new, and possibly foreign, way of thinking about planning and implementing instruction. We know that in order to develop a deep understanding of how to implement a new paradigm and the accompanying skills and techniques, it takes time and both cognitive and emotional energy. So, to try out UDL and co-teaching is, in a way, a "leap of faith"—a statement that "I am going to try this, even though it may take time and energy, because I believe each student is an individual who can and will learn, and has a right to effective and motivating instruction."

We also share our beliefs and convictions about teachers and administrators at this point because we know from our research of the organizational change literature that teachers and administrators do innovate, given infrastructures of professional support and development. Researchers (e.g., Fullan, 1993; Joyce & Showers, 1980) have consistently shown that to change schooling practices requires far more than mere exposure to new ideas. Like their students, teacher innovators need ongoing modeling, guided practice, permission to "do it in their own way," and recognition for "not only the *success* teachers are experiencing implementing strategies in their classrooms, but also the *sheer effort* they are putting into making substantive change in their classrooms" (Marzano, Pickering, & Pollock, 2001, p. 157).

Ongoing professional development is key. For example, Tomlinson (2005) argued eloquently for staff development that provides models for teachers regarding the beliefs, attitudes, and practices that differentiation offers their students. It is important that teachers experience powerful images of what the practice looks and feels like and how it benefits individual human beings.

But how does an administrator sandwich these new developments into an already packed school day, week, and year? Of course, there are many professional development formats (e.g., schoolwide inservice training, in-class coaching); and teachers do have various preferences. We suggest administrators consider the bite-sized approach used by administrators who have adopted co-teaching as a practice and that is discussed in our book on co-teaching (Villa, Thousand, & Nevin, 2004) as the professional development catalyst. Administrators have organized brief, frequent, ongoing events such as breakfast clubs or coaching corners in which co-teachers can systematically engage in chapter-by-chapter book studies, co-planning, lesson sharing, and problem solving. This approach has the potential of decreasing stress while increasing motivation because it builds in real-life application, natural interpersonal supports through face-to-face interaction, and individual accountability—features of effective cooperative groups (Johnson & Johnson, 1999).

How should you begin? The first of the four design points in a UDL approach involves thinking first about the students. So, let's do it! Let's take a risk, and give UDL and co-teaching a try! The research promises that not only can these methods make a difference in the lives of students, but they can "make your day" as well!

Resources

Table 1   Gathering the Facts About the Learner and the Classroom Demands

Facts About the Learner	Facts About the Classroom Demands
Strengths *Background Knowledge & Experiences* *Interests* *Learning Style(s)* *Multiple Intelligences* *Important Relationships* *Other:* _____ *Other:* _____	*Content Demands* How is the content made available to the learners?
	Process Demands What processes do the teachers use to facilitate student learning?
Goal Does this learner have any unique goals related to academic learning, communication, English language acquisition, and/or social-emotional functioning? Are there particular concerns about this learner?	*Product Demands* How do the students demonstrate what they have learned? How are they graded?

Table 2 Blank Co-teaching Universal Design Lesson Plan Template

PLANNING PHASE:

Lesson Topic and Name: _____   Content Area(s) Focus: _____

Step #1: Facts About the Student Learners

Step #2: Content (What will students learn?)

Step #3: Products (How will students show success?)

Step #4: Process of Instruction (How will students be instructed?)

Instructional Formats	Instructional Arrangements	Social and Physical Instructional Strategies	Environment	Co-teaching Approach(es)

IMPLEMENTATION PHASE:

Date(s) of the lesson: _____

Who are the co-teachers? _____ _____

What does each co-teacher do before, during, and after implementing the lesson?

Co-teacher Name:		
What are the specific tasks that I do BEFORE the lesson?		
What are the specific tasks that I do DURING the lesson?		
What are the specific tasks that I do AFTER the lesson?		

REFLECTION PHASE:

Table 3 Top Nine Research-Based Strategies for Increasing Student Achievement

Strategy	We can use this strategy when...
1. Identifying similarities and differences	
2. Summarizing and note taking	
3. Reinforcing effort	
4. Homework and practice at appropriate level of difficulty	
5. Nonlinguistic representations, graphic organizers	
6. Cooperative group learning	
7. Setting objectives and providing feedback	
8. Generating and testing hypotheses	
9. Questions, cues, and advance organizers	

Table 4   A Matrix for Note Taking

Similarities Among the Four Approaches

Supportive Differences	Parallel Differences	Complementary Differences	Team Teaching Differences
Supportive Cautions	**Parallel Cautions**	**Complementary Cautions**	**Team Teaching Cautions**

References

Apple, M., & Beane, J. (1995). *Democratic schools.* Alexandria, VA: Association for Supervision and Curriculum Development.

Armstrong, T. (2000). *Multiple intelligences in the classroom* (2nd ed.). Alexandria, VA: Association for Supervision and Curriculum Development.

Artiles, Λ., & Trent, D. (1994). Overrepresentation of minority students in special education: A continuing debate. *The Journal of Special Education, 27*(4), 410–437.

Bardwell, G. (2005). *Algebra I: Explorer.* Potomac, MD: Cognitive Technologies, Inc. Retrieved October 11, 2006, from http://www.mathrealm.com/CD_ROMS/Algebra_1.php

Barnett, H. (2003). *Investing in technology: The payoff in student learning.* Washington, DC: ERIC Clearinghouse on Information & Technology. ED479843. Retrieved March 16, 2006, from http://www.ericdigests.org/2005–2/technology.html

Bartolo, P., & Ale, P. (2005, October). *DTMp: A Comenius 2.1 project to produce a Differentiated Teaching Module for primary school trainee teachers.* Proceedings of the 30th Annual Conference of the Association for Teacher Education Europe. Retrieved March 16, 2006, from http://www.atee2005.nl/search/paperworks.php?contrid=150

Beech, M. (2005). *IEP Team Guide to Florida's Comprehensive Achievement Test (FCAT) Accommodations.* Tallahassee, FL: Florida Department of Education, Bureau of Exceptional Education and Student Services. Retrieved June 7, 2006, from http://www.myfloridaeducation.com/commhome/fcat/fcat-par.pdf

Beecher, R. (2006*). Integrating the visual arts in first grade writing lessons.* Starksboro, VT: Robinson Elementary School.

Blankenship, C., & Lilly, M. S. (1981). *Mainstreaming students with learning and behavior problems.* New York: Holt, Rinehart and Winston.

Bloom, B. S. (1984). The two sigma problem: The search for methods of group instruction as effective as one-to-one tutoring. *Educational Researcher, 13*(6), 4–16.

Bloom, B. S., Englehart, M. B., Furst, E. J., Hill, W. H., & Krathwohl, D. R. (Eds.). (1956). *Taxonomy of educational objectives: The classification of educational goals. Handbook I: Cognitive domain.* New York: McKay.

Boykin, W., Albury, A., Tyler, K., Hurley, E., Bailey, C., & Miller, O. (2005). Culture-based perceptions of academic achievement among low-income elementary students. *Cultural Diversity and Ethnic Minority Psychology, 11*(4), 339–350.

BSCS biology: A human approach (2nd ed.). (1997). Dubuque, IA: Kendall-Hunt.

Buswell, B. E., & Schaffner, C. B. (2002). Families as creative and resourceful collaborators in inclusive schooling. In J. S. Thousand, R. A. Villa, & A. I. Nevin (Eds.), *Creativity and collaborative learning: The practical guide to empowering students, teachers, and families* (pp. 13–20). Baltimore: Paul H. Brookes.

California Department of Education. (1999). *Mathematics contents standards for grades 8–12: Algebra 1.* Sacramento, CA: CDE. Retrieved June 6, 2006, from http://www.cde.ca.gov/re/pn/fd/documents/math-stnd.pdf

Carnegie Learning. (2005). *The cognitive tutor.* Pittsburgh, PA: Carnegie Mellon University. Retrieved March 16, 2006, from http://www.carnegielearning.com/company.cfm

Carr, E. G., & Ogle, D. (1987). K-W-L-plus: A strategy for comprehension and summarization. *Journal of Reading, 21*(8), 684–689.

Carter, C. (1997, March). Why reciprocal teaching? *Educational Leadership, 54*(6), 64–68.

Center for Applied Special Technology. (2005). *Universal design for learning.* Retrieved March 16, 2006, from http://www.cast.org/about/index.html

Center for Applied Special Technology. (2006). *About CAST.* Retrieved June 5, 2006, from http://www.cast.org/about/index.html

Chadwick, F., & Hood, A. (2005, October). *The infusion and confusion of standards: Visual and performing arts in the core curriculum.* Proceedings of the 30th Annual Conference of the Association for Teacher Education Europe, Amsterdam, The Netherlands.

Chadwick, F., Hood, A., Lorimer, M., Norman, K., Santamarie, L., Woo, K., & Stall, P. (2005, April). *Understanding through collaboration.* Paper presented at annual conference of the American Association for Educational Research, Montreal.

Compton, M., Stratton, A., Maier, A., Meyers, C., Scott, H., & Tomlinson, T. (1998). It takes two: Co-teaching for deaf and hard of hearing students in rural schools. In *Coming together: Preparing for rural special education in the 21st century.* Conference Proceedings of the American Council on Rural Special Education, Charleston, SC. (ED 417901)

Cramer, E. D., & Nevin, A. I. (2007). A mixed methodology analysis of co-teacher assessments: Implications for teacher education. *Teacher Education and Special Education, 30*(1).

Cramer, E., Nevin, A., Salazar, L., & Landa, K. (2004, April). *Co-teachers who loop: A case study of an urban multicultural co-teaching team.* Presented at the Council for Exceptional Children, Baltimore.

Cramer, E., Nevin, A., Salazar, L., & Landa, K. (2006). Co-teaching in an urban, multicultural setting: Research report. *Florida Educational Leadership. 7* (1), 42–50.

Cramer, E., Nevin, A., Voigt, J., & Salazar, L., (2006, April). *The accomodated learner in a multicultural setting.* Presented at the Council for Exceptional Children, Salt Lake City, UT.

Crossley, R. (1997). *Speechless: Facilitating communication for people without voices.* New York: Dutton.

Daunci, A. P., Correa, V. I., & Reyes-Blanes, M. E. (2004). Teacher preparation for culturally diverse classrooms: Performance-based assessment of beginning teachers. *Teacher Education and Special Education, 27*(2), 105–118.

Dieker, L. (1998). Rationale for co-teaching. *Social Studies Review, 37*(2), 62–65.

Dill, E. M., & Boykin, A. W. (2005). The comparative influence of individual, peer tutoring, and communal learning contexts on the text recall of African American children. *Urban Education, 40*(5), 521–549.

Dolan, R. P., Hall, T. E., Banerjee, M., Chun, E., & Strangman, N. (2005). Applying principles of universal design to test delivery: The effect of computer-based read aloud on test performance of high school students with learning disabilities. *Journal of Technology, Learning, and Assessment, 3*(7). Retrieved June 5, 2006, from http://www.bc.edu/research/intasc/jtla/journal/v3n7.shtml

Doyle, M. B. (2002). *The paraprofessional's guide to inclusive education: Working as a team* (2nd ed.). Baltimore: Paul H. Brookes.

Duda, M., & Utley, C. (2006). Culturally responsive techniques for positive behavior supports. *Multiple Voices*, 21–35.

Duda, M., & Utley, C. (2006). Positive behavioral support for at-risk students: Promoting social competence in at-risk culturally diverse learners in urban schools. *Multiple Voices, 8*(1), 128–143.

Dunn, R., & Dunn, K. (1987). Dispelling outmoded beliefs about student learning. *Educational Leadership, 44*(6), 55–61.

Echevarria, J., & Graves, A. (2003). *Sheltered content instruction: Teaching English language learners with diverse abilities* (2nd ed.). Boston: Allyn & Bacon.

Echevarria, J., & McDonough, R. (1995). An alternative reading approach: Instructional conversations in a bilingual special education setting. *Learning Disabilities Research and Practice, 10*(2), 108–119.

Educational Resources Information Clearinghouse (ERIC). *Welcome to the ERIC data base.* Retrieved June 5, 2006, from http://www.eric.ed.gov/ERICWebPortal/resources/html/about/about_eric.html

Faltis, C. (1993). Critical issues in the use of sheltered content teaching in high school bilingual programs. *Peabody Journal of Education, 69*(1), 136–151.

Falvey, M., Forest, M., Rosenberg, R., & Pearpoint, J. (2002). Building connections. In J. S. Thousand, R. A. Villa, & A. I. Nevin (Eds.), *Creativity and collaborative learning: The practical guide to empowering students, teachers, and families* (pp. 29–54). Baltimore: Paul H. Brookes.

Federal Register. (1999, March 12). *Rules and regulations, 64*(48).

Fenna, E., Carpenter, T., Levi, L., Franke, M., & Empson, S. (1977). *Cognitively guided instruction: Professional development in primary mathematics.* Madison, WI: Board of Regents of the University of Wisconsin System.

Fortini, M., & Fitzpatrick, M. (2000). The universal design for promoting self-determination. In R. Villa & J. Thousand (Eds.), *Restructuring for caring and effective education: Piecing the puzzle together* (2nd ed., pp. 575–589). Baltimore: Paul H. Brookes.

Foster, M. (2002). *Using call-and-response to facilitate language mastery and literacy acquisition among African-American students.* EDO–FL–02–04. Retrieved June 7, 2006, from http://www.cal.org/resources/digest/0204foster.html

Fuchs, D., Fuchs, L., Mathes, P., & Martinez, E. (2002). Preliminary evidence on the social standing of students with learning disabilities in PALS and No-PALS classrooms. *Learning Disabilities Research and Practice, 17*(4), 205–215.

Fuchs, D., Fuchs, L., Thompson, A., Al Otaiba, S., Nyman, K., Yang, N., & Svenson, E. (2000). *Strengthening kindergartners' reading readiness in Title 1 and non-Title 1 schools.* Paper presented at the Pacific Coast Research Conference, La Jolla, CA.

Fuchs, L. S., & Fuchs, D. (1999). Monitoring student progress toward the development of reading competence: A review of three forms of classroom-based assessment. *School Psychology Review, 28*(4), 659–671.

Fullan, M. G. (1993). *Change forces: Probing the depths of educational reform.* Bristol, PA: Falmer.

Gansle, K., Noell, G., Vanderheyden, A., Slider, N., Hoffpauir, L., Whitmarsh, E., & Naquin, G. (2004). An examination of the criterion validity and sensitivity to brief intervention of alternate curriculum-based measures of writing skill. *Psychology in the Schools, 41*(3), 291–300.

Gardner, H. (1983). *Frames of mind: The theory of multiple intelligences.* New York: Basic Books.

Gardner, H. (1997). Are there additional intelligences? The case of naturalistic, spiritual, and existential intelligences. In J. Kane (Ed.), *Education, information, and transformation* (pp. 135–152). Upper Saddle River, NJ: Prentice-Hall.

Garrigan, C. M., & Thousand, J. S. (2005, Summer). Enhancing literacy through co-teaching. *The New Hampshire Journal of Education, 8,* 56–60.

Gest, S., & Gest, J. (2005). Reading tutoring for students at academic and behavioral risk: Effects on time-on-task in the classroom. *Education and Treatment of Children, 28*(1), 25–47.

Giangreco, M., Clonninger, C., & Iverson, V. (1993). *Choosing Options and Accommodations for Children (COACH): A guide to planning inclusive education.* Baltimore: Paul H. Brookes.

Glasser, W. (1999). *Choice theory: A new psychology of personal freedom.* New York: Perennial.

Goldsmith, O. (Irish playwright, 1728–1774). Cited in Quotable Quotes. Retrieved June 11, 2006, from http://littlecalamity.tripod.com/Quotes/QRS.html

Good, T. L., & Brophy, J. G. (1997). *Looking into classrooms* (7th ed.). New York: Harper & Row.

Gregorc, A. F. (1982). *Gregorc style delineator: Development, technical, and administrative manual.* Maynard, MA: Gabriel Systems.

Gregory, G., & Chapman, C. (2002). *Differentiated instructional strategies.* Thousand Oaks, CA: Corwin Press.

Gronlund, N. E. (1995). *How to write and use instructional objectives* (5th ed.). Englewood Cliffs, NJ: Merrill.

Grossman, H., Utley, C., & Obiakor, F. (2003). Multicultural learners with exceptionalities in general and special education settings. *Effective Education for Learners with Exceptionalities, 15,* 445–463.

Hall, T. (2002). Differentiated instruction. *CAST: National Center on Accessing the General Curriculum: Effective classroom practices report.* Retrieved June 5, 2006, from http://www.cast.org/ncac/index.cfm?i=2876

Hall, T., & Mengel, M. (2002). *Curriculum-based evaluations.* Center for Applied Special Technology (CAST). Retrieved June 7, 2006, from http://www.cast.org/publications/ncac/ncac_curriculumbe.html

Harry, B. (1994). *The disproportionate representation of minority students in special education: Theories and recommendations.* Miami, FL: University of Miami, Project FORUM Final Report.

Hasselbring, T., Kinsella, K., & Feldman, K. (n.d.). *READ 180.* Retrieved March 16, 2006, from http://teacher.scholastic.com/products/read180/

Hess, M. A. (1999). Teaching in mixed-ability classrooms: Teachers guide students down many paths to a common destination. *Newsletter of the Wisconsin Educational Association Council.* Retrieved June 5, 2006, from http://www.weac.org/kids/1998–99/march99/differ.htm

History Alive! *Curriculum.* Retrieved October 11, 2006, from http://www.teachtci.com/resources/onlHistory.aspx

Hourcade, J., & Bauwens, J. (2002). *Cooperative teaching: Re-building and sharing the school-house.* Austin, TX: Pro-Ed.

Idol, L., Nevin, A., & Paolucci-Whitcomb, P. (1996). *Curriculum based assessment: A blue-print for learning* (4th ed.). Austin, TX: Pro-Ed.

Idol, L., Nevin, A., & Paolucci-Whitcomb, P. (1999). *Models of curriculum-based assessment* (3rd ed.). Austin, TX: Pro-Ed.

Individuals with Disabilities Education Improvement Act (IDEIA) of 1990, 20 United States Congress 1412[a] [5]), Reauthorized 1997; 2004.

IDEIA (P.L. 108–446, Part B, Sec. 682 [c] Findings [5]) Public Law 108-446. (2004). The Individuals with Disabilities Education Improvement Act. 20 USC 1401.

Johnson, D. W., & Johnson, F. P. (1997). *Joining together: Group theory and skills* (6th ed.). Needham Heights, MA: Allyn & Bacon.

Johnson, D. W., & Johnson, R. T. (n.d.). *Cooperative learning, values, and culturally plural classrooms.* Retrieved March 16, 2006, from http://www.co-operation.org/pages/CLandD.html

Johnson, D. W., & Johnson, R. T. (1989). *Cooperation and competition: Theory and research.* Edina, MN: Interaction Book Company.

Johnson, D. W., & Johnson, R. T. (1996). The role of cooperative learning in assessing and communicating student learning. In T. R. Gusky (Ed.), *1996 ASCD yearbook: Communicating student learning* (pp. 25–46). Alexandria, VA: Association for Supervision and Curriculum Development. Also available on the Cooperative Learning Web Site. Retrieved June 5, 2006, from http://www.co-operation.org/pages/assess.html

Johnson, D. W., & Johnson, R. T. (1999). *Learning together and alone: Cooperative, competitive, and individualistic learning.* Boston: Allyn & Bacon.

Johnson, D. W., & Johnson, R. T. (2002). Ensuring diversity is positive: Cooperative community, constructive conflict, and civic values. In J. S. Thousand, R. A. Villa,

& A. I. Nevin (Eds.). *Creativity and collaborative learning: The practical guide to empowering students, teachers, and families* (2nd ed., pp. 197–208). Baltimore: Paul H. Brookes.

Johnson, D. W., & Johnson, R. T. (2005). *The Cooperative Learning Center at the University of Minnesota*. Retrieved October 11, 2006, from http://www.co-operation.org/

Joyce, B., & Showers, B. (1980). Improving inservice training: The messages of research. *Educational Leadership, 37*(5), 379–385.

Kagan, S. (1995). *Cooperative learning*. San Clemente, CA: Kagan Publishing.

Kagan, S., Kyle, P., & Scott, S. (2004). *Win-win discipline: Strategies for all discipline problems*. San Clemente, CA: Kagan Publishing.

Karayan, S., & Gathercoal, P. (2003). Service-learning: Empowering students with special needs. *Academic Exchange Quarterly, 7*(2), 151–157.

Keller, N., & Cravedi-Cheng, L. (2004). A retrospective on developing a shared voice through co-teaching. In R. A. Villa, J. S. Thousand, & A. I. Nevin (Eds.), *A guide to co-teaching: Practical tips for facilitating student learning* (pp. 103–110). Thousand Oaks, CA: Corwin Press.

King, Martin Luther, Jr. (1963). *I have a dream (Yo tengo un sueno . . .)*. (Jose R. Tejada, Trans.). Retrieved October 11, 2006, from http://www.mlkonline.net/dream_spanish.html

King-Sears, M., Cummings, C., & Hullihen, S. (1994). *Curriculum-based assessment in special education*. Florence, KY: Wadsworth.

Kleiner, B., & Chapman, C. (1999). Youth service-learning and community service among 6th–12th grade students in the United States: 1996 and 1999. *Education Statistics Quarterly, 2*(2). Retrieved June 13, 2006, from http://nces.ed.gov/programs/quarterly/vol_2/2_1/q4–2.asp

Klingner, J., Artiles, A., Kozleski, E., Utley, C., Zion, S., Harry, B., Zamora-Duran, G., & Riley, D. (2004). *Theoretical assumptions for addressing the disproportionate representation of culturally and linguistically diverse students in special education*. Denver, CO: National Center for Culturally Responsive Educational Systems (NCCRES).

Klingner, J. K., & Edwards, P. (2006). Cultural considerations with response to intervention models. *Reading Research Quarterly, 41*(1), 108–117.

Klingner, J. K., Vaughn, S., Arguelles, M. E., Hughes, M. T., & Leftwich, S. A. (2004). Collaborative strategic reading: Real world lessons from classroom teachers. *Remedial and Special Education, 25*(5), 291–302.

Klingner, J. K., Vaughn, S., Hughes, S., Schumm, J., & Elbaum, B. (1998). Outcomes for students with and without learning disabilities in inclusive classrooms. *Learning Disabilities Research & Practice, 13,* 153–161.

Kluth, P., Diaz-Greenberg, R., Thousand, J., & Nevin, A. (2002). Teaching for liberation: Promising practices from critical pedagogy. In J. S. Thousand, R. A. Villa, & A. I. Nevin (Eds.), *Creativity and collaborative learning: The practical guide to empowering students, teachers, and families* (pp. 71–84). Baltimore: Paul H. Brookes.

Kneedler, R., & Hallahan, D. (1981). Self-monitoring of on-task behavior with learning disabled children. *Attention Disorders: Implications for the Classroom, 2*(3), 73–82.

Kolb, D. (1984). *Experiential learning: Experience as the source of learning and development.* Englewood Cliffs, NJ: Prentice Hall.

Krathwohl, D. R., Bloom, B. S., & Masia, B. B. (1964). *Taxonomy of educational objectives: Handbook II: Affective Domain.* New York: McKay.

Kunc, N., & Van der Klift, E. (1994). Benevolence, friendship, and the politics of help. Retrieved June 5, 2006, from http://www.normemma.com/arhellbe.htm

Lloyd, J. (1982). Reactive effects of self-assessment and self-recording on attention to task and academic productivity. *Learning Disability Quarterly, 5*(3), 216–227.

Luckner, J. (1999). An examination of two co-teaching classrooms. *American Annals of the Deaf, 144*(1), 24–34.

Lyons, C. (1998). More than a decade of data. *Literacy Teaching and Learning: An International Journal of Early Reading and Writing, 3*(1). Retrieved February 23, 2006, from http://www.readingrecovery.org/sections/reading/decade1.asp

Mager, R. F. (1997). *Preparing instrumental objectives.* Palo Alto, CA: Fearon.

Magiera, K., Smith, C., Zigmond, N., & Gabauer, K. (2005). Benefits of co-teaching in secondary mathematics classes. *Teaching Exceptional Children, 37*(3), 20–24.

Mahoney, M. (1997). Small victories in an inclusive classroom. *Educational Leadership, 54*(7), 59–62.

Marzano, R. (2000). *Designing a new taxonomy of educational objectives.* Thousand Oaks, CA: Corwin Press.

Marzano, R., Pickering, D., & Pollock, J. (2001). *Classroom instruction that works: Research-based strategies for increasing student achievement.* Alexandria, VA: Association for Supervision and Curriculum Development.

McCarthy, B. (1990). Using the 4MAT system to bring learning styles to the schools. *Educational Leadership, 48*(2), 31–37.

McMaster, K., Fuchs, D., & Fuchs, L. (2002). Using peer tutoring to prevent early reading failure. In J. S. Thousand, R. A. Villa, & A. I. Nevin (Eds.), *Creativity and collaborative learning: The practical guide to empowering students, teachers, and families* (pp. 235–246). Baltimore: Paul H. Brookes.

McTighe, J., & Wiggins, G. (2004). *The understanding by design professional workbook.* Alexandria, VA: Association for Supervision and Curriculum Development.

McWilliams, P. (2000). *Life 101: Everything we wish we had learned about life in school—but didn't.* Los Angeles, CA: Prelude Press.

Meyer, A., & Rose, D. (2002, December). Universal design for individual differences. *Educational Leadership, 58*(3), 39–43.

Miller, A., Valasky, W., & Molloy, P. (1998). Learning together: The evolution of an inclusive class. *Active Learner: A Foxfire Journal for Teachers, 3*(2), 14–16.

Moffat, H. (2002). *Expressing nonverbal encouragement: A social skills lesson.* San Marcos, CA: California State University–San Marcos.

Morgan, P., & Ritter, S. (2002). *An experimental study of the effects of Cognitive Tutor® Algebra I on student knowledge and attitude.* Pittsburgh, PA: Carnegie Learning.

Morrocco, C., & Aguilar, C. (2002). Co-teaching for content understanding: A school-wide model. *Journal of Educational and Psychological Consultation, 13*(4), 315–347.

Multiple Intelligences Research and Consulting, Inc. (2005). *MIDAS: A professional manual.* Kent, OH: Author.

Murawski, W., & Dieker, L. (2004). Tips and strategies for co-teaching at the secondary level. *Teaching Exceptional Children, 36*(5), 53–58.

National Center for Educational Restructuring and Inclusion. (1995). *National Study on Inclusive Education.* New York: City University of New York.

National Council of Teachers of Mathematics. (2000). *Principles and standards for school mathematics.* Reston, VA: Author.

National Information Clearinghouse for Handicapped Children & Youth. (2005). Disability specific information. Retrieved June 5, 2006, from http://www.nichcy.org/disabinf.asp

Neal, L. I., McCray, A. D., Webb-Johnson, G., & Bridgest, S. T. (2003). The effects of African American movement styles on teachers' perceptions and reactions. *Journal of Special Education, 37,* 49–57.

New Jersey Science Standards. (2002). *Life Sciences.* Retrieved June 6, 2006, from http://www.nj.gov/njded/cccs/s5_science.htm

New Mexico State Standards. (2000, June). *High school language arts.* Retrieved October 11, 2006, from http://www.ped.state.nm.us/

No Child Left Behind. (NCLB). (2002). HB1. Retrieved March 16, 2006, from http://www.ed.gov/policy/elsec/leg/esea02/beginning.html#sec1

Noddings, N. (1992). *The challenge to care in schools.* New York: Teachers College Press.

Noeth, L. C. (2004, September 9). Co-teaching system boosts special education test scores in Tennessee district. *Commercial Appeal.* Memphis, TN. Retrieved September 11, 2004, from www.contactscommercialappeal.com/mca/local_news/article/0,1426,MCA_437_3168716,00.html

Nunley, K. (1998). *The layered curriculum.* Boston: Nunley Associates.

O'Neil, R. E., Homer, R. H., Albin, R. W., Sprague, J. R., Storey, K., & Newton, N. S. (1997). *Functional assessment and program development for problem behavior: A practical handbook.* Pacific Grove, CA: Brooks/Cole.

Orkwis, R., & McLane, K. (1998). *A curriculum every student can use: Design principles for student access.* (ERIC/OSEP Topical Brief # ED423654)

Ortiz, A. (2001). *English language learners with special needs: Effective instructional strategies.* Washington, DC: ERIC Education Reports.

Padrón, Y., Waxman, H., & Rivera, H. (2002, August). *Educating Hispanic students: Effective instructional practices. Practitioner Brief #5.* Santa Cruz, CA: University of California, Center for Research on Education, Diversity & Excellence (CREDE). Retrieved June 6, 2006, from http://repositories.cdlib.org/crede/practbrfs/practitioner_brief05/

Paige, R. (2004). *A guide to education and No Child Left Behind.* Washington, DC: U.S. Department of Education, Office of the Secretary, Office of Public Affairs.

Palinscar, A. S., & Brown, A. (1984). Reciprocal teaching of comprehension: Fostering and monitoring activities. *Cognition and Instruction, 1*(2), 117–175.

Palinscar, A. S., & Brown, A. (1987). Advances in improving the cognitive performance of handicapped students. In M. Wang, M. Reynolds, & H. Walberg (Eds.), *Handbook of special education: Characteristics and adaptive education.* NY: Pergamon.

Peer-Assisted Learning Strategies Web site. (2005). *Strategies for successful learning.* Retrieved March 16, 2006, from http://kc.vanderbilt.edu/pals/

Pickett, N., & Dodge, B. (2001). *Rubrics for web lessons.* Retrieved February 5, 2006, from http://edweb.sdsu.edu/webquest/rubrics/weblessons.htm

Plato Math Expeditions Program. Retrieved October 11, 2006, from http://www.plato.com/products.asp?cat=Instructional&mark=elem&subj=math&ID=27

Poplin, M. S., & Stone, S. (1992). Paradigm shifts in instructional strategies from reductionism to holistic/constructivism. In W. Stainback & S. Stainback (Eds.), *Controversial issues confronting special education: Divergent perspectives.* Boston: Allyn & Bacon.

Renaissance Learning. (2004). *STAR early literacy.* Wisconsin Rapids, WI: Author.

Rice, D., & Zigmond, N. (1999, December). Co-teaching in secondary schools: Teacher reports of developments in Australia and American classrooms. *Resources in Education.* (ERIC Document Reproduction Service No. 432558)

Ritter, S., & Morris, S. (2005, August). *Meeting the needs of diverse learners in the general education class.* Paper presented at the Inclusive and Supportive Education Congress International Special Education Conference—Inclusion: Celebrating Diversity? Glasgow, Scotland. Retrieved June 5, 2006, from http://www.isec2005.org.uk/isec/abstracts/papers_r/ritter_s.shtml

Riverdeep. (n.d.). *Riverdeep: Your path to success.* Retrieved March 16, 2006, from http://www.riverdeep.com/

Salazar, L., & Nevin, A. (2005). Co-teachers in an urban multicultural school. *Florida Educational Leadership, 5*(2), 15–20.

Salend, S. (2005). Report card models that support communication and differentiation of instruction. *Teaching Exceptional Children, 37*(4), 28–34.

Scheckley, B. G., & Keeton, M. T. (1997). Service learning: A theoretical model. In J. Shine (Ed.), *Service learning* (pp. 28–35). Chicago: The National Society for the Study of Education.

Schumm, J. S., Vaughn, S., & Harris, H. (1997). Pyramid power for collaborative planning. *Teaching Exceptional Children, 26*(6), 62-66.

Schwartz, J., & Exeter, T. (1989). All our children. *American Demographics, 1*(5), 34–34.

Science Learning Network. (1997). *Leonardo's Perspective.* Retrieved October 11, 2006, from http://www.mos.org/sln/Leonardo/LeonardosPerspective.html

Shepard, L. A. (2005). Linking formative assessment to scaffolding. *Educational Leadership, 63*(3), 66–70.

Shinn, M. (Ed.). (1998). *Advanced applications of curriculum-based measurement.* New York: Guilford.

Shuflitowski, R. (2005). *Collecting data to correct classroom disruptive behavior.* Miami, FL: Florida International University, College of Education: Report submitted in partial fulfillment of requirements for EDP 7058: Behavioral Interventions Research and Evaluation.

Silver, H., Strong, R., & Perini, M. (2000). *So each may learn: Integrating learning styles and multiple intelligences.* Alexandria, VA: Association for Supervision and Curriculum Development.

Simpson, E. J. (1972). *The classification of educational objectives: Psychomotor domain.* Urbana, IL: University of Illinois Press.

Slavin, R. (1994). *Cooperative learning: Theory, research, and practice* (2nd ed.). Boston: Allyn & Bacon.

Stainback, S., & Stainback, W. (1996). *Inclusion: A guide for educators.* Baltimore: Paul H. Brookes.

Starr, L. (2004). Strategy of the Week: Differentiated instruction. Education World. Retrieved August 26, 2006 from http://www.education-world.com/a_curr/strategy/strategy042.shtml

Sternberg, R. (1997a). What does it mean to be smart? *Educational Leadership, 5*(6), 20–24.

Sternberg, R. J. (1997b). *Thinking styles.* New York: Cambridge University Press.

Taba, H. (1962). *Curriculum and practice.* New York: Harcourt Brace & World.

Tharp, R., & Gallimore, R. (1991). *The instructional conversation: Teaching and learning in social activity.* Santa Cruz, CA: National Center for Research on Culture Diversity and Second Language Learning.

Thomas, C., Correa, V., & Morsink, C. (1995). *Interactive teaming: Consultation and collaboration in special programs.* Englewood Cliffs, NJ: Prentice-Hall.

Thousand, J. S., & Villa, R. A. (2000). Collaborative teaming: A powerful tool in school restructuring. In R. A. Villa & J. S. Thousand (Eds.), *Restructuring for caring and effective instruction: Piecing the puzzle together* (2nd ed., pp. 254–293). Baltimore: Paul H. Brookes.

Thousand, J. S., Villa, R. A., & Nevin, A. I. (2002). *Creativity and collaborative learning: The practical guide to empowering students, teachers, and families.* Baltimore, MD: Paul H. Brookes.

Thousand, J. S., Villa, R. A., Nevin, A. I., & Paolucci-Whitcomb, P. (1995). A rationale and vision for collaborative consultation. In W. Stainback & S. Stainback (Eds.), *Controversial issues confronting special education: Divergent perspectives* (2nd ed., pp. 223–232). Baltimore: Paul H. Brookes.

Tomlinson, C. A. (1995). Deciding to differentiate instruction in middle school: One school's journey. *Gifted Child Quarterly, 39,* 77–87.

Tomlinson, C. A. (1999). *The differentiated classroom: Responding to the needs of all learners.* Alexandria, VA: Association for Supervision and Curriculum Development.

Tomlinson, C. A. (2001a). Grading for success. *Educational Leadership, 58*(6), 12–15.

Tomlinson, C. A. (2001b). *How to differentiate instruction in mixed-ability classrooms* (2nd ed.). Alexandria, VA: Association for Supervision and Curriculum Development.

Tomlinson, C. A. (2005). Traveling the road to differentiation in staff development. *Journal of Staff Development, 26*(4). Retrieved June 7, 2006, from http://www.nsdc.org/library/publications/jsd/tomlinson264.cfm

Tomlinson, C. A., Kaplan, N., Renzulli, J., Purcell, J., Leppien, J., & Burns, D. (2002). *The parallel curriculum.* Thousand Oaks, CA: Corwin Press.

Tomlinson, C. A., & McTighe, J. (2006). *Integrating differentiated instruction & understanding by design* (2nd ed.). Alexandria, VA: Association for Supervision and Curriculum Development.

Townsend, B. (2002). Leave no teacher behind: A bold proposal for teacher education. *International Journal of Qualitative Studies in Education, 15,* 727–738.

Trent, S. (1998). False starts and other dilemmas of a secondary general education collaborative teacher: A case study. *Journal of Learning Disabilities, 31*(5), 503–513.

Udvari-Solner, A. (1996). Examining teacher thinking: Constructing a process to design curricular adaptations. *Remedial and Special Education, 17*(4), 245–254.

Udvari-Solner, A. (1998). Adapting curriculum. In M. Giangreco (Ed.), *Quick guides to inclusion 2: More ideas for educating students with disabilities* (pp. 1–27). Baltimore: Paul H. Brookes.

Udvari-Solner, A., Thousand, J. S., Villa, R. A., Quiocho, A., & Kelly, M. (2005). Promising practices that foster inclusion. In R. A. Villa & J. S. Thousand (Eds.), *Creating an inclusive school* (2nd ed., pp. 97–123). Alexandria, VA: Association for Supervision and Curriculum Development.

Udvari-Solner, A., Villa, R. A., & Thousand, J. S. (2002). Access to the general education curriculum for all: The universal design process. In J. S. Thousand, R. A. Villa, & A. I. Nevin (Eds.), *Creativity and collaborative learning: The practical guide to empowering students, teachers, and families* (2nd ed., pp. 85–103). Baltimore: Paul H. Brookes.

Udvari-Solner, A., Villa, R. A., & Thousand, J. S. (2005). Access to the general education curriculum for all. In R. A. Villa & J. S. Thousand (Eds.), *Creating an inclusive school* (2nd ed., pp. 134–155). Alexandria, VA: Association for Supervision and Curriculum Development.

U.S. Department of Education. (2001). *Twenty-third annual report to Congress on the implementation of the Individuals with Disabilities Education Improvement Act.* Washington, DC: Author.

U.S. Department of Education Office of Special Education and Rehabilitative Services. (1999). *IDEA '97: The Regulations.* Washington, DC: Author. Retrieved October 11, 2006, from http://www.ed.gov/news/fedregister/finrule/1999-1.html

Van Den Broek, P., & Kremer, K. (2000). The mind in action: What it means to comprehend during reading. In B. Taylor, M. Graves, & P. Van Den Broek (Eds.), *Reading for meaning: Fostering comprehension in the middle grades, language and literacy series* (pp. 1–32). New York: Teachers College Press.

VanDerHayden, A., & Burns, M. (2005). Using curriculum-based measurement to guide instruction: Effect on individual and group accountability scores. *Assessment for Effective Intervention, 30*(3), 15–31.

Van der Klift, E., & Kunc, N. (2002). Beyond benevolence: Supporting genuine friendships in inclusive schools. In J. S. Thousand, R. A. Villa, & A. I. Nevin (Eds.), *Creativity and collaborative learning: The practical guide to empowering students, teachers, and families* (2nd ed., pp. 21–28). Baltimore: Paul H. Brookes.

Villa, R. (2002). *Collaborative teaching: The co-teaching model.* Videotape. Port Chester, New York: National Professional Resources.

Villa, R., & Thousand, J. (2004). *Creating inclusive schools* (2nd ed). Alexandria, VA: Association for Supervision and Curriculum Development.

Villa, R. A., & Thousand, J. S. (2005). *Creating an inclusive school* (2nd ed.). Alexandria, VA: Association for Supervision and Curriculum Development.

Villa, R. A., Thousand, J. S., & Nevin, A. I. (2004). *A guide to co-teaching: Practical tips for facilitating student learning.* Thousand Oaks, CA: Corwin Press.

Villa, R. A., Thousand, J. S., Nevin, A. I., & Liston, A. (2005). Successful inclusion practices in middle and secondary schools. *American Secondary Education Journal, 33*(3), 33–50.

Villa, R. A., Udis, J., & Thousand, J. S. (2002). Supporting students with troubling behavior. In J. S. Thousand, R. A. Villa, & A. I. Nevin (Eds.), *Creativity and collaborative learning: The practical guide to empowering students, teachers, and families* (2nd ed., pp. 135–156). Baltimore: Paul H. Brookes.

Vygotsky, L. (1987). *The collected works of L. S. Vygotsky.* (R. W. Rieber & A. S. Carton, Trans.). New York: Plenum Press. (Original works published in 1934, 1960)

Walter, T. (1998). *Amazing English!* New York: Addison-Wesley.

Webb-Johnson, G. C. (2002). Strategies for creating multicultural and pluralistic societies: A mind is a wonderful thing to develop. In J. S. Thousand, R. A. Villa, & A. I. Nevin (Eds.), *Creativity and collaborative learning: The practical guide to empowering students, teachers, and families* (2nd ed., pp. 55–70). Baltimore: Paul H. Brookes.

Webb-Johnson, G. C. (2003). Behaving while black. *Beyond Behavior, 12*(2), 3–7.

Weiss, M., & Lloyd, J. (2002). Congruence between roles and actions of secondary special educators in co-taught and special education settings. *Journal of Special Education, 36*(2), 58–68.

Welch, M. (2000). Descriptive analysis of team teaching in two elementary classrooms: A formative experimental approach. *Remedial and Special Education, 21*(6), 366–376.

Weldall, K., & Panagopoulou-Stamatelatou, A. (1991). The effects of pupil self-recording of on-task behavior on primary school children. *British Educational Research Journal, 17*(2), 113–127.

Wiggins, G. (1992). Foreword. In R. A. Villa, J. S. Thousand, W. Stainback, & S. Stainback. *Restructuring for caring and effective education: An administrative guide to creating heterogeneous schools* (pp. xi–xvi). Baltimore: Paul H. Brookes.

Wiggins, G., & McTighe, J. (2005). *Understanding by design* (2nd ed., expanded). Alexandria, VA: Association for Supervision and Curriculum Development.

Willis, S., & Mann, L. (2000, Winter). Curriculum update. *Newsletter of the Association for Supervision and Curriculum Development.* Retrieved August 26, 2006, from http://www.ascd.org/ed_topics/cu2000win_willis.html

Wisconsin Department of Public Instruction. (2005). *Social studies model academic standards.* Retrieved June 6, 2006, from http://dpi.wi.gov/standards

Index

**CORWIN
PRESS**

The Corwin Press logo—a raven striding across an open book—represents the union of courage and learning. Corwin Press is committed to improving education for all learners by publishing books and other professional development resources for those serving the field of PreK–12 education. By providing practical, hands-on materials, Corwin Press continues to carry out the promise of its motto: **"Helping Educators Do Their Work Better."**